The City: inside the great expectation machine

Myth and reality in institutional investment and the stock market

Tony Golding

FT Prentice Hall
FINANCIAL TIMES

An imprint of Pearson Education

London • New York • Toronto • Sydney
Tokyo • Singapore • Hong Kong • Cape Town • New Delhi
Madrid • Paris • Amsterdam • Munich • Milan • Stockholm

332.6322

PEARSON EDUCATION LIMITED

Head Office:
Edinburgh Gate
Harlow CM20 2JE
Tel: +44 (0)1279 623623
Fax: +44 (0)1279 431059

London Office:
128 Long Acre
London WC2E 9AN
Tel: +44 (0)20 7447 2000
Fax: +44 (0)20 7447 2170
Website: www.financialminds.com

First published in Great Britain in 2001
Second edition published in Great Britain in 2003

© Pearson Education Limited 2003

The right of Tony Golding to be identified as Author of this work has been
asserted by him in accordance with the Copyright, Designs and Patents Act 1988.

ISBN 0 273 66104 3

British Library Cataloguing in Publication Data
A CIP catalogue record for this book can be obtained from the British Library.

This publication is designed to provide accurate and authoritative information in
regard to the subject matter covered. It is sold with the understanding that neither
the authors nor the publisher is engaged in rendering legal, investing, or any other
processional service. If legal advice or other expert assistance is required, the service
of a competent professional person should be sought.

The publisher and contributors make no representation, express or implied, with
regard to the accuracy of the information contained in this book and cannot accept
any re-sponsibility or liability for any errors or omissions that it may contain.

10 9 8 7 6 5 4 3 2 1

Typeset by Northern Phototypesetting Co. Ltd, Bolton
Printed and bound in Great Britain by Bell & Bain Ltd, Glasgow

The Publishers' policy is to use paper manufactured from sustainable forests.

About the author

After graduating from Cambridge and the University of Sussex, where he gained a doctorate in industrial economics, Tony Golding spent several years with an international electronics company. He entered the City in 1974 and spent 24 years there, starting as an investment analyst with a small, research-based firm of stockbrokers. In 1978 he joined Flemings, the London-based investment bank, becoming a director and head of research in the asset management division. Before Big Bang in 1986 he took responsibility for setting up the research and sales functions in Flemings' newly established securities operation. In 1989 he moved over to investment banking, where he specialized in the generation and marketing of acquisition and equity-financing ideas in several industry sectors, both in the UK and internationally. He left in 1998 to write this book.

Many people in the City can lay claim to an in-depth knowledge of institutional investment or securities or investment banking, but very few have first-hand experience of working at director level in all three. In writing this book, Tony Golding has drawn extensively on the all-round perspective that his varied career has given him.

This book is dedicated to my late father.

Contents

List of figures

List of tables

Preface and acknowledgements to the Second Edition

The first edition of this book grew out of my long-held conviction that there was a 'gap in the market' for a book about the inner workings of the investment part of the City. A book that explained the relationships between the different segments in terms understandable to anyone with a basic knowledge of stock exchange investment, that didn't avoid contentious issues, that considered dispassionately what the City does well – and what it does less well.

Fortunately, a considerable number of people with an interest in investment and the City shared my original 'gap' perception. So, less than two years after my initial foray into print, here I am putting the finishing touches to a second edition, fully updated, revised and extended (including an additional section on the mergers and acquisitions business, an area I know well from personal experience).

In the financial world change comes thick and fast. The stock market, institutional investors and investment analysts have all hit the headlines in the last two years – not necessarily for the right reasons! This new edition takes full account of these developments, particularly the analysis and conclusions of the landmark Myners Review on institutional investment and the fascinating – if less than edifying – insight into fund management provided by the Unilever court case against Merrill Lynch Investment Management in the last weeks of 2001. Since the abrupt end of the 'dotcom' boom, the role of investment analysts has (rightly) been the subject of much public scrutiny. Hedge funds have risen from nowhere to become a potent force in the market place. I have, accordingly, updated and substantially extended the chapter on the securities business and how it works. More generally – and beyond the scope of this book – the collapse of Enron has cast a shadow over the entire financial system, calling into question the validity of the raw numbers that are fed daily to the City's army of information-crunchers – what I call 'The Great Expectation Machine'.

As ever, I am indebted to many people still active in the City for helping me keep up to date with trends and developments. Once again, John Hatherly has been a constant source of information, advice and support. I particularly wish to thank the following for being kind enough to read and comment on sections of the revised text: Morfydd Evans, Andrew Hawkins, Keith Hodgkinson, Jeff Hooke, Andrew Moffat, John Pierce, Ian Ramsay, Chris Russell, Fred Stone, Jeremy Tasker, Richard Taffler and Tony Zucker. My wife, Gill, prompted by her reading of the first edition to become a trustee of her former employer's pension fund, again read through the text and made some valuable comments. Any views expressed are mine and mine alone.

Tony Golding
June 2002

Acknowledgements to the First Edition

Many people inside and outside the City contributed to this book. Those who found time in their busy schedules to talk to me about present-day institutional equity investment include former colleagues, clients and competitors, in investment management, securities and investment banking. Several were also kind enough to read and comment on sections of the draft. I cannot name everyone who gave me the benefit of their knowledge and advice. I do, however, particularly wish to thank Philip Bradley, Jane Brook, Peter Constable, Jim Cox, Oliver Ellingham, Morfydd Evans, John Ford, Laura Hickman, Neil Honebon, Peter Lehmann, Brian Matthews, Graham Meek, Luke Nunneley, Tim Owen, Michael Rawlinson, John Richards, Chris Russell, Jonathan Simon and Alan Towers. Any opinions expressed in the text are entirely my own and not those of my informants. I am grateful to Flemings, my former employers, for allowing me continued use of the excellent Asset Management research library.

Among those who helped me, one person merits far more than a passing mention. If this book is a faithful reflection of the City's current modus operandi – as I believe it to be – it is due in large part to John Hatherly. John, a friend from stockbroking days in the 1970s, was an enthusiastic supporter of the project right from the start. Always ready with sensible advice and practical assistance, he was a constant source of encouragement. Our regular meetings allowed me to check both facts and perceptions with someone who remains actively involved in the cut and thrust of institutional investment and equity markets.

Last, but not least, I am indebted to a group of readers who fall into an important category I call 'intelligent laypersons'. Rennie Sinclair, Andrew Ellam and my wife, Gill, all read through the text, providing valuable feedback and preventing those (occasional) lapses into City jargon! I am also grateful to Richard Stagg, my publisher, for his consistent support and guidance throughout the writing process.

Preface to the First Edition

When I – nervously – entered the City from industry in 1974 it took me two years to work out why share prices fell after good results! The answer is, of course, 'expectations'. Shares are valued on what people think the future holds – not on what has happened. Investor psychology is a fascinating subject, if only because it is fundamental to an understanding of how to make money in the stock market. Equities are all about guessing other people's future reactions. In today's market, these 'other people' are almost invariably investment institutions.

As I progressed from investment analysis to fund management (and, in time, to investment banking) I came to realize that I was but a small cog in a gigantic machine dedicated to generating and disseminating these expectations. I dubbed it – purely for my own private purposes – 'the Great Expectation Machine'. The way it worked intrigued me and still does. Equity markets have changed dramatically since those cozy pre-Big Bang days. But, in essence, the way in which City institutions approach investment and analysts 'create' the expectations that fund managers need in order to function has not changed.

In writing this book I set myself the task of explaining in as simple and direct a manner as possible how all the separate but interrelated elements in 'the machine' fit together and work with each other. The large investment institutions (pension funds, insurance companies, unit trusts) are the source of the power that moves the cogwheels and shifts the levers. To an extent that few outside the City appreciate, they dominate the UK (and the US) stock market, both in terms of ownership and activity. Yet remarkably little has been written about these institutions, about how fund managers invest and the implications of their investment behaviour, on either side of the Atlantic. The average beginner's guide to stock market investment – of which there are at least 30 in the UK and literally hundreds in the US – accords them a passing reference, as if they were peripheral rather than central to the whole process. It is rather like trying to explain the Catholic church in terms of the priesthood, without mentioning the Pope, the Vatican and the cardinals! My purpose is not to replicate what many of these books already do extremely well but to build on what they contain. Anyone who has an elementary understanding of the City and its ways should be able to read what follows without difficulty.

I count myself fortunate that I was taught my investment analysis by Roger Nicholas, one of the early practitioners of equity research in London. His thoroughly conventional dress and manner belied an acute mind with a strong independent streak. In his analysis of companies he was fearless in his pursuit of managerial incompetence or evasion. As head of research, he exhorted us to accept nothing at face value, to analyze companies without fear or favour. Somewhat improbably, he had adopted the battle cry of the 1960s' protest movement as his own. 'Tell it like it is!', he urged us, 'Tell it like it is!' In writing this book I have tried to follow his instruction. The objective is to analyze the City as it really operates, not how it purports or is perceived to operate – but 'like it is'.

Conscious of gender sensibilities – and so as not to offend the rising number of women in professional City jobs – I must make it clear that, throughout the text, 'he' should be regarded as synonymous with 'he or she'. 'He' is merely a convenience.

Tony Golding
August 2000

Introduction: What this book is all about

Britain is a country with an exceptionally large and well-developed 'financial tail' that frequently wags an underweight 'industrial dog'. The City of London is such a dominant and pervasive part of UK life that it is easy to forget that this is not the natural order of things. No other nation has so successful a financial sector – and in no other nation is the financial centre so powerful relative to the rest of the economy.

How did the City achieve this status? Exactly how do the big investment institutions exercise their controlling influence over British industry and commerce? Does the City still have a life of its own or, in a reversal of history, does the overwhelming influence of the American investment banks mean that London has become little more than a colonial outpost of Wall Street?

This book tackles these broad issues and, through a step-by-step analysis of the current institutional investment and investment banking scene, offers answers to several important questions including:

- What motivates institutional fund managers and how do they make their decisions?
- What do investment analysts actually do and why do they get paid so much for doing it?
- What is it about companies that turns institutional investors on – and off?
- Why does the City neglect smaller companies?
- What is the 'New Industrial Compact' between 'UK plc' and the City, and how does it work?

The City: inside the great expectation machine is aimed at anyone who is already conversant with the absolute basics of stock market investment and City practice but wants to know much, much more. Chapter 1 looks at how the City got to where it is now, focusing on the remarkable rise of the investment institutions who control 75 per cent of the UK equity market and the steady invasion of the Wall Street investment banks. In Chapter 2 we explain how institutional fund managers view the assets – mostly equities and bonds – in which they invest and the way in which they determine their expectations of the returns these assets might produce. For those unfamiliar with modern financial terminology and usage, Chapter 3 explains the arcane and often confusing vocabulary of what we call CitySpeak. (A glossary at the end of the book provides a quick reference guide.) Chapter 4 analyzes the huge money flows that continue to pour into investment institutions, looking at the sources of those funds – pensions, insurance policies, unit trusts – and the impact they have on the behaviour of the fund managers who run them. Chapter 5 moves on to the actual practice of investment management – the shape of the industry, the way in which fund managers make their investment decisions and the pressures on them to perform. Building on the analysis done so far, Chapter 6 provides answers to several of the critical questions just posed: What do fund managers want from companies? How do companies communicate with their institutional shareholders, especially with regard to the all-important task of managing expectations? And what are the reasons for the difficulties experienced by smaller quoted companies? Chapter 7 covers the securities industry, concentrating on the dramatic change in the role of the investment analyst during the last decade, from independent commentator to promoter. Chapter 8 summarizes several key themes and draws some conclusions on the current state of the investment management industry.

Readers will approach this book with different degrees of knowledge and areas of interest. Some may find the content of the earlier chapters covers ground with which they are already familiar. Based on over two decades of first-hand experience, *The City: inside the great expectation machine* offers everyone, whatever their knowledge base, genuinely fresh and original insights into the closed and closely connected worlds of institutional investment and investment banking.

From then to now

How the tail came to wag the dog

- Is the City still 'the City'?

- Compartments and connections

- Making the grade in international financial services

- Never underestimate the power of history

- The key role of the outsider

- How the Euromarkets saved the City

- The remarkable rise of the investment institutions

- How the Street swept over the City

- International equities and the Anglo-Saxon effect

Take a walk to Broadgate one cool summer's day. Milling around in cafés and bookshops you will find Italian derivative traders, American corporate financiers, Lebanese arbitrageurs, Dutch brokers, Moroccan rocket scientists, German bond salesmen, Swiss equity market makers, Japanese swappers and even the stray Essex forex boy. There is no other financial centre in the world with a talent pool to match that of the City.

(Margareta Pagano, 'A matchless talent pool',
Financial News, 14 June 1999)

Is the City still 'the City'?

To the great majority of outsiders the City of London is a monolith. It may contain a variety of activities – many with a minimal or non-existent public profile – but these are viewed as interrelated and interconnected. After all, how often do the media make use of that convenient phrase 'the City view' in the context of interest rates, stock market prices, exchange rates and other key economic variables?

'City' reality is very different from perception. The diversity of activities is much greater than commonly supposed. More important still, these activities are highly fragmented and compartmentalized. The image of the monolith needs to be replaced by a different image: a series of circles of different sizes, some overlapping, some just touching, many making no contact at all. For example, institutional investors (principally pension funds, insurance companies and unit trusts) invest in the stock market using securities firms to buy and sell for them, so these activities clearly overlap. These same institutions may invest indirectly in the financing of, say, a power project in China which has been arranged by the project finance department of an investment bank. In terms of our image, the circles only touch in this instance. The project financiers do not sell the project to the investors – this is the job of others in the investment bank – but a relationship exists between the investors and the project finance team.

> The image of the monolith needs to be replaced by a different image: a series of circles of different sizes, some overlapping, some just touching, many making no contact at all.

But between many City activities there is no relationship at all. A trader in the equity market will know nothing of the workings of the London Metal Exchange (where world prices are set daily for the likes of copper and aluminium) let alone the Baltic Exchange, which is the pre-eminent international shipping services marketplace. Equally, participants in these specialized markets will have little knowledge of the job of a stock exchange market maker or an institutional equity salesman. There is no point at which these activities touch, even though they are functionally similar.

Given this degree of diversity, what then defines 'the City'? A precise definition is practically impossible. Certainly, there is an emphasis on wholesale (corporate and institutional) activity rather than retail (personal) financial services. The Bank of England, the Stock Exchange and Lloyd's of London are clearly part of the City but where do we place the lawyers and accountants who provide essential support services for City activity? They may have branches elsewhere and do much work that is unrelated to the City. For many journalists at the popular end of the media spectrum these definitional niceties are not a problem – 'City' is synonymous with pretty well anything financial (it has the additional merit of being a short word, which makes it ideal for headlines!).

Nor can 'the City' any longer be defined geographically, in terms of the area administered by the Corporation of London (the local authority responsible for 'the Square Mile'). Several of the largest investment institutions are not and have never been based in the City. Edinburgh is home to Standard Life, one of the largest insurance companies in the UK and a leading equity investor. Some firms of stockbrokers 'defected' to the fringes of the City in the early 1980s. Salomon Brothers, the US investment bank, chose in 1984 to move to a building next to Victoria Station in central London. A 1998 report commissioned by the Corporation of London sensibly conceded defeat on the geographical front. It conveniently defined 'the City' as covering all 'City-type' activities that take place in Greater London.

As a general rule, until the late 1980s, both domestic and foreign financial institutions preferred to have their London base inside the City proper where the UK merchant banks, insurance companies, stockbrokers and other key participants were located. The soaring rents of 1986/87, together with the need for larger offices and advances in communications technology, caused an exodus both westwards (to the West End of London) and eastwards (to Canary Wharf in Docklands). Many of the big investment banks are now located at Canary Wharf (Morgan Stanley and Crédit Suisse First Boston were founder members). Today 'the City' is a financial rather than a physical entity.

> The soaring rents of 1986/87, together with the need for larger offices and advances in communications technology, caused an exodus both westwards and eastwards.

The bit of the City that is visible to the world at large is the one talked about in the business pages of the quality newspapers, in which the emphasis is on macroeconomic trends and British quoted companies. News relating to UK companies and their share prices dominates because that is what is directly relevant to the great majority of readers, as investors or employees. How much press coverage is given to the City's role in the flotation of Polish Telecom or the financing package for an iron ore mine in India? None, except possibly deep inside the 'Companies & Markets' section of the *Financial Times*.

Investment banks consciously use their equity activities – because they are visible – as the 'shop window'. But behind the scenes lie many other City activities that have little or no public profile, which are often larger in scale and quite possibly more profitable. A good example is the Eurobond market (nowadays more properly called the market for 'international securities'). In short, it is important not to lose sight of the fact that the greater part of the City functions quietly out of the limelight – and that these 'invisible' operations are actually more important to its continuing prosperity.

Most of these 'invisible' operations are international in focus. In fact, it is this international orientation that truly defines the City, not the services it supplies to the UK domestic market. Much of what the City does has little or no connection with the British economy. Martin Taylor, the former chief executive of Barclays, neatly encapsulated this view in a tongue-in-cheek article for the *Financial Times* in which he suggested that:

> The best way to think about the City ... is essentially [as] an off-shore phenomenon, half-way between a Caicos Island and an oil rig.

('If only the City would secede from Europe', *Financial Times*, 23 December 1999)

As we shall see, the City's raison d'être has always been, and indeed still is, the provision of financial services to an international marketplace. It remains the largest centre for international financial transactions.

In this book we explore the workings of the equity market and the institutions that today dominate that market. Equity is the generic term for what in the UK are called 'ordinary shares' and in the US 'common stocks' (or mostly just 'stocks'). The two terms are used interchangeably. Equity is risk capital. It confers ownership rights but, in exchange for these, no guarantee of income (in the form of dividends) and certainly no commitment to repay the original sum invested. The investor has to take his chances on both counts. Bonds, by contrast, offer a reasonably high degree of assurance on both income and capital.

This book covers investment institutions and fund managers, securities firms and analysts, and the investment banks that today embrace so many of these equity-related activities. In all of these areas the international dimension is vitally important. We compare the City with Wall Street and also, to a lesser extent, with the equivalent centres in continental Europe.

Compartments and connections

Figure 1.1 shows the essential relationships between the parts of the City covered in this book (with the addition of venture capital). The four boxes

Figure 1.1 The Institutional Equity Nexus

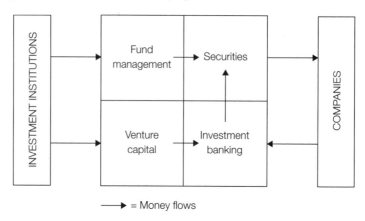

⟶ = Money flows

are all connected by the use of equity and rely on funds that derive from an institutional source, principally pension funds, insurance companies and unit trusts (flowing in from the left-hand side of the page). The lines linking the boxes show the major business flows between them. This group of connected activities is the 'Institutional Equity Nexus'. Nowadays all four activities represented by the boxes can often be found, together with many others, inside a single organization. This organization was once called a merchant bank but is now called an investment bank.

The essential direction of flow is from the investment institutions to companies, via the City, which acts as an intermediary. Within the City, the prime movers, who shape and influence the Institutional Equity Nexus, are the fund managers who invest in quoted companies. The funds they manage on behalf of the investment institutions flow 'downstream' into securities, investment banking and venture capital. Quite often, institutions manage their investments themselves so that, in practice, there is a considerable overlap between the box marked 'fund management' and the bar marked 'investment institutions'. It is the fund managers (also called asset managers, investment managers or portfolio managers) who determine the volume and the direction of these flows. They buy new issues sponsored by investment banking using the securities function. A venture capital firm floating an investment on the stock market does so with the help of both investment banking and securities but relies on fund managers to buy the shares.

We look closely at these flows and analyze the often subtle relationships between the functions. We focus on the investment institutions and fund management, in view of the 'engine room' role they fulfil in the Institutional Equity Nexus. The emphasis is on how things work in practice, not how they are purported to work, or how the media would have us believe they work.

Surprisingly perhaps to an outsider, many operations within an investment bank are quite compartmentalized. In part, this is due to the existence of 'Chinese walls', designed to ensure information flows between departments do not confer an unfair advantage. Some areas will, of necessity, be in regular contact, such as fund management and securities. But managing an equity portfolio has nothing in common with, for example, the provision of specialized, tax-driven leasing services to companies. Investment bankers, except at a senior level, rarely have more than a superficial understanding of fund management. Fund managers usually know nothing about investment in unquoted companies (known as venture capital or, increasingly, by the US term, 'private equity') even though this activity may be part of the same investment banking organization, perhaps operating from another floor of the same building. This will seem particularly odd as they are performing exactly the same function: fund managers invest in public companies, venture capitalists in private. The process may be different but the objectives are the same – maximizing the value of the investment. Yet there is no reason for them to communicate.

> The emphasis is on how things work in practice, not how they are purported to work, or how the media would have us believe they work.

These activities are separate because they serve distinct, specialized requirements. 'The City' is shorthand for myriad products and markets. One fundamental reason for this compartmentalization is the divide in terms of customer base between institutional and corporate clients. As Figure 1.1 shows, the City performs a valuable 'middleman' role between these two types of customer, between the providers of capital and the consumers of capital. The result of this divide is that some activities sell a range of products to the institutional (investment and banking) community while others face the corporate world, marketing an equally diverse range of specialized products to companies, governments and similar organizations.

Within this diverse set of services niche product areas abound. A typical one is securities lending, in which a bank takes a fee for arranging for market makers who have 'gone short' (sold stock they do not own, in the hope of buying it back at a lower price) to borrow that stock from an institutional investor for a payment. All these specialized product areas are constantly changing, as a consequence of shifting client needs, innovation and changes in the external environment. Today's niche can quickly become tomorrow's commodity business, or (like securities lending) it can stay as a niche because it is too small to attract more than a few suppliers. It can grow but become less profitable as competitors move in and drive down margins. Or it can disappear suddenly as a result of a change in the regulatory environment, as when, in 1979, the business of trading in the investment currency premium (known colloquially as 'the dollar premium') vanished overnight when Margaret Thatcher abolished exchange controls. An investment bank will seek to cover many or all of these specialized areas but only a few senior people will be capable of taking an overall view of the total product range, let alone possessing a detailed operational under-standing of each one.

It should be clear by now that there is no single 'City view', in the literal sense of a collective view of all of the City. The 'City view' favoured by the media is the view of a particular segment of the City – for example, econ-omists employed by investment banks (or other organizations) on the course of interest rates, or strategists (as they are now known) in those same investment banks on future trends in equity markets.

> Even today, in a global financial marketplace that is moving rapidly towards the American model – current City practice is still influenced by what has gone before.

From the standpoint of the City there is absolutely nothing new about this degree of specialization. It has always operated in this way. London honed its skills during the 19th century on the back of Britain's position as the dominant power in world manufac-ture and trade. An impressive study by two historians charts the decline in the UK's industrial and trading might in the final quarter of the 19th century and the simultaneous emergence of the City as the financial capital of the world, commenting on the way it was organized at the end of that period.

> By 1900 [the City] had grown spectacularly and was populated mainly by hordes of specialists each making their own peculiar contribution to an increasingly complex process that few understood in the round.

(Cain and Hopkins, 2001, p. 126)

As the quote makes clear, the City of London had, by the turn of the cen-tury, developed its own unique and successful modus operandi. Even today, in a global financial marketplace that is moving rapidly towards the Amer-ican model – spearheaded by an advance guard of well-financed, aggres-sive and ambitious American investment banks – current City practice is still influenced by what has gone before.

Making the grade in international financial services

The City of London is the pre-eminent centre for international financial services of all kinds. (The term 'cross-border' is also widely used, meaning that
at least one end of a transaction is located outside the UK.) No one can
doubt the City's success, with a growth rate in the last 25 years that has
been well above that for the UK domestic economy. Nor can the City's contribution to the British economy be denied. Figures cited by Roberts and
Kynaston in their book, *City State* (2001), show that it accounts for about
3 per cent of GDP but contributes a disproportionate 7.5 per cent of total
tax revenues. London is one of the three most important global financial
centres. However, New York and Tokyo exist primarily to serve their large
domestic markets.

New York is ahead of London by most measures – size of markets, volume
of transactions and so on – but it is smaller by at least two significant measures in the context of equities: value of funds under management and the
volume of trading in non-domestic equities. According to the Thomson
Financial Investor Relations 2001 *International Target Cities Report*, London
is a larger centre for institutional investment management than New York,
though only just. This comparison is, however, more than a little flattering to
London and does scant justice to the scale and strength of the US asset management industry. Fund management in the US is much more dispersed
geographically than in the UK. New York is an important but not dominant
centre – it accounts for perhaps a quarter of US institutional assets. Boston,
in particular, is home to Fidelity, the largest US equity investor, and several
other large asset management firms and insurance companies. In foreign
equity trading, the City retains a market-leading position. Typically, a fund
manager wanting to buy, say, Siemens or Ericsson, may prefer to deal in London rather than in Frankfurt or Stockholm. However, the City's position in
this business is eroding as other centres improve their skills.

How substantial is the City's commitment in terms of resources? And is
it possible to quantify London's growth rate and competitive position
versus the other world financial centres? Fortunately, there is a reasonable
amount of material available that goes some way towards answering both
these questions. International Financial Services, London (the new name for
what used to be called, rather oddly, British Invisibles) publishes regular
reports on the UK's position in international financial markets. IFSL has a
brief to promote the international activities of UK-based financial institutions and professional and business services. Additionally, during the
1990s, the Corporation of London, concerned by 'location leakage' from

the Square Mile and the increased competitive threat from Frankfurt and Paris, commissioned several reports on the City's position and prospects.

Lombard Street Research especially has done some valuable work for the City Corporation on this subject. Employment in 'City-type' activities in London in 1995 was estimated (in a 1998 report) at 250,000, split 195,000 in the Square Mile and 55,000 in Canary Wharf and the West End. (Nearly all those who work in the City commute there daily: the Square Mile has only 11,000 residents.) Other centres, notably Edinburgh, probably employ a further 25,000. By 2000 City-type employment was estimated to have risen to over 300,000, though it has since declined with the downturn in financial markets. Although City-type employment has risen consistently since the early 1970s there were two big surges, in the 1980s and again in the mid-1990s. The Corporation of London estimates that around 45 per cent of City jobs are in firms whose ultimate owner-ship lies outside the UK. A report for the Corporation in 2000 estimated that non-UK European Community firms accounted for 14 per cent of employment – which leads to the unsurprising conclusion that the predominant non-domestic City employers are American.

> The reason for the strength of international financial services is the increasing internationalization of production and investment, reflecting the global trend towards deregulation and free markets.

What proportion of this workforce is concerned solely or primarily with servicing international clients? This is an extremely difficult question to answer, if only because some jobs involve selling to both overseas and domestic clients (this would be true of investment banking advisory work, for instance). The only clue lies in an estimate made by a report for the City Corporation by the Centre for Economics and Business Research in 2000 which estimated that just under a fifth of City-type jobs were dependent on customers in other European Community economies. At a guess, adding in the rest of the world would push this figure above 50 per cent and perhaps as high as 70 per cent. London's usage by other European countries reflects the large proportionate share of City-type services in the British economy.

The Lombard Street Research report *Growth Prospects of City Industries*, published in 1998, made some interesting calculations on the growth rate the City has enjoyed since the 1970s, which help to explain why it has been such a successful part of the British economy. Since 1945 the worldwide growth rate for financial services output is estimated at 5 per cent per annum. But *international* financial services output has grown faster over the same period, at perhaps 7 to 8 per cent annually (which implies domestic financial services growth of only 4 per cent per annum). The reason for the strength of international financial services is the increasing internationalization of production and investment, reflecting the global trend towards deregulation and free markets. This, in turn, has generated an increased demand for a diverse range of financial services that are needed to 'oil the wheels' of trade and the movement of capital. Over the past 25 years the UK's output of international financial services – predominately from the City – has been growing by at least 7 per cent a year in real terms. Full credit to the City for retaining its historically high market share over the past three decades, but let us not forget that it happens to be a participant in one of the 20th century's major, long-term growth industries.

Drawing on a variety of sources, IFSL has been making a regular assessment of the City's competitive position since 1989. It is a long way from being comprehensive but does indicate a British view – rather than the view of an independent organization – of market shares in several key areas (see Table 1.1).

Each year IFSL also produces what it calls the 'City' table, with the aim of showing the net overseas earnings of the UK financial sector. The figure is, as one would expect, massively positive: a surplus of £31.1 billion in 2000. The UK records a larger surplus in trade in financial services than any other nation, well ahead of Switzerland, the US and Germany.

Table 1.1 UK share of certain international financial markets

	UK	USA	Japan	France	Germany
Cross-border bank lending (March 2001)	20%	10%	11%	6%	9%
Foreign equities turnover (2000)	48%	36%	–	–	6%
Foreign exchange dealing (April 2001)	31%	16%	9%	3%	5%
Derivatives turnover:					
exchange traded (2000)	8%	43%	5%	8%	15%
over-the-counter (April 2001)	36%	18%	3%	9%	13%
Insurance net premium income (1998):					
marine	19%	13%	13%	5%	12%
aviation	31%	23%	3%	14%	3%
International bonds (2001):					
primary market	60%				
secondary market	70%				

Source: International Financial Markets in the UK, IFSL, November 2001

Never underestimate the power of history

The City of London has been a success story for two centuries. How did it achieve and retain its leading position in international financial services? Wall Street, a significantly larger financial centre located in the world's dominant economy, has been a potential challenger since the early 1900s. Amsterdam, Berlin, Zurich, Frankfurt and Paris have all had aspirations to overtake London at one time or another – the last two still harbour such ambitions. As ever, there are many reasons. Several are rooted in history. Some are due to chance (for example, the fact that London sits in the European time zone, an important advantage over New York, and the use of the English language, a distinct attraction in an American-dominated industry).

> Originally, exporters went to their local bank to raise cash in exchange for the bill but often found them reluctant to provide them with cash, or were only prepared to do so after taking a large discount from the sum due.

It was after the Napoleonic wars that the City first achieved pre-eminence in international trade. The war removed Amsterdam as a threat and also drove continental merchants to settle in London. At this point, in the early 1800s, the City was essentially a city of merchants, who bought and sold physical commodities from all over the world. The financing of that trade as yet played a minor role. The trade that flowed through London had three main elements: a growing domestic demand for American, Asian and North European consumer goods and raw materials; a developing European market for the re-export of American and Asian products; and a rapidly expanding outlet for British manufactured goods in the protected markets of the British Empire. A high proportion of world trade either entered Britain or was shipped via London. This pivotal position was reinforced during the Victorian era as the international economy 'took off'. By 1870 international trade was five times larger than it had been in 1840.

The need to finance this trade grew naturally out of the City's involvement in this elaborate system of buying and selling globally. Before the emergence of an effective international banking system, exporters used a financial instrument that had evolved over centuries called a 'bill of exchange' to ensure that they received payment. This system of payment allowed them to receive a high proportion of the money due to them in advance of delivery of the goods. A bill is a promise to pay a certain sum on a particular date. Originally, exporters went to their local bank to raise cash in exchange for the bill but often found them reluctant to provide them with cash, or were only prepared to do so after taking a large discount from the sum due. Clearly, the bank had to take the risk that the importer might not pay.

Smaller merchants began to ask larger merchants to guarantee (or 'accept') their bills for them. This made sense as, in their role as traders, often specializing in a particular part of the world, they were in a good position to assess the credit standing of the importer. These larger merchants made their money by charging a percentage acceptance commission on the value of the bill. Once it had been guaranteed by an 'accepting house', the exporter could sell the bill for cash. Soon the accepting houses had taken over the business of trade finance from the banks and, over time, they evolved from pure merchants into 'merchant bankers', a term that only came into common usage in the 1890s. (In Chapter 3 we see how 'merchant banks' evolved into 'investment banks'.)

By the late 19th century, London's pivotal position in world trade had been eroded by the US and Germany, but it had secured for itself the leading position in the financing of that trade. The majority of the industrialized world financed its exports and imports through sterling-denominated bills drawn on London, even though much of that trade no longer passed through London or had any connection with Britain. The accepting houses at the centre of this system of short-term trade finance were firms that had originated as merchants, often merchants who had come from overseas to do business in London with their native country. (Firms of foreign origin, who often retained strong family ties and an associated intelligence network in the 'old country' were, after all, much better placed to assess local creditworthiness than an Englishman.)

By 1900 the leading names among the accepting houses were Kleinworts, Brown Shipley, Morgans, Barings, Schroders, Rothschilds and Hambros. Although they now operated worldwide, the traditional geographical specialization often remained important. For instance, apart from Germany, Schroders also focused on the fast-growing US economy, where it supplied credit to many of the larger New York-based sugar refiners who needed to import supplies from Cuba.

It was but a small step for these firms to move on from the provision of (short-term) trade finance to the provision of (long-term) capital for governments and companies – generically referred to as 'corporate finance'. The accepting houses entered the business of raising money for foreign governments, and subsequently foreign companies (especially railway ventures), with energy and enthusiasm. David Kynaston, in the first volume of his comprehensive and detailed history of the City of London, neatly summarizes the background to this development.

Although Paris to the end of the 1860s offered keen competition, London during the third quarter of the century consolidated and immeasurably strengthened its position as the world's leading international capital market, providing a string of foreign loans to capital-hungry states seeking to enjoy the fruits of scientific progress and industrialisation. British overseas investments, some £200m in the mid 1850s, increased about fivefold over the next twenty years and, in conjunction with the permanent effects of the railway boom, a fully-fledged rentier class was born.

(Kynaston, 1994, p. 167)

Originally an exercise carried out by an accepting house on its own, by the 1860s the business of 'loan contracting' (as it was called) for foreign governments had become too large for any single house and syndicates were formed for each issue. In contrast to the low-profile, steady business of acceptance credits, raising foreign loans was a variable but glamorous activity. It was also highly profitable and discouraged the accepting houses from seeking comparable business in the UK domestic market, where the issues were generally small and viewed as high risk and low return. This situation was mirrored by the stock exchange, where the emphasis was equally on government stocks and overseas issues (foreign railways became a favourite in the second half of the 19th century). British industrial shares were consigned to a 'miscellaneous' category, a nomenclature that speaks volumes about City attitudes of the time! Periodically during the 19th century the City was accused of neglecting British industry in favour of foreign business (a familiar, and recurrent, theme in the 20th century).

The key role of the outsider

It is not difficult to identify the advantages the City has, largely as a consequence of its history, over its international rivals: a pool of skilled labour, political stability, its location in an 'international', capital city (compare, for example, Frankfurt, a much smaller city which feels 'provincial'), the use of English, time zone location, an effective legal and regulatory environment and so on. But, above all else, the one thing that has enabled it to prosper over two centuries is the City's willingness to adapt and its capacity to absorb new ideas and new techniques. In other words, its 'openness'. The history of the City, and the chief reason for its remarkable resilience over time, is one of continuous self-renewal, not from within but from without.

Frequently this injection of outside talent has been foreign. Such waves of immigration have occurred roughly every generation, effectively starting with Schroders (from Hamburg) and Rothschilds (from Frankfurt via Manchester) in 1800–1809. The backgrounds were mixed. Germans (both Jew and gentile) have been an important source of 'new blood', as have Huguenots. Alexander Kleinwort was a church-going German who had spent time in Cuba and realized there were big opportunities in financing the sugar trade. Cazenove, the archetypal London 'establishment' stockbroking partnership (until its incorporation in April 2001), is of Huguenot origin. Later in the century Americans, such as George Peabody who founded the City branch of what became J.P. Morgan, became an important source of fresh talent. Firms with foreign antecedents often 'imported' young men from their home country to work in London as clerks and translators, so giving the City a strong international flavour. In the 1890s Schroders employed twice as many Germans as Englishmen.

> The history of the City, and the chief reason for its remarkable resilience over time, is one of continuous self-renewal, not from within but from without.

There are distinct parallels with today's City, as the American and continental European investment banks bring in able individuals from all over the world to work in London, usually for a few months or a few years but sometimes permanently. In many of these organizations – and especially the concentration of US banks at Canary Wharf – the majority of the professionals employed there are not British. For the US investment banks, London is the focal point of their pan-European business, typically employing 80 per cent of the total headcount. Due to the activities of these banks the City retains the international atmosphere that has characterized it for two centuries.

The City's willingness to absorb outsiders was not confined to foreigners but extended to compatriots of humble origin, often from the provinces. A good example is Samuel Montagu, the son of a Liverpool watchmaker, who, after gaining experience in the City, founded his own firm in 1853. Paradoxically, although from the earliest times the City had been dominated by a few families who looked after their own, the importance of fresh talent and new ideas was recognized. Change generally occurred through new entry rather than via an injection of new blood into existing organizations. But, while new entrants were not resisted, they were often resented, particularly if they threatened to undermine the existing business structure through innovation and/or price competition.

As so often happens in an essentially tolerant environment, within two or three generations the outsider is absorbed into the host society and becomes an integral part of it. This is what happened to the immigrants into the City, a process that was accelerated at the end of the 19th century by mutual self-interest. The rent rolls of the aristocracy were falling and they needed access to an alternative source of income. Fortunately, stockbroking especially had a requirement for those with the right social background and schooling to sell securities to the rich and well connected, as well as to the solid, prosperous Victorian and Edwardian upper middle and middle class who, for the most part, lived on income from interest and dividends. It was this rentier class that formed the backbone of the investing public. This was the group that the merchant bankers relied on to act as the natural 'takers' of foreign government and other issues, bought through a stockbroker. The City provided (in Kynaston's words) 'well-paid, light duty' jobs. In return, merchant bankers, and especially stockbrokers, acquired the respectability and status that had eluded them so far. They bought land and country houses, married into the aristocracy and achieved social acceptance.

The net result of all this was that 'the City' became synonymous with solidity, social status and respectability, a situation that persisted into the 1980s. The term 'the stockbroker belt' (conjuring up visions of substantial detached houses surrounded by greenery within commuter distance of London) was in widespread usage over this period. More recently, as the investment institutions came to dominate stock exchange business, the concept of a 'stockbroker' has had to be redefined, a process that came to a head in the freewheeling 1980s. In today's environment, the word no longer throws up an image of a middle-aged man in pinstripes and a bowler hat dispensing sage investment advice to well-heeled private clients. For the investment banks, traditional private client business has come to be regarded as a small but profitable backwater.

During the interwar period the City suffered from the contraction in international trade, which led to lower foreign loan activity, together with increased competition from New York and Paris. Domestic equity issues became relatively important and several merchant banks became involved as promoters of new issues. As other markets closed, the City became more and more dependent on the Empire for overseas business. The City that emerged from World War II was little different from the City of the 1930s – smaller and much less international than in its heyday, and essentially dependent on the Empire and the sterling area. And, at the beginning of the 1970s, even this role was under threat. However, by a remarkable stroke of good fortune, a substantial new market had already started to develop, basing itself on London. As Cain and Hopkins put it graphically and succinctly:

> As the good ship sterling sank, the City was able to scramble
> aboard a much more seaworthy young vessel, the Eurodollar.

(Cain and Hopkins, 2001, p. 641)

In terms of wider English society, between the wars and until the 1960s, the City retained its pivotal position in what Cain and Hopkins call 'gentlemanly capitalism'. It remained socially cohesive, with ties based on education and family, an emphasis on personal relationships and an unspoken but universally accepted system of shared values. But the rise of the institutions forced the merchant banks and the stockbrokers to extend their recruitment horizons beyond family and the public schools. Institutional clients were far more demanding in their approach to investment. Good breeding, in the absence of anything else, was no longer a sufficient qualification. True to its history, the City adapted once again, by recruiting bright young men (and a few women) from grammar school and industrial backgrounds to work as investment analysts and fund managers as well as in a variety of other roles.

But, while the City of the 1960s and 1970s successfully absorbed fresh talent and adjusted its ideas, certain structures had become ossified. This applied particularly to stockbroking which had effectively, as a result of a vote by the members of the stock exchange in 1912, chosen to preserve itself as a 'cottage industry' for all time, by imposing fixed commissions, ensuring the strict separation between brokers and jobbers (now called market makers), retaining a partnership structure and restricting new entry. Additionally, no outside firm was permitted to own a stockbroking partnership, preventing the merchant banks with their superior resources from entering a business that was, in modern business terms, a means of securing direct access to their suppliers. On Wall Street, as we explain in Chapter 3, there was never any such division: the investment banks sold and traded securities as an integral part of their business.

> Institutional clients were far more demanding in their approach to investment. Good breeding, in the absence of anything else, was no longer a sufficient qualification.

The straitjacket that the City had placed itself in – motivated by undiluted self-interest – inhibited innovation and adaptation. By the early 1980s the Bank of England and the government had became seriously concerned at the obvious mismatch between a newly resurgent City and the stock exchange's cozy Edwardian timewarp. This situation could not be allowed to continue if London were to retain its primary position in international financial transactions. The result was the City's 1986 'Big Bang', when all these barriers came down (further details in Chapter 7).

How the Euromarkets saved the City

We saw in the last section how the less vibrant and more inward-looking City that existed after 1918 began to change in the 1960s, for two main reasons. The first of these was the creation of the so-called 'Eurobond' market, pioneered and developed by outsiders but with the City of London as its base. The second, which is a principal subject of this book, is the emergence of the investment institutions as a potent force in UK securities markets. Both developments are absolutely crucial to an understanding of the modern-day City.

The Eurobond market revitalized the City, allowing it to regain its historic role as the place where overseas companies and governments came to raise money. In doing so, it revived the City's function as a supplier of wholesale financial services to an international market. By contrast, the emergence of pension funds, insurance companies and unit trusts as significant investors is not solely a British phenomenon – it happened in the US a little earlier and on a larger scale. Rather than create a new business, it forced the established merchant banks and stockbroking firms to adapt their existing operations to servicing a new, and much more demanding, customer base.

The 'Eurodollar' market first emerged in the late 1950s. It arose because European exporters to the US had ended up with surplus dollars. If the exporting company decided to hold these dollars in an account outside the US for future use (rather than convert them into the domestic currency or use them to buy American products) they became 'Eurodollars'. The same principle could be applied to other currencies – Euromarks or Euroyen for example – but, in practice, the big accumulation of deposits in Europe was of dollars. These large-scale deposits, placed in European banks or the European branches of American banks, represented a new source of funds for lending, just at a time when the world economy was starting to recover. This process was helped along by a US Federal Reserve regulation that imposed ceilings on the interest earned by US bank deposits during the 1960s, making Eurodollar deposits relatively more attractive.

Initially, the Eurodollar market was a lending market – from banks to companies – but it soon developed into a market for capital as the banks realized that the techniques used for lending could be used to tap financial institutions and wealthy individuals directly as a source of capital for companies. For longer-term loans of substantial size the banks came together in an ad hoc 'club' in which several participated, as no single bank was prepared to stand the whole exposure. This became known as a 'syndicated loan'. The approach used in arranging a syndicated loan, with one bank taking the lead and procuring other banks (often in several different countries) to participate, could just as well be applied to procuring international investors. This extension of the banks' function, from straight lending to acting as an intermediary, was conceptually nothing new, especially for the US investment banks, but turned out to be highly significant. It gave birth to the Eurobond market.

A bond, as we consider in detail in the next chapter, is merely a piece of paper issued by a borrower (government or corporate) that promises to pay regular interest over its life and return the sum invested at the end of that period. Bond markets exist in domestic economies. However, companies and governments wanting to raise bond finance, particularly in smaller economies, can often find that the local investor base is too small or simply unprepared to provide finance on the scale required, and/or at a price (the rate of interest charged) that is acceptable. In the austerity that characterized the post-1945 period, what bond borrowing there was tended to be in domestic markets. The Eurobond market provided borrowers with immediate access to an international investor base. Once again, the US authorities gave the nascent market an (unintended) push in 1963, by instituting a tax that discouraged foreign companies from raising bond finance in the US. They then compounded this by imposing a withholding tax (which took 30 per cent off the interest paid at source) on overseas investors in US bonds. (This tax existed until 1984.) Eurobonds, by contrast, paid interest without any deduction. Borrowers and investors alike turned naturally to the Eurobond market.

> For longer-term loans of substantial size the banks came together in an ad hoc 'club' in which several participated, as no single bank was prepared to stand the whole exposure. This became known as a 'syndicated loan'.

These factors gave the Eurobond market a favourable initial start but they do not explain its subsequent success. The market has certain characteristics that mark it out from any other.

■ First and foremost, it is truly borderless. There is no physical market. Marketing of new issues and subsequent trading take place over the telephone. Many Eurobonds are listed on a stock exchange – London and Luxembourg are favourites – but this is merely a nominal listing, to meet the requirements of those institutional investors who can only invest in listed securities. Most of the activity occurs in London but, particularly with modern communications, the business could be conducted from any significant financial centre. It is an 'offshore' market in the sense that it is a 'place' in which borrowers and investors choose to be brought together by international banks, outside their normal home market jurisdiction.

- Eurobonds lie outside any domestic regulatory environment. The market is self-regulating, with the approval of several domestic regulatory authorities on the basis that it meets national standards. This testifies to the fact that it is considered to run efficiently, using a settlement mechanism it created for itself outside the existing stock exchange-based systems. For borrowers, the Euromarkets represent a relatively light regulatory regime in terms of disclosure, certainly compared with the rigours of the US Securities and Exchange Commission (known universally as the 'SEC').

- The market effectively tapped a new investor base, initially in Europe and subsequently worldwide. Eurobonds are 'bearer' bonds which means that the interest is paid without any deduction to whoever presents the bond (or, more accurately, the tear-off 'coupon' from the bond) to the paying bank. Bearer bonds permit complete anonymity – there is no register of holders. In the beginning, the typical buyer was an individual, probably a middle-class professional (the 'Belgian dentist' of Eurobond mythology) seeking to avoid tax. Today, the principal buyers are investment institutions and they account for 90 per cent of Eurobond ownership. For them, the tax issue is more a matter of convenience. A pension fund that is exempt from tax avoids the bother of reclaiming it. However, some of these institutions – particularly the Swiss banks – manage large funds on behalf of private clients for whom anonymity and 'tax minimization' are still priorities.

Who were the prime movers in the Eurobond market? And what have been the implications for London of its phenomenal growth? The first Eurobond was organized by S.G. Warburg for the company that built and operated the Italian motorways in 1963. True to the City's history, the innovator was an outsider. Siegmund Warburg came to Britain in 1934 as a refugee and founded what was to become S.G. Warburg. One of the main reasons for Warburg's success in this field was that several of his partners were, like him, immigrant financiers who had been active in the international bond market in the 1920s and 1930s. A good number of foreign-owned international banks entered the new market with enthusiasm, from the continent and especially from the US. For the US commercial banks it represented a golden opportunity to do in Europe what legislation (the ground-breaking Glass–Steagall Act, which separated commercial from investment banking, of which more later) prevented them from doing at home.

London soon became the centre of the Eurobond market, reinforced by the natural preference of the Americans, who set up offices and sent over staff, for a familiar language and culture. In doing so, they and the other overseas banks were instrumental in recreating the dynamism that was the hallmark of the City before World War I. Characteristically, the London Stock Exchange ignored the new market (presumably because it felt that it could not possibly qualify as a real market in the absence of a trading floor!). None of the UK merchant banks was prepared to make a serious commitment to this new source of business – with the notable exception of Warburgs.

Together with the continental Europeans, the American banks soon assumed leadership of a market that (as Figure 1.2 demonstrates) has gone from strength to strength. Today the leaders in international bond issuance are Schroder Salomon Smith Barney (SSSB, part of Citigroup, the merger of Citibank and Travelers Corporation), Morgan Stanley, Deutsche Bank, J.P. Morgan Chase

> London soon became the centre of the Eurobond market, reinforced by the natural preference of the Americans, who set up offices and sent over staff, for a familiar language and culture.

Figure 1.2 Eurobond market new issue trend 1993–2001 ($bn equivalent)

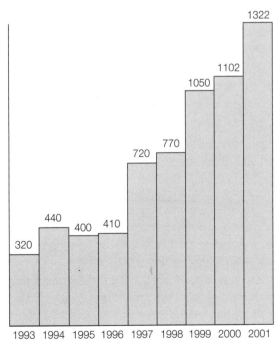

Source: International Securities Markets Association

(the new name for Chase, after its takeover of J. P. Morgan at the end of 2000), Merrill Lynch and Swiss-owned Credit Suisse First Boston (invariably abbreviated to CSFB).

Today reference is often made to the 'Euromarkets' or, more properly, the market for 'international securities'. The term 'capital markets' is also widely used, although, to be precise, it covers any market in which fresh money is raised by companies or governments from investors, via bonds, equity or any other financial instrument. In fact, the securities sold and traded on the Euromarkets are no longer just bonds but are much more diverse and complex, endeavouring to satisfy every conceivable corporate and investment need. In the 1990s the market extended its reach into international equities, as it became clear that, as with bonds, it made sense for the larger issuers of equity – particularly privatizations – to seek funds from institutional investors based outside their own country. We explain how this business works in Chapter 3.

The remarkable rise of the investment institutions

As we observed earlier, investment in Victorian and Edwardian times was essentially the preserve of private individuals. Institutional investors, especially insurance companies, did exist but on a small scale. In the late 19th century investment trusts became important, followed by unit trusts in the 1930s. Merchant banks developed fund management expertise in their private client departments, managing the money of the partners' families and friends. But the real growth started in the 1960s when pension funds took off and the life insurance industry reinvented itself as an investment medium. Then, in the 1980s, the abolition of exchange controls gave the fund management industry a further boost. Over the same period, both the UK and the US saw a massive shift in the investment preferences of these newly expanding institutions, from bonds to equities. The combined effect was the rapid emergence during the 1960s and 1970s of a stock market dominated by institutions rather than individuals which, as this book explores, has had profound economic consequences.

A 'snapshot' view of UK equity ownership in 1963, 1981 and 2000 shows the impact of these changes (Figure 1.3). In 1963 individuals owned 54 per cent of shares by value but by 1981 this figure was down to 28 per cent. According to the comprehensive survey published by the Office for National Statistics in June 2001 it reached a low of 16 per cent in December 2000. The number of private shareholders may have been swollen by privatizations and

Figure 1.3. UK equity market ownership by type of holder, 1963, 1981 and 2000

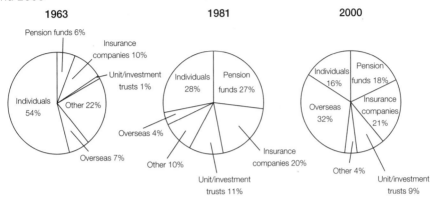

Source: Share Ownership, Office for National Statistics, June 2001

demutualizations but, of the 11.5 million individuals who are directly invested in UK equities, over two-thirds own shares in five companies or fewer.

The trend in the US has been similar but with two notable differences. First, the major shift towards institutional ownership of equities occurred later than in the UK, in the 1980s. Second, and much more important, even today, institutions account for around 55 per cent of the value of US equities, compared with an estimated 75 per cent institutional ownership in the UK. It is difficult to be more precise about UK equity ownership, as it is impossible to allocate the overseas holder segment – which is now very large – between institutions and individuals. What is clear is that the personal investor remains a significant force in the US, unlike the UK where for years he has been regarded as a dying breed in need of nurture and encouragement. Indeed, the US individual investor staged a revival during the 1990s, partly due to an influx of personal pension fund money (a development we cover in Chapter 4).

Beyond the Anglo-Saxon landscape the situation is rather different. Elsewhere, equity markets have historically been viewed as less important as a source of capital and, as a consequence, tend to be smaller in relation to the size of the economy. Equally – and clearly related to the size of equity markets – few other countries have experienced anything like the same growth in institutional assets, driven largely by the 'pensions revolution'. On top of this, investment managers in these countries have, in any event, generally favoured bonds over equities. Finally, in many non-Anglo-Saxon economies, the issue of equity ownership is confused by large family stakes, extensive corporate cross-holdings and residual government holdings. The net result is that local investment institutions typically hold

10–30 per cent of the domestic equity market, considerably lower than in the UK or the US. During the 1980s and 1990s, foreign institutional investors, mainly from the US and the UK, became big buyers of equities outside their home market and have become a major factor in continental Europe and in emerging markets. We trace these developments in more detail later in this chapter and in Chapter 4.

Even from this brief analysis, one salient fact emerges – the exceptional level of institutional shareholder power in the UK. In no other major economy – including the US – do investment institutions exert such a grip on the corporate sector as they do in the UK. It is not uncommon for large and medium-sized British companies to have 80 or 90 per cent institutional ownership (the equivalent figure in the US is 60–65 per cent).

Compounding the phenomenon of institutional dominance is the fact that investment decision-making is becoming more and more concentrated, as the size of fund management organizations increases and the absolute number declines. It is popularly supposed that institutional investors all react in the same ('herd-like') manner. This may be so but it does not work in quite the way most people imagine. Certain critical differences exist between funds in terms of their investment decision-making. Source of funds – where the money comes from – significantly influences investment behaviour. As we shall see in Chapter 4, the manager of a pension fund is subjected to a different set of pressures from those experienced by a unit trust manager. Equally, an insurance fund manager has constraints that mean that he has to adopt an investment strategy different from that of a pension fund manager.

> During the 1980s and 1990s, foreign institutional investors, mainly from the US and the UK, became big buyers of equities outside their home market and have become a major factor in continental Europe and in emerging markets.

The single overwhelming reason for this institutional hegemony is the emergence, particularly over the last 30 years, of a funded pension sector. 'Funded' is the key word here. In the US and the UK, occupational pension schemes are generally financed by contributions from employers and employees: this creates an identifiable 'pot' of money for investment. In other countries the pension bias is significantly less in favour of the funded approach. The alternative, in which pensions are paid from current income, creates no such 'pot' for investment. Funded pension schemes became significant institutional investors in the 1970s, grew very rapidly in the 1980s and continued to advance in the 1990s. The US and the UK, therefore, ended up with huge pools of money seeking an investment home. A professional fund management industry evolved to invest this money, together with support services such as those provided by the securities firms. London and Edinburgh fund managers have a long tradition of overseas investment, dating from the 19th century. When the opportunity to invest freely abroad returned in the early 1980s, they embraced it with enthusiasm and soon re-established a reputation for expertise in international fund management, attracting substantial funds from non-UK (mainly American) sources.

How the Street swept over the City

To anyone involved in investment banking, and especially those in the international equity and bond markets, Wall Street is 'the Street'. It is also used more broadly to refer to the securities industry – those firms (or 'houses') that act as intermediaries in the process of transferring capital between investors and corporate borrowers. Institutional equity investors talk about 'Street estimates', referring to the consensus earnings estimates of Wall Street (or London) analysts. Companies are sometimes described by analysts and investors as 'Street sensitive', when management is known to be desperately anxious to please Wall Street (in terms of meeting earnings forecasts and in every other way).

The Wall Street-based investment banks had a profound impact on global financial markets during the 1990s. For the securities and investment banking departments of the investment banks, this expansion into international markets was a deliberate – and well-publicized – strategy. Institutional investors based in the US also exerted a significant influence on non-domestic companies and markets during the decade, but this occurred quietly and without fanfare. For those US-based funds that moved heavily into international equities, this was a response to the strong flow of new money into their funds, combined, of course, with a perception of opportunity.

These two parallel trends have been mutually self-reinforcing. American institutions became more comfortable with the idea of foreign investment in the 1990s when there was an on-the-ground presence of a familiar Wall Street name. Equally, the big US securities houses felt more confident about pursuing business in foreign markets when they knew there was real interest in buying overseas stocks from investment clients they already serviced back home. And both benefited immeasurably from the long bull market on Wall Street, until it ended so abruptly when the 'New Economy' boom turned to bust.

The leading American investment banks, such as Goldman Sachs, Merrill Lynch and Morgan Stanley, enjoy a huge competitive advantage over investment banks based in the City or any of the other European financial centres – a large, active and innovative domestic market that, in several areas, provides them with levels of profitability above those prevailing in the rest of the world. To an extent, this reflects economies of scale. But, in certain parts of the business, fee levels on Wall Street are actually above those obtainable elsewhere, specifically in fund management, mergers and acquisition advice (invariably abbreviated to M&A) and new equity issues. Not only does this provide them with a substantial ongoing cash flow for investment elsewhere, but the variety, speed of change and innovative vigour of US markets has allowed these banks to hone their skills domestically before exporting them to the rest of the world.

US superiority in investment banking is also a product of history, specifically American history. Legislation passed in the New Deal era imposed a strict division between commercial and investment banking: between deposit taking and lending money to companies, and raising money for companies on the markets. These functions had to be carried out by separate organizations. The new structure was a reaction to the 1929 stock market crash. It was designed, in part, to protect depositors from having their funds used in (risky) securities transactions. In reality, the Banking Act of 1933 (universally known as Glass–Steagall) that imposed this division did the embryo US investment banks, operating mostly as subsidiaries of commercial banks, a big favour. As independent entities, they were able to create and mould the business free from the restraints of the traditional, slow-moving commercial banking culture. Put simply, the US investment banks wrote the rules while everyone else, struggling in the bowels of a commercial bank, was busy trying to work out what investment banking was all about! With such a head start, it is hardly a surprise that they remain so dominant.

> In certain parts of the business, fee levels on Wall Street are actually above those obtainable elsewhere, specifically in fund management, mergers and acquisition advice (invariably abbreviated to M&A) and new equity issues.

Global expansion for the American investment banks over the last decade of the 20th century was the result of a fortuitous coincidence of resources and opportunity. Despite the excesses of the 1980s, most of the major US investment banks emerged from the economic downturn of the early 1990s in good shape. This happened to coincide with the final defeat of Communism. For the next decade, the US liberal, laissez-faire model of capitalism swept all before it. Other forms of capitalism do exist. Charles Hampden-Turner and Fons Trompenaars (1993) analyze what they describe as 'the seven cultures of capitalism'. But stagnation in Japan, the reversal of the Asian capitalist growth machine and a lacklustre economic performance in Europe eroded the appeal of these alternative versions of capitalism. Then, in 2000, it became clear that the Americans had not, after all, succeeded in inventing the economic equivalent of a perpetual motion machine. Post the internet boom and post-Enron the 'US model' of capitalism is looking decidedly tarnished. None of this, however, has been sufficient to deflect the underlying trend. Today, the generally accepted rules of capitalism are American rules. Deregulation, reduced social taxes, and free and flexible markets for both capital and labour represent conventional economic wisdom. Economies everywhere continue to move, whether by choice or as a consequence of events, towards the 'US model'.

During the 1990s, the triumph of American values and American ways provided an ideal background for the Wall Street investment banks. What more powerful message can there be than: 'If you want to compete in an American-style marketplace and secure access to the vast pool of American capital, who better to service you than an organization that is imbued with these practices and epitomizes these values?' This message has been effective in the mature economies of Europe and in the vigorous economies of Asia. It has also been effective in all those developing countries that decided that, in the New World order, they should follow the capitalist path (motivated in part, no doubt, by a desire to open the capitalist purse!). Countries in Eastern Europe, Africa, Latin America and Asia deregulated, set up stock markets and sought advice on privatization and raising finance. The early 1990s saw an explosion of interest on the part of Western institutional investors in 'emerging markets', keen to participate in growth rates well above those in the mature economies.

All this provided the Wall Street houses with a vastly enhanced range of opportunities internationally during the 1990s, which they were not slow to exploit. At the same time, the victory of the 'US model' gave them both a strong selling point and a new-found confidence in their ability to market their skills internationally. They did not, however, have everything their own way. British investment banks, much more familiar than their continental counterparts with the Anglo-Saxon rules of the game, provided considerable competition, particularly on privatization (a UK invention). Confronted with the need to compete with American investment banks playing by American rules, the continental European banks bought London investment banking expertise. Deutsche Bank bought Morgan Grenfell, Swiss Bank Corporation acquired Warburgs, Dresdner Bank bought Kleinwort Benson, ING of the Netherlands bought Barings and Société Générale of France acquired Hambros. Of the traditional City merchant banks, only Schroders (stripped down to its fund management business after the sale of its investment banking business to Citigroup), Lazards and Rothschilds remain in independent hands. The two UK commercial banks with original aspirations in this field, Barclays and NatWest, sold most of their investment banking operations to CSFB and Bankers Trust (now Deutsche Bank) respectively.

The inexorable march of the legions of Wall Street can, in fact, be traced back to the early 1980s. However, not all the activities that we cover in this book have been equally affected. The London securities firms were first to succumb, following the long overdue Big Bang reforms in 1986. The business of researching and trading equities in London is today dominated by a handful of American and continental European investment banks, headed by UBS Warburg, Merrill Lynch, Deutsche Bank, Morgan Stanley, SSSB, CSFB and Goldman Sachs. (Interestingly, few of these chose to participate in the scramble to acquire London stockbroking firms that accompanied Big Bang, leaving it to the likes of Chase Manhattan and Citibank to buy – expensively – in haste and retreat soon afterwards.) Chapter 7 looks closely at the workings of the modern-day securities markets.

By contrast, fund management in the UK has been least affected by competition from across the Atlantic. In view of the size and strength of the American asset management business, it is surprising that the leading contenders were not tempted to try to penetrate the large UK pensions industry together with its well-developed unit trust sector. But, with a few exceptions, this did not happen. Some, like Morgan Stanley Asset Management, set up in London in the early 1980s but decided to concentrate on obtaining continental European money to manage rather than tackle the well-developed and competitive UK market. However, starting in the mid-1990s, American asset management firms have mounted a determined assault on the UK pension fund market, with considerable success. While sharing a common base, the structure and approach of the investment management industry in the UK and the US have diverged considerably over the last three decades. We explain the differences, and consider the implications, in Chapters 4 and 5. Chapter 6 considers how and why fund managers behave as they do.

> The inexorable march of the legions of Wall Street can, in fact, be traced back to the early 1980s. However, not all the activities that we cover in this book have been equally affected.

Extensive reference has been made to 'investment banking' in this chapter rather than another term that is in common currency, 'corporate finance'. This is deliberate. Like many financial terms, 'corporate finance' can mean different things to different people. It has a narrow definition in the UK and a wider one from an American perspective. The corporate finance department of a British merchant bank traditionally provides advice to companies on mergers and acquisitions (note that M&A also includes advice on the sale of companies) and raises equity for them on the London stock market. In an American investment bank corporate finance means something much broader. It is actually about the myriad ways in which companies can finance themselves. A US bank seeks to offer the finance director or treasurer of a corporate client a smorgasbord of financing options. Not only is the British conception of corporate finance too narrow, it is misleading because M&A advisory work does not, as such, involve finance (although it may have financing consequences). That is why throughout this book the term 'investment banking' is used instead. Where the context refers specifically to M&A work, we prefer the American term 'corporate advisory'. Investment banking is, admittedly, an ill-defined concept (we consider the various definitions in Chapter 3) but it does have the merit of encompassing a very wide range of activities, including corporate finance and corporate advisory.

In investment banking, the American contenders began to influence traditional City practice in the early 1980s. But it was not until the late 1990s that the persistence of the major US investment banks really started to pay off. They began to take significant corporate advisory work from the established UK merchant banks on what they regarded as their home ground, namely advising British companies on acquisitions, and were even more successful in continental Europe. Morgan Stanley's successful defence of Marks & Spencer against a hostile bid from the entrepreneur, Philip Green, in February 2000 was a landmark deal – the first time a significant British company had appointed an American investment bank to repel boarders. The Americans had earlier made greater inroads into the business of raising equity finance in the Euromarkets for those UK companies that had decided they wanted to tap an international, rather than a purely domestic, institutional investor base.

International equities and the Anglo-Saxon effect

Why have the Wall Street (and to a much lesser extent London) investment banking houses been so successful in international markets over the last decade? The principal reason should be clear by now. Quite apart from any other advantages, US investment bankers have achieved superiority because they are players in a game that they invented and others now want to join. It is as if the rest of the world suddenly decided it wanted to take on the Americans at baseball! The UK version of capitalism is an attenuated form of the US model (perhaps equivalent to the British school game of rounders?). Both countries have emphasized the role of capital markets, especially equity markets, in raising money for industry and commerce. This market-based approach is in stark contrast to the reliance on bank lending everywhere else.

But, as we noted in the previous section, there is another important subsidiary reason which is a reflection of the Anglo-Saxon model of capitalism – the existence of a large and rapidly growing pool of institutional money looking for things in which to invest, initially at home and then abroad. During the 1980s in the UK, and the 1990s in the US, investment managers started to invest in the equity of quoted companies outside their own country to a significant degree.

> During the 1980s in the UK, and the 1990s in the US, investment managers started to invest in the equity of quoted companies outside their own country to a significant degree.

The actual process whereby the US and the UK became the two key sources of investment in the equity of foreign companies is a three-stage one:

1 Lacking a funded pensions structure, the absolute amount of institutional money available for investment from continental Europe and elsewhere around the world (but not Japan) is much lower than in the US or the UK. Globally, the position of the US as a manager of institutional assets is overwhelming.

2 The Anglo-Saxon economic system emphasizes the use of equity raised on a stock market rather than debt. This built-in bias towards equity was reinforced in the inflationary 1970s when – following the so-called 'cult of the equity' – institutional investors in the US and the UK moved heavily out of bonds. Continental Europeans, the Japanese and others have retained their bank debt and bond culture (although it is changing). Institutional funds in these countries consequently contain low levels of equity.

3 With high levels of funds and high levels of equity investment in the Anglo-Saxon economies, it was only a matter of time before foreign equities became the focus of attention. In the UK, this occurred in the 1980s. US investors also started to look abroad in the 1980s, often using a British-based investment manager. But the American overseas equity boom really took off in the 1990s when asset managers began to invest directly in foreign markets.

The net result, in terms of equity investment in third markets, has been a 'double dominance' effect. So large are the sums involved that the actions of American and, to a lesser extent, British institutional investors have had, and do have, major consequences for national stock markets and individual companies.

The British foreign portfolio investment boom in the early 1980s reflected a hectic period of 'catch-up' after 40 years of enforced restraint. Holdings of overseas securities rose from £6.5 billion in 1978 to £30 billion in 1985. By that point the typical UK pension fund had 16 per cent of its assets in overseas equities. The current figure is around 22 per cent. By contrast, in 1988, US institutional investors were buying a modest $2 billion a year of foreign equities and the average pension fund commitment was under 3 per cent of assets. By the mid-1990s this figure had leapt to $60 billion a year. For all types of funds, the allocation by American institutions to non-US equities is now around 11 per cent (see Figure 1.4). The key point is that, while the UK is still much more oriented towards overseas investment, American investors are now the dominant external factor in all markets by virtue of the sheer size of the US fund management industry.

A small band of large US institutional investors have been in the vanguard of this trend. As part of this process, they have exported the US approach to equity investment, encouraged by the worldwide trend towards the 'US model'. Pressure is applied on management to improve

Figure 1.4 US and UK overseas equities as a percentage of institutional assets, 1985–2001

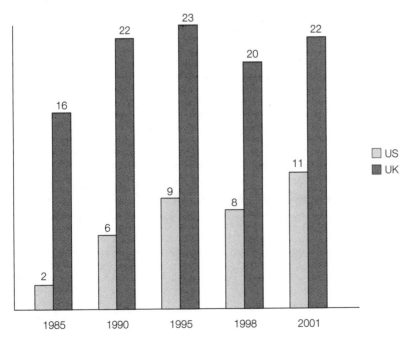

Note: For UK, pension funds only
Sources: Federal Reserve Board, WM Company

earnings via restructuring, cost-cutting, divestments and all the other things American companies do as a matter of course to enhance their status (and their stock price) in the eyes of Wall Street. With few exceptions, this has been done quietly and discreetly in the one-to-one meetings that all large investors insist on holding regularly with top management.

For British companies this is nothing new – they have for some time been subjected to similar pressures from UK-based institutional shareholders. However, it is a new element for many large companies in continental Europe. Germany, in particular, has experienced wrenching change at some of its largest and most traditional companies. Of course, it would be misleading to suggest that direct pressure from American institutional investors has been the only factor, or even the single most important factor. Other active ingredients have been increased global competition, intensified pressure from local institutional investors, the desire to access the US market and the need to secure access to American capital. For example, Hoechst, one of the three big German chemical/pharmaceutical companies, listed its shares in New York in September 1997 to encourage greater US ownership and has since behaved much as a US company would, with massive restructuring and M&A to bring about a complete change of profile. Amid the clamour surrounding Vodafone's successful hostile bid for the German mobile phone company, Mannesmann, in 2000 little attention was paid to the fact that two-thirds of Mannesmann's equity was held outside Germany, with 25 per cent in the hands of American institutions. The decision to accept was not a *German* decision. Pressure from foreign shareholders played a key role in securing Mannesmann's agreement to the deal.

> Many continental European companies believe they have no alternative but to play the game the American way if they are to survive in the new 'US model' environment.

The 'push effect' of US institutional investors in the 1990s has been complemented by the 'pull effect' of the US investment banks, who research, trade in and offer advisory services to those same companies. Many continental European companies believe they have no alternative but to play the game the American way if they are to survive in the new 'US model' environment. They seek American investors and when they do major deals – even deals without any US component – they increasingly use American advisers. When pitching for investment banking business in Europe, the US investment banks are not averse to using the argument that only they truly understand the requirements of US institutional investors and that their involvement will give comfort to these same investors. To an extent then, continental European economies are being 'Americanized' from within, not as a result of any deliberate strategy but simply through the constant search for equity investment opportunities that characterize a 'US model' capitalist economy.

The Big Decision

How institutional investors handle assets and expectations

- Selecting from the asset agenda

- For some, bonds are beautiful

- No bonds for the Brits

- The excitement of equities

- Equities go up because institutions buy them

- The Holy Grail of low risk, high reward

- Trust me, I'm an analyst!

- Inside the Great Expectation Machine

Before thinking about managers, the [pension fund] investor must first choose an appropriate mix from the available asset classes. This is the way in which you express whether you prefer to eat well in retirement, or sleep well in the interim. You cannot achieve both, unfortunately.

(Don Ezra, Director of European consulting at Frank Russell Company, investment consultants, quoted in *Financial News*, 15 March 1999)

Too many corporate managers, auditors and analysts are participants in a game of nods and winks. In the zeal to satisfy consensus earnings estimates and project a smooth earnings path, wishful thinking may be winning the day over faithful representation.

(Arthur Levitt, former Chairman, Securities and Exchange Commission, September 1998)

Selecting from the asset agenda

A fund manager has a sum of money entrusted to him. Sometimes when a professional fund manager takes over a fund it arrives in the form of cash, which is extremely convenient as cash can easily be converted into anything else. Much more common nowadays is the situation where an existing fund is transferred to a new manager. This fund will probably already be invested in a variety of securities, typically equities and bonds. The new manager will have the job of changing the structure of the portfolio (as the composition of the fund is referred to in the industry) into a mix that he thinks is appropriate. It is rare for a manager to take over a fund and not make changes – because the fund usually moves on the basis that the new manager has convinced those who are responsible for the fund that the stock selection has been poor or, indeed, that the entire portfolio structure is misconceived.

In simple terms, the objective of any fund manager is to maximize over time the value of the money he is contracted to manage, with due allowance for risk. The difference between where he is now and where he is in, say, 12 months' time, is his 'performance'. If the fund manager does better than the standard against which he has agreed to be judged, he is said to have 'outperformed'. If he falls below this level, he has 'underperformed'. (The terminology used is a little curious to an outsider. Surely 'overperformed' would have been more logical than 'outperformed'? On the other hand, 'inperformed' sounds distinctly odd.) The fund manager invests in certain types of asset, many of which will produce a regular income. Maximizing the value of those assets over time will involve increasing the capital value of the assets and, if it is part of his 'mandate' (or 'brief'), reinvesting the income generated by these assets to enhance further the value of the fund. Sometimes those responsible for a fund will want or need to use the income for current expenditure (a charity is usually in this position, as is a pension fund that has a high proportion of retirees) so the income will not be available to add to the portfolio.

> If the fund manager does better than the standard against which he has agreed to be judged, he is said to have 'outperformed'. If he falls below this level, he has 'underperformed'.

What assets can a fund invest in? Virtually anything can be regarded as an asset. Those responsible for the fund merely need to agree that it is an asset. Fine art, for example, can certainly be considered a legitimate asset. Between 1974 and 1980 British Rail Pension Fund, one of the largest pension funds in the UK, invested £40m in paintings and various objets d'art. In 1987 the trustees of the fund decided to dispose of the portfolio, which turned out to be a lengthy process (the last item was not sold until 2001). Gold, especially at times of high inflation, has also been a popular asset. However, a major problem with gold, fine art and other physical assets is that they not only produce no income, they actually cost money to store and insure. Despite these disadvantages, 'alternative assets' remain an area of interest for many funds, particularly in the US where the idea of investing in less conventional assets is far more widely accepted.

For the most part, in practice, funds invest in quoted securities. A security is simply written evidence of ownership, in the form of a certificate (or nowadays the electronic equivalent). The owner holds a right in a financial asset that he can buy and sell at will (at least in theory). For a fund manager the ability to convert into cash has enormous attractions. It provides flexibility and a means of adjusting the portfolio on a continuous basis in a constantly changing world. In other words, a security has the crucial advantage of liquidity – the ability to exchange into cash with ease – compared with other types of asset.

Liquidity is an absolutely crucial issue in the context of institutional investment and in the operation of modern-day securities markets (a point we consider more fully in the next chapter and, indeed, throughout the book). In an ideal world, every security could be traded freely in any quantity as and when a fund manager desired. In practice, liquidity is highly imperfect – not only does it vary from security to security, it also varies according to time. But even imperfect liquidity is better than no liquidity at all, which is why securities form such a high proportion of the assets in a typical fund.

What does the 'asset agenda' look like to a professional fund manager? Institutional investors invest primarily in four classes of assets (the term used is always class of assets, never anything else):

- bonds (also called 'fixed income' or 'fixed interest')
- equities
- property ('real estate' in the US)
- cash and 'money market' (very short-term) securities.

It may be that a few per cent of the value of a fund will be invested in other assets, such as a venture capital fund or a commodities fund (as is common in the US). Such 'alternative assets' are not regarded as a mainstream asset class. The first decision a fund manager has to take is how to allocate his fund between these four classes of assets. This is the Big Decision. However, not all fund managers are asked to invest in all asset classes. Some specialize in one class only or indeed part of a class, such as smaller continental European companies or index-linked bonds. Greater specialization is, in fact, a fast-developing trend in fund management.

For those with the freedom to invest across all asset classes, the asset allocation decision is a crucial decision in terms of performance. Paddling a canoe is a good analogy. The distance travelled is determined not by how well you paddle but by which river your canoe is in! A small extra percentage allocation to, say, bonds at the beginning of a year at the expense of equities will drag down the overall performance of the fund if equities have performed well and bonds have produced a poor return. As we shall see in Chapter 5, mere fractions of 1 per cent difference in overall performance can be highly significant in the race to win new business (or avoid the loss of existing business!).

In practical terms, cash is viewed mostly as a residual asset class. Few funds keep a significant proportion of their assets in cash: 5–10 per cent is typical. Cash will, of course, reflect at any given time the proceeds from securities just sold and intended for reinvestment. But it can also be a part of a strategy. A fund manager who believes securities markets are going down may decide to protect himself from the expected fall by selling securities for cash. However, the big disincentive for fund managers going too heavily into cash is that this is something that any fund or investor can do directly. It risks undermining their rationale. Those responsible for pension funds, for example, do not like paying fees to managers who do no more than put cash on deposit in the wholesale money markets, something the pension fund could do just as well for itself.

> Those responsible for pension funds, for example, do not like paying fees to managers who do no more than put cash on deposit in the wholesale money markets, something the pension fund could do just as well for itself.

Property is often called 'the forgotten asset class'. Direct investment in commercial property – as opposed to buying the equity of quoted property companies – was once a significant asset for UK insurance companies and pension funds but has fallen out of favour in recent years. It has certain major disadvantages, the main one being lack of liquidity – it can take months to sell a building. The present level of allocation to property by UK pension funds is around 5 per cent. In the US real estate is classified as an 'alternative asset'.

In reality, for most professional fund managers, the Big Decision is the asset allocation between bonds and equities. Getting this mix right in the first instance is frequently critical to the performance of the portfolio. It is often more important than selecting the right companies for the equity portfolio. A typical British pension fund will have 70 per cent of its assets in (UK and foreign) equities and 20–25 per cent in bonds. In the early 1990s the equity allocation was over 80 per cent. Historically, US pension funds held a lower percentage of their assets in equities (40–45 per cent) but the strong rise in stock prices during the 1990s pushed the equity content closer to 60 per cent. In continental Europe institutional portfolios are heavily weighted towards bonds, predominately domestic government bonds, although equities are gaining ground. For many countries in Europe a 70:30 bond:equity allocation would not be unusual.

How does a fund manager make the allocation decision between equities and bonds? In an institution of any size this decision will be made by a committee, based on inputs from bond and equity managers and other in-house executives whose specific function is to advise on asset allocation strategy. Ultimately, it depends on the internal projection of the expected relative performance from both these asset classes over the relevant period, probably the coming 12 months. In making this judgment the institutional investor is deluged with advice from strategists and economists employed by the securities houses. The interplay between bonds and equities is, in large part, a function of interest rates. Whole forests are felled each year to provide fund managers with every conceivable interest rate and return scenario!

Funds contain assets that are invested with the express purpose of achieving an increase in value, but this does not necessarily happen in a vacuum. There may be a need to meet certain projected future liabilities. This is usually true of pension funds and insurance funds. It does not apply to funds sold to the retail investor where the objective is simply to maximize value. The need to meet specified future liabilities introduces a further element of complexity into the investment decision-making process, particularly in regard to the portfolio mix between bonds and equities. These two asset classes are viewed as essentially complementary. Bonds offer a guaranteed return (if held until they are due to be repaid) so are particularly useful for funds with a known future liability. Equities can usually be expected to produce a better performance than bonds over the long run – but with higher risk.

A fund that is required to meet certain future obligations needs to consider the risk that the performance of the fund will fall short of its objectives. In an extreme instance, a pension fund that is badly invested may not have enough money to pay out all those who are entitled to a pension when everyone wants to draw out of the fund. Asset classes, and the assets within them, have different risks attached to them – essentially the risk that they will not achieve a projected level of appreciation. A highly sophisticated industry has developed to measure this risk. An equally highly sophisticated industry has evolved to help fund managers protect themselves from this risk, in the form of derivatives (futures and options) products available on one of the specialized exchanges or marketed by the securities arms of the investment banks. Today, risk quantification and risk management are critical components in professional investment management.

For some, bonds are beautiful

For fixed income aficionados, bonds have a certain mathematical symmetry that appeals. Equity investors often take the opposite view. For them, bonds are like peas in a pod, lacking that essential element of variety (and the opportunity for really large capital gains). Equities are so different from each other while bonds are, quite frankly, boring! In fact, bonds are an extremely significant class of asset with a vital role to play in any portfolio. Indeed, in a low-inflation, low equity yield environment, interest in bonds is increasing.

Bonds are fixed income securities because, unlike a cash deposit account, the income received is always the same every year. A bond therefore produces a steady and secure stream of income throughout its life, which is normally a fixed period of time. The amount received each year (usually twice a year) is defined as a percentage (the 'coupon' rate) of the original issue ('face') value. The bond's face amount (also called 'the principal') is repaid to the investor at the end of its life (known as 'maturity'), unless the issuer has defaulted. So, £10 million worth of a 10-year bond issued with a coupon of 5 per cent will always produce an income of £500,000 annually for however long it is held. At the issue price the yield is therefore 5 per cent. After 10 years the bond reaches maturity and the borrower must repay the original £10 million.

> A bond therefore produces a steady and secure stream of income throughout its life, which is normally a fixed period of time. The amount received each year (usually twice a year) is defined as a percentage (the 'coupon' rate) of the original issue ('face') value.

During the lifetime of a bond the income may be fixed but the value of the bond can vary from the face value. This is because all bonds are affected by the general level of interest rates. When interest rates go up the prices of outstanding bonds decline and when interest rates go down prices increase. The reason for this lies in the need for existing bonds to offer a yield that is competitive with newly-issued bonds. In our example, if the issue were priced at £100 but the 'going rate' coupon for a comparable new bond after, say, six months has elapsed has moved up to 6 per cent because interest rates generally have risen, no one in their right mind would want to buy at a 5 per cent yield! To be attractive to investors, the price of the old bond needs to adjust to a 6 per cent yield (which means a fall in price to £83.33 – and a 17 per cent decline in the current value of the £10 million).

The other risk to which a bondholder is exposed is credit risk. This is the risk that the borrower will default, either by not meeting the scheduled interest payments or, worse still, not being able to repay the principal when the bond matures. A whole industry has developed to help investors make a judgment on the credit risk they run if they decide to buy a particular bond. Credit ratings agencies assign credit ratings to larger bond issues to help investors assess this risk. The two best known are Standard & Poor's and Moody's, both US based, and founded in 1916 and 1909 respectively. The fees for this service come partly from the borrower, keen to obtain an independent stamp of approval that will reassure investors.

In general, all bonds rated AAA to BBB are considered to be 'investment grade' and bonds rated BB or lower are regarded as 'below or sub-investment grade' (or 'junk' in Street parlance, although those who promote them prefer us to call them 'high yield bonds').

The credit ratings business is American dominated because the US has a long-established tradition of bond raising for both governmental and corporate purposes. The US domestic bond market is, as a consequence, extremely large and varied, and has allowed the US-based ratings agencies to gain a depth of experience which non-US agencies find difficult to match. Institutional investors and the investment banking houses who arrange and trade in the bonds rely primarily, however, on their own internal credit research.

The credit rating feeds through to the yield that investors demand before they are prepared to put money into a bond. In the first instance they will look at the prevailing interest rate (coupon) offered by existing bonds with similar characteristics, especially the term to maturity. The next step is an evaluation of credit risk – if the issuer's credit rating is high they will accept a low yield but if it is low they will demand a higher yield to offset the perceived risk of default. The yield acts, in effect, as a form of price mechanism, balancing supply and demand.

In all developed economies central government bonds – 'gilts' in the UK, 'treasuries' in the US, 'bunds' in Germany and so on – are considered to be totally secure with no risk of default. (Governments, after all, have, in extremis, the option of printing more money.) States or state agencies (known generically as 'sovereign' issuers) consequently borrow at a lower interest rate than anyone else. Because it is considered to be risk free the relevant government bond is treated as a reference point ('benchmark') for all other bonds. Investors talk of the 'spread' or the 'yield pick-up' (expressed in 'basis points' – each point is one hundredth of 1 per cent) that a corporate or municipal bond needs to offer over the comparable government bond. The bond of a highly rated company will typically pay interest of between 0.5 per cent and 2 per cent more than a gilt with an equivalent maturity. In the Eurobond market each new issue has a published spread associated with it: against US treasuries if it is a dollar issue; against the

> A government with a heavy borrowing requirement is in a good position to pre-empt the corporate sector, by issuing bonds that 'soak up' the demand from institutions.

appropriate gilt-edged issue if it is issued in sterling; against Japanese government bonds if in yen. The spread is very sensitive to perceptions of credit risk because it is measured against a benchmark with no risk. In the wake of the 11 September terrorist attacks bondholders became nervous and this was immediately reflected in the spreads they demanded. The yield difference between European BBB-rated corporate bonds and US treasuries rose from 1 per cent to 2 per cent in a matter of weeks.

Supply and demand play an important role in any understanding of the bond markets. It is not difficult to 'design' a bond to meet a known institutional demand. This kind of responsiveness is much less possible in the equity market, where the security must reflect a particular company and business rather than a set of financial parameters. Investment institutions often have a known demand for a bond with certain characteristics – coupon, maturity, liquidity and so on. Companies will seek to construct a bond with these specific features, aided and abetted by the ever-attentive investment banks, for whom this is a significant business. In addition, the actions of government have an important indirect influence on supply and demand. A government with a heavy borrowing requirement is in a good position to pre-empt the corporate sector, by issuing bonds that 'soak up' the demand from institutions. Or, as in the UK in recent years, the reverse may happen: the supply of gilts dries up and the institutions scan the corporate bond market for alternatives.

A bond is a 'loan' made by an investor to a borrower, who may be a company, a government or some other kind of public body. It is a form of debt obligation which is why the bond market is often viewed as part of the wider debt market, including bank debt. Figure 2.1 is a simple matrix showing the relationship between loans, bonds and equity from the perspective of a company looking to obtain funding.

Capital market and bank debt are conceptually similar. Indeed, the line between bonds and loans is becoming increasingly blurred. (We saw in the

Figure 2.1   Corporate funding options in the bank and capital markets

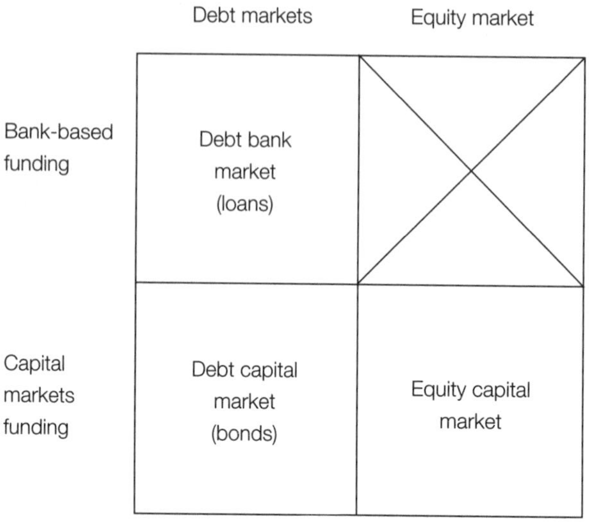

last chapter how the London merchant banks developed a large foreign business as 'loan contractors' even though what they were doing was issuing bonds.) Both bonds and loans involve regular interest payments and repayment of the principal at maturity. Neither a bondholder nor a bank making a loan has any ownership rights in that company. The risks are essentially the same. But a bank will make its own internal credit assessment rather than rely (even in part) on an outside agency. If it is concerned about the creditworthiness of a borrower it will charge a higher interest rate to reflect the higher risk.

From the point of view of the finance director or treasurer of a company there is no difference in principle between taking a loan from a bank or issuing a bond. Indeed, the process of arranging bank debt in the syndicated loan market is now very similar to the issuing procedure in the bond market. From a smaller base, the European corporate bond market has grown faster than the syndicated loan market over the last decade.

The essential practical difference between these two forms of debt from the point of view of the provider is that a bank is lending its own money (procured from retail or institutional deposits) whereas an investment bank promoting a bond issue obtains the money from investors. If a borrower defaults the bank has to write off the loan against its balance sheet. In the case of a bond it is the investors who suffer (quite possibly not the original investors). An investment bank that sponsored a bond in default has no financial liability but may find investors reluctant to put up money for the next issue!

The process whereby companies bypass banks and go straight to the capital markets for funding is called 'disintermediation'. (Quite apart from its inelegance, disintermediation is a curious word as no one in banking ever previously described themselves as being involved in intermediation!) It simply means 'cutting out the middleman'. Disintermediation is not confined to the banking business. With the growth of the internet it afflicts a whole range of industries, as when customers buy directly from a manufacturer, cutting out the retailer. A closely related concept is 'securitization', a process by which financial institutions that originate loans can turn them into marketable securities (called generically 'asset-backed securities', or ABS). Effectively, the interest payable on the loan is diverted from the bank to bondholders. For securitization to work, the asset must be capable of generating a reliable income stream to pay the coupon. Almost anything can – and has been – securitized, from credit card debt to future royalties on music sales. Bonds are a growth business.

No bonds for the Brits

Bond markets have a lower profile than equity markets. Gilt prices are not the stuff of headlines. Bonds are – correctly – viewed as a safe but unexciting class of asset. For long periods interest rates move little either way and bonds attract hardly any attention. This lack of enthusiasm for bonds has been particularly marked in the UK. Since the 1960s, fixed income investment has been overwhelmed by the 'cult of the equity', high inflation and big government deficits (although low inflation and the outperformance of bonds against equities in 2000 and 2001 has rekindled interest).

> Until inflation took off in the late 1960s, fixed income assets formed the bulk of any investment portfolio.

This built-in bias against bonds during the last 30 years applies almost as much to the UK institutional investment community as to the investing public. Yet, until inflation took off in the late 1960s, fixed income assets formed the bulk of any investment portfolio. For much of the 19th and early 20th centuries, a typical new issue on the London Stock Exchange involved a simultaneous offering of three types of asset: debenture stock, preference shares and ordinary shares. The first two (fixed income) components often accounted for most of the issue.

Britain has a large-scale market for government bonds but the market for other types of bond, especially corporate bonds, has historically been small and unimportant. In part, the absence of a significant domestic corporate bond market reflects the past reluctance of UK institutional investors. It also reflects the proximity of the Euromarkets which are, in effect, an extension of the domestic bond market. Many large UK companies have opted to borrow via this route. However, the situation has changed dramatically since 1997. With low inflation and a scarcity of government bonds, institutions are keen to promote the development of a UK corporate bond market. Sterling corporate bond issuance has expanded strongly, with companies encouraged to issue by demand from pension funds and, in 2001, the non-government bond market overtook the (shrinking) gilt market in terms of size.

In the US, by contrast, bonds of all types – federal, municipal, corporate – are extremely important. Unlike the UK, the US has a deeply ingrained 'bond culture' that sits alongside the vibrant 'equity culture' that has been a feature of the US scene since the 1950s. The New York Stock Exchange originated in 1792 as a *bond* exchange. Bonds were used extensively to finance the industrialization of America. Until the 1970s US investors tended to buy bonds and hold them until maturity but bonds have since become much more actively traded. Taken as a whole, the US bond market reflects over $16 trillion in outstanding debt obligations. This is larger than the US equity market, which it dwarfs in terms of activity.

While it is undoubtedly true that continentals prefer bonds, the European 'bond culture' is more of a government bond culture. Domestic corporate bond markets exist but only on a small scale. By and large, firms in continental Europe – particularly in Germany – rely on bank debt to finance themselves rather than the corporate bond market (although, like their UK counterparts, the larger ones do make use of Euromarkets). However, things are changing. With the advent of the euro in 1999, European companies have turned to the bond market in greater numbers, resulting in a surge in euro-denominated debt issuance. Individual and institutional investors in continental Europe have traditionally distrusted equities, preferring the relative safety of bonds, whether government bonds or Eurobonds. Even in the Eurobond market the emphasis is on low-risk, first-class companies. As the 'US model' gains ground, however, continental investors are starting to become more adventurous. The emergence of a single European-wide capital market has encouraged cross-border investment. Equity, corporate and high-yield bonds – in which there is an emerging market in Europe – are beginning to attract greater investment interest.

In the US the size, sophistication and competitiveness of the domestic bond market has enabled it to capture around 70 per cent of corporate borrowing, relegating the commercial banks to a minor role. The situation in continental Europe is almost exactly the reverse: corporate relationships with lending banks remain important. Loans have remained price competitive, reinforced by the fragmented state of the banking industry and the presence of banks with a public sector involvement. This is true of Germany especially, where companies have been slow to make use of the debt capital markets post the euro. Equally, European bond investors have not in the past been prepared to look down the 'credit curve' (in Wall Street jargon). The concept of a trade-off between credit risk and yield is an unfamiliar one. As a consequence, companies lacking instant investor name recognition have been unable to 'buy' money in the bond market, leaving them, until recently, with no alternative but to stay with the banks.

In America big companies barely use banks. They use the markets for all their financing requirements: the equity market, the bond market, or the 'money market' (such as the 'commercial paper' market) for shorter-term financing needs. Nearly all the massive growth in US corporate borrowing since the early 1980s has been captured by the debt capital markets. Since 1980 the value of US corporate bonds outstanding has grown more than fivefold.

As American industry disintermediated the commercial banks sought out customers in other sectors, notably real estate and individuals. In doing so they faced higher risks (in real estate particularly) and intensified competition, both from their fellow banks and from other, newer types of lending institution like credit card issuers (the so-called 'non-bank banks', an inelegant and inadequate description if ever there was one!). Confronted with a situation in which the investment banks were 'eating their lunch', the US commercial banks – and to a lesser degree banks everywhere – have, over the past two decades, been obliged to rethink their entire strategy. The traditional core money-lending business of commercial banking (making a margin on the difference between the interest rate paid for funds and the interest rate charged to borrowers) is under serious threat. Not only has the 'interest margin' (as the difference between these two rates is called) been squeezed but bad debts have, because they are 'on the books', the potential to bring down the whole bank.

> The traditional core money-lending business of commercial banking (making a margin on the difference between the interest rate paid for funds and the interest rate charged to borrowers) is under serious threat.

Entry into the issuing business that was capturing much of their traditional core activity was an obvious response (to the extent that they were permitted by Glass–Steagall). Commercial banks, after all, retain extensive corporate contacts they can build on to sell investment banking services. The appeal of moving into debt capital markets was further enhanced by the fact that arranging and marketing bonds to institutional investors produces fees and commissions – with no attendant balance sheet exposure. Commercial banks have adopted a variety of strategies in the face of the bond market challenge. Many, as we see in the next chapter, have been tempted into the unfamiliar territory of investment banking, with interesting – and frequently disastrous – consequences.

The excitement of equities

Nearly all investment involves some risk but investing in shares places the investor at the higher end of the risk spectrum. Unlike bonds, equities offer no assurance of income, either in terms of the scale or the regularity of dividends paid. The whole point about equities is that dividends are paid when times are good but can be reduced or eliminated altogether when times are bad, so helping the company to conserve resources. Nor is there any commitment to repay the sum invested after a specified time, or indeed at all. And, in a bankruptcy situation, the ordinary shareholders are at the bottom of the pile. Share prices can be volatile, in the absence of the support that the high and guaranteed yield gives to bond prices (although some, like utility shares, tend to have higher yields and bond-like characteristics).

There are, however, some offsetting advantages: notably the right of ownership. Ordinary shareholders are in a position, unlike bondholders, to influence the management of the company, even substitute one management for another. But, although this power is being exercised more freely now, it is a cumbersome mechanism and can take considerable time (during which the situation may deteriorate further). All in all, looked at in this way, equity investment appears to represent little more than 'a leap of faith' on the part of the investor.

In spite of all this, in recent decades, both individuals and institutions have found equities as an asset class to be a more attractive investment than bonds. We saw earlier that this was not always so. During the 19th century and much of the 20th century the natural choice for the investor was bonds. Companies issued fixed interest stock alongside equity to 'soak up' the considerable demand for securities that would provide the (private) investor with a high and stable income. Shares were distrusted and, remarkably from our perspective, actually yielded more than bonds for long periods to compensate for the higher risk. Today bond yields are almost invariably higher than equity yields, standing the concept that shares should offer more in terms of yield – to offset the risk the dividend might be cut or cancelled – on its head.

Why are modern investors prepared to tolerate a situation in which high-risk equities yield less than low-risk bonds? The reason for this lies in the evidence of recent history – simply that the returns from investing in equities are higher. In the City 'return' has two alternative meanings. It can simply refer to the percentage capital gain from a share over a specified period. More often, though, it is the combination of two items: capital appreciation and dividends. Adding these together gives what – for equities or bonds – is called total return. To take an example, if a share increased in value by 20 per cent in a year and the dividend yield was 3 per cent in that year its total return would be 23 per cent. Similarly, if the equity market as a whole produced a capital gain of 15 per cent over a year and the yield was 2 per cent the total return would be 17 per cent. In principle, it is no more complex than that. But these two components are qualitatively different. Capital appreciation depends on the value of the investor's holding on the accounting date. It is merely a paper profit until he actually sells and realizes cash for it. (Fortunately for the managers, fund performance does not depend on the conversion of the capital appreciation achieved into cash.)

Asset class statistics calculated by Barclays Capital show that, since 1902 and adjusted for inflation, UK equities have generally produced a better return than bonds or cash. However, Table 2.1 shows that these superior returns, sliced into 10-year bands, are highly variable. The past decade has seen a narrowing of the long-term gap, as gilts outperformed equities in 2000 and 2001.

For more than a generation equities have been the natural choice of the investor, the 'default'. Any other asset class has had to prove itself against equities. Equities are affected in the short term by numerous factors but, over the long run, share values reflect the past and projected growth in earnings and dividends of individual companies. The perceived superiority of equities as an asset class is based purely on experience – mid- to late

Table 2.1 Real investment returns generated by major asset classes in the UK since 1902 (% p.a)

	Equities	Gilts	Cash
1902–11	4.2%	–0.3%	1.6%
1912–21	–5.1%	–6.4%	–2.9%
1922–31	7.6%	8.5%	6.9%
1932–41	5.9%	4.3%	–2.2%
1942–51	4.1%	–2.6%	–2.0%
1952–61	12.2%	–3.3%	0.6%
1962–71	6.6%	1.4%	1.2%
1972–81	–2.4%	–5.6%	–2.7%
1982–91	13.2%	8.4%	5.8%
1992–2001	8.6%	8.0%	4.0%

Source: Barclays Capital Equity-Gilt Study, February 2002

20th-century history tells us that, for all the risks and short-term fluctuations, they are the better long-term bet.

What persuaded investors to shake off the belief that bonds were best in all circumstances? In Britain, one man was primarily responsible for changing the thinking of the emerging institutional fund management industry. George Ross Goobey, the son of a non-conformist lay preacher, was employed as the first in-house actuary of the Imperial Tobacco Pension Fund. In 1947 he came up with the radical idea that, with inflation gaining hold, investment in equities offering a 4 per cent yield was a better bet than investing in fixed income government stock yielding 2.5 per cent. He was so convinced that equities were cheap that he likened himself to:

A child in a sweetshop who discovers that everything is for sale at knock-down prices.

(*Financial Times*, 22 March 1999)

Equity investment really came into vogue in the late 1960s when inflation started to take off in the developed world. In contrast to bonds, equities are 'real' assets. A real asset is one that is capable of protecting the owner from inflation. Bonds cannot do this because the sums involved are fixed, whatever happens to the general level of prices. Companies, on the other hand, can raise prices to compensate for increases in their costs (subject to competitive and other influences, of course) and generally have a fighting chance of raising profits and dividends in line with the general level of prices. In fact, dividends have generally risen faster than inflation and it is this, as much as anything, that underpins the case for equity investment. Property is also a 'real' asset as rents can be raised, although in practice it has produced disappointing long-term returns.

> Essentially, what investors want from equities is future growth – growth in profits and dividends. Growth is the god. Growth is the reason for buying.

Essentially, what investors want from equities is future growth – growth in profits and dividends. Growth is the god. Growth is the reason for buying. In the City the tag 'ex-growth' is synonymous with a fall from grace. The key advantage that shares have over bonds is the ability to increase dividends (and thus the yield) when profits are doing well. The effect of continuous increases in dividends is very powerful.

Take our example of a £10 million bond investment at a 5 per cent yield. Suppose instead this sum were invested in a share yielding 2.5 per cent. In the first year the dividend would produce an income of £250,000, versus £500,000 from the bond. If, however, dividends grow at 15 per cent per annum for five years the income received in Year 5 has doubled to £500,000 – the same as the bond. If the share price of the equity has not moved (and the company is still worth the original £10 million) then the yield on the equity is now 5 per cent – the same as the bond. But, in practice, because share prices reflect expectations of future dividend growth, it is highly probable that the share price will have increased, provided investors think this rate of dividend increase will continue. Very simplistically, if, in Year 5, investors believe that this kind of growth rate will continue, the price may well have doubled, in which case the yield (the £500,000 dividend now as a percentage of £20 million) will still be 2.5 per cent. Because they believe that profits and dividends will grow at this rate, investors are prepared to buy the equity on a 'permanent' 2.5 per cent yield, even though it is intrinsically riskier than the bond. If, for example, market expectations were for dividend increases in the 5–10 per cent range rather than 15 per cent, then it is likely that the value of the equity would reflect this and the yield would be somewhere between the high-growth yield and the bond yield, say 3–4 per cent. History – the fact that the company has done well until now – clearly gives the company a headstart in the minds of investors but the key element is the anticipation of future growth, however this is formed.

Bonds can be defined, categorized, compared and valued with ease. Equities cannot. Valuing a bond, or assessing the coupon at which a new issue will sell, is a relatively quantifiable and mechanical exercise. Companies, by contrast, differ too much, in size, product range, geographical spread, quality of management and in a host of other ways. Their share prices are affected by a multitude of variables, from interest rates and currencies to things like the specific industry situation, perceived management competence, bid rumours and the weather. Try as they might, most professional investors do not look upon equities and bonds in a wholly dispassionate way. Equities have foibles, bonds just have figures. And in volatility lies both interest and opportunity.

Equities go up because institutions buy them

Bond prices change because investors buy or sell them, but they do so according to certain well-defined 'rules'. There is no comparable framework for equities. Share prices go up because other investors decide to buy the shares based on their perception of future profit and dividend prospects. And, except in the case of quite small companies, these other investors are invariably institutions.

This leads to a crucial point: equity returns are vitally dependent on the actions of other investors. This may sound obvious but, in an age when 'the market' is regarded as the ultimate arbiter of pretty well everything, it is easy to forget that there is nothing supernatural about the single figure that represents a share price. A market price is no more than a coalescence of hopes, fears, perceptions and misconceptions at an instant in time. It is a manmade process – not something delivered to humanity from on high by a Solomon-like market deity. This statement has even greater force in a stock market dominated by institutional investors, needing to buy or sell millions of pounds' worth of stock every time they deal. It is the fund managers in a small number of big institutions who determine share prices. The nostalgic idea that price setting in the stock market is the result of a multitude of individual decisions is a dangerous illusion. No one can dispute that the institutions are the price makers now.

> Management has a choice – it can pay out earnings in dividends or retain the money inside the company.

Equity valuation is a tricky business. Ultimately, there are no 'rules' – simply what people are prepared to pay (although, in practice, there tends to be a consensus of what constitutes 'fair value' among institutional investors). Strenuous efforts are made to find comparable shares, rather in the way that bond analysts use government stocks or similar maturity corporate bonds as benchmarks. But this is much more difficult in the heterogeneous equity environment. There are no universally accepted benchmarks, which is why assessing the 'right' price for an equity is, unlike valuing a bond, much more of an art than a science.

As if this were not enough, there is an additional element of complexity in valuing equities. In our simple model we made the implicit assumption that dividend growth would faithfully reflect profit growth. If that were true, yield would be a helpful valuation tool. Reality is, unfortunately, less straightforward. Investors actually focus their attention on earnings (after-tax profit) growth, not dividend growth. More specifically, institutional investors look above all else at earnings per share (EPS), which is simply the earnings in a trading period divided by the number of shares a company has in issue. The reason for this is that dividends do not necessarily rise in line with earnings. Management has a choice – it can pay out earnings in dividends or retain the money inside the company.

In the UK a company that does increase its dividends in line with earnings is described in City jargon as pursuing 'a progressive dividend policy'. Companies that reject the notion of such a policy are much more common in the US (partly for tax reasons). American investors are more prepared to accept the argument that retaining the cash in the business will be of greater benefit to shareholders in the long run than paying it out now. To some extent, the prevalence of this view reflects the higher proportion of growth companies in the US economy, with substantial internal funding requirements to finance that growth.

Many American listed companies, particularly in the high-tech sector, pay no dividend at all. Microsoft, for example, pays no dividend, even though it could easily afford to do so. (At the end of 2001 the company had $36 billion sitting in its balance sheet and was generating cash at a rate of $1 billion a month). More recently, the link between earnings and dividends has been further undermined by the fashion for companies to buy back their stock, which rewards shareholders in a different way. Stock buy-backs used to attract negative comment but institutional investors no longer perceive a company that is returning capital to them as one that has run out of ideas.

Dividends come in regularly and are received in the form of cash which cannot be taken away. Capital appreciation, on the other hand, reflects a figure that is inherently transient. It reflects earnings that are intrinsically 'soft'. Earnings can be managed or – depending on your point of view – manipulated. The monetary value implied by the share price can quickly disappear. Even if the price does not move, there is no guarantee of liquidity if the investor wants to sell. Combining capital appreciation and dividends into something called 'total return' is a bit like combining apples and oranges – it is a rather strange conjunction. One component is fundamentally more reliable and secure than the other. Dividends indeed are a significant component in historic equity returns, especially when invested in additional shares.

At certain times – the latter half of the 1990s and the late 1920s being two such periods – equity investors are prepared to forego the 'secure' element in total return in exchange for the alluring prospect of unlimited capital appreciation. On Wall Street, in the raging bull market of the late 1990s, dividends became more or less irrelevant – many popular internet-based US equity screening systems did not even accept yield as a possible criterion! However, since the market hit its peak in early 2000, dividends have returned to fashion. In a bear market a regular payout from a solid company is the one return you can count on. Some US investors are beginning to demand dividends as tangible proof of a corporation's earning power.

Capital appreciation in equities only works because other investors are prepared to buy the shares, so pushing up the paper value of the holding. The system functions because everyone plays the game by the same rules – everyone chases potential earnings. This process is self-reinforcing.

Investors chase earnings growth because they know that other investors will chase earnings growth. The evidence of the past 50 years is that this is a profitable exercise. It is a brave person who argues against the power of human experience.

Earnings are important because they demonstrate the *capacity* a company has to pay increased dividends. It need not actually do so, or it may increase the dividend by substantially less than the rise in earnings. From this perspective, earnings represent a crucial 'comfort zone' for investors. The higher the earnings growth the greater the level of comfort.

All this helps to explain why the price–earnings ratio (P/E or sometimes PER) remains the principal method of valuing and comparing equities. (In the City, the P/E is also called the 'multiple' or the 'rating': Wall Streeters tend to talk about 'the valuation'.) The current share price divided by the EPS gives the P/E ratio, which measures the number of years' worth of that year's earnings investors are prepared to pay for a stake in that company. If a company has a share price of 300p and last year it earned 15p per share it is on a historic P/E of 20. A forecast EPS of 20p for the current year will bring the P/E down to 15. Dividend yield is still important for some companies but, overall, yield is very much a secondary consideration. Investors seek earnings growth above all else and the P/E quickly and efficiently measures the past and expected growth rate of earnings. As earnings go up the P/E falls – information that can be seen at a glance.

In practice, the forward P/E is what matters. Investors base their valuation on projected earnings. Past earnings (reflected in the historic P/E or, on Wall Street, the trailing P/E) are of limited value as a valuation tool. Other forward-looking criteria are extensively used, especially cash flow-based valuation methodologies, as these are less liable to be distorted by differences in accounting and make for easier international comparisons. Two measures currently favoured by professional investors are EBIT (earnings before interest and tax) and EBITDA (earnings before interest, tax, depreciation and amortization). But, even in the US where most of these alternative valuation tools originate, the P/E still commands wide acceptance in the investment community. It benefits from both simplicity and transparency. Earnings are, after all, what companies actually report. Other valuation tools are generally used to supplement it, not to supplant it.

> Investors chase earnings growth because they know that other investors will chase earnings growth. The evidence of the past 50 years is that this is a profitable exercise. It is a brave person who argues against the power of human experience.

The Holy Grail of low risk, high reward

The measurement of returns – usually total returns – is obviously a key element in investment performance. But what about risk? Most assets have some risk attached to them. Risk in an investment context is rather different from risk in the usual sense: say, the risk of an accident or the risk of a fire. Risk in fund management means the uncertainty as to whether an asset will produce its expected return. Equity prices are more variable than bond prices, so there is more chance of an unpleasant surprise. A fund manager needs to be able to measure the level of risk associated with any particular portfolio mix – not just bonds and equities but the risks associated with individual stocks. Just as insurance companies use historic data to assess the probability of, say, a car accident, so institutional investors use historic data on share prices to measure the volatility (expressed as the standard deviation) of the equity market or of individual share prices. In this way it is possible to assess at the beginning of a period the probability of a share failing to meet an expected return. The process is clearly less finite and much more complicated than our standard insurance example. However, both are based on the same assumption – that the past is a reliable guide to the future.

Institutional investors as a breed are deeply risk averse. They hate uncertainty. They like to minimize risk. But, having said that, they like high returns. In the real world, they have to weigh potential return and risk for each class of asset and each security. If government stock with a one-year maturity produces an annual (risk-free) return of 5 per cent, corporate bonds a relatively secure 7 per cent over the same period, and equities a less reliable potential 9 per cent, the investor might well conclude that, given the variability, the prospective equity return is not enough to offset the extra risk. At, say, a 15 per cent prospective equity return it may well be worth it. Investment decision-making is a constant series of trade-offs between potential return and the associated risk.

It should be clear by now that these trade-offs are not independent, isolated events but exist within a framework. Investment risk and potential reward generally march in step with each other. Low-risk investments have low returns while high-risk investments have high potential returns. This makes obvious sense. Why would anyone put money into a high-risk investment – with prospect of losing some or all of it – if there were only the prospect of a 10 per cent return? They might be prepared to do it for a 50 per cent prospective return. Figure 2.2 identifies the relationship between risk and return. In investment circles this fundamental principle has been known for years as the 'risk–reward ratio' (rather than, as one might expect, the 'risk–return ratio').

Figure 2.2 The risk–reward ratio

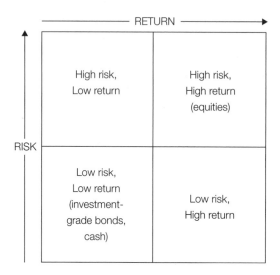

Equities fall into the high-risk, high-return box while investment-grade bonds generally fit into low risk, low return. Of course, no one in their right mind would want to enter the area marked high risk, low return. The investment equivalent of the Holy Grail lies in the low-risk, high-return quadrant. It is a constant and unrelenting search, even though, in a deregulated, instant information world, common sense would suggest that there is no such promised land. But who can be certain? It is at least conceivable that someone, somewhere has found a sure-fire way of making substantial returns with low risk and is sensibly keeping quiet about it.

> There is one type of investor who, as a matter of strategy, tries to position himself in the low-risk, high-return category. It is the 'hedge fund'.

There is one type of investor who, as a matter of strategy, tries to position himself in the low-risk, high-return category. It is the 'hedge fund'. Hedge funds, as a species, are maligned and misunderstood in just about equal measure, particularly in the UK where the concept is unfamiliar, although attitudes are changing. Invented in the US in the 1960s, the original idea literally involved allowing fund managers to 'hedge their bets' with the goal of preserving capital. In other words, the classic hedge fund is all about risk control. The aim is to make a consistent return of, say, 10 per cent per annum, whatever markets are doing. Hedge funds employ a variety of strategies. One popular strategy, faithful to the original concept, is called 'market neutral'. Another similar approach is 'long–short' (as it involves managing both 'long' positions and 'short' sales). Some hedge fund strategies make extensive use of derivatives. A sizeable number rely heavily on computer-based models that attempt to replicate the world and identify pricing disparities that represent temporary investment opportunities. Attempting to profit by exploiting price differences in similar securities on different markets or in different forms is known as 'arbitrage'. It would be more accurate to describe hedge funds as low risk, modest return. In fact, the record suggests that these funds, if managed along classic lines, can produce a steady return with low risk.

Hedge funds are essentially a US phenomenon. In all, there are around 6,000 such funds, unregulated and mostly based in Caribbean tax havens. The principal investors are wealthy American individuals. Some US institutions do place money with them (hedge funds fall into the alternative assets category) but, with the exception of university endowment funds, these tend to be modest amounts. British institutional and private investors have generally been deeply suspicious of the hedge fund concept and avoided any involvement. Attitudes are, however, changing, assisted no doubt by the prospect of a 'certain' return in uncertain markets. A few large pension schemes have invested small amounts in hedge funds. Retail asset managers are increasingly offering their clients access to hedge funds, run internally or by external specialists. London is home to a growing band of newly established hedge fund managers, often run by refugees from large fund management and securities firms, attracted by the idea of running their own business and by the high incentive fees that hedge funds command.

As so often happens, the original concept has been extended and abused. A hedge fund has come to mean any kind of fund pursuing an alternative investment approach. Some may not even hedge risk. Some do no more than buy equities – 'go long' in the jargon – using large quantities of borrowed money. These highly leveraged 'long-only' funds are, without doubt, highly risky investments.

When Long-Term Capital Management (LTCM), the New York-based hedge fund, had to be rescued so spectacularly in the third quarter of 1998, the suddenness of the reversal raised some serious questions. LTCM had a first-class pedigree and numbered among its partners two Nobel prize winners in economics (a virtual guarantee of outperformance!). Like others, it seemed to have found a way of earning good returns with low risk. The fund pursued a classic 'market-neutral' approach but was forced to resort to exceptionally high levels of leverage, resulting from the need to buy into a vast number of tiny market disparities thrown up by a highly sophisticated computer model built and maintained by a bunch of super-bright 'rocket scientists'.

What went wrong was that security prices moved in ways that did not conform to historical patterns – on which inevitably the model was based. Interest rates went the wrong way, equity and bond prices that were supposed to converge instead diverged. Spreads between government and corporate bonds widened drastically. Then, in addition to being wrongfooted by an unforeseen set of circumstances, LTCM was hit by a drying up of liquidity (the ability to trade easily) in many securities. A clever deal is of no use if there is no buyer when you want to sell, or vice versa. Huge amounts of debt brought LTCM down. The LTCM crisis does not invalidate the hedge fund concept. But it does demonstrate that even a low-risk, modest-return strategy – especially one based on a mathematical model that claims to replicate the universe – has its limitations. Less ambitious, well-managed hedge funds continue to produce consistent returns in uncertain markets.

> A ratings agency is measuring something that is relatively stable – the balance sheet numbers broadly convey the degree of risk.

Trust me, I'm an analyst!

We noted earlier the key role played by the credit ratings agencies in the bond market, interposing themselves as independent and objective arbiters of value. Clearly, there is a need for a comparable function for equities. It should, however, be obvious by now that any attempt by the ratings agencies to set up a similar system would have been doomed to failure. Bonds and equities are very different animals. A ratings agency is measuring something that is relatively stable – the balance sheet numbers broadly convey the degree of risk. In equities, risk is endemic. It is not just a matter of financial ratios. Each share has its own set of imponderables. It would be impossible to set up a generally acceptable grading system, let alone ensure that each grade meant exactly the same thing to all investors. Two analysts using the same information can easily arrive at radically different views on whether the current share price represents good value or poor value, whether the shares are a 'buy' or a 'sell'.

In the absence of a neutral organization the equity system evolved in a different way. Stockbrokers – who were already acting as intermediaries between issuers and investors for the purpose of buying and selling – set up research departments to 'grade' stocks. This began to happen on Wall Street in the 1920s and gathered momentum in the 1930s. A similar process occurred in London but not until the 1960s. Although this system of evaluating equities could hardly be described as independent it was undoubtedly better than no system at all. Often those who advised on the investment merits of an issue were the promoters of that issue. But, at minimum, research into companies and industries provided additional intelligence on which personal, and later institutional, investors could base their own judgment. The research departments of the securities houses also covered shares for which their competitors were responsible, so their input into the institutions acted as a counterweight to that of the promoter.

Despite its defects, the system worked tolerably well. Investment analysts ('financial analysts' or 'securities analysts' in Wall Street parlance) provided both insight and advice on companies and their share prices which professional fund managers found useful. The pressures on them to be less than objective were not regarded as undue and, for the most part, would be disclosed to investors (such as the fact that the firm was acting as an issuer for a company under review). The institutions rewarded those who gave reliable and objective advice with bigger commissions, which flowed through to higher salaries and bonuses for the analyst concerned.

With the rise of the investment bank in the 1980s this imperfect but reasonably effective system of guidance for institutional investors began to break down. As trading for institutions in existing equities became less profitable, the investment banks began to view the analyst as a key element in the generation of business for all parts of the organization, but particularly new equity issues and M&A. In today's investment bank, equities are consciously used as the 'shop window', with the analyst as the strikingly dressed figure at the centre of the display! From this perspective, the analyst's primary role is to help generate business from the bank's corporate clients while continuing to maintain credibility with institutional investors – a difficult balancing act given the inherent conflicts. The role of the analyst has also become more difficult for other reasons, including the requirement to support the market-making function in an investment bank and the regulatory pressure on companies to provide equal access to information. Companies, especially large companies, control the flow of financial information much more tightly than in the past. Chapter 7 explains how the system works in much more detail.

The consequence of all this is that professional investors no longer trust the equity analysts employed by the investment banks. (The usage of credit research is, by contrast, on a rising curve.) Fund managers know that equity analysis is often driven more by the pressure to create profitable business opportunities for the bank as a whole – focusing on its corporate clients – than by the provision of solid, objective advice for institutional clients. During the 1990s, the institutions responded by moving heavily into expanding or setting up their own internal equity research departments ('buy-side' research in the jargon, to differentiate it from securities, or 'sell-side', research). External analysts are still used, but more sparingly and with greater circumspection.

Inside the Great Expectation Machine

How do the investment institutions use all this research – both internal and external – to make decisions on the shares of particular companies? Before tackling this question we need to take a look at the underlying psychology of institutional fund managers and what drives them. As we observed earlier, investors abhor uncertainty. They have a deep-rooted desire to make the world a more predictable place. Much effort is expended by the institutions in an attempt to reduce the uncertainty element in the complex and unstable world that surrounds them. Institutional investors know they cannot control the future but they do believe they can, to some degree, tame the future.

> Advance knowledge should allow time for avoiding action. For obvious reasons, investors are much less concerned about positive surprises.

In practice, what investors really want to avoid is negative surprises – interest rates going up without warning, a lower than expected rise in a company's reported earnings, a corporate announcement about the loss of an important customer and so on. ('Negative surprise' is Street parlance: Brits often make do with that old-fashioned word 'disappointment'.) Advance knowledge should allow time for avoiding action. For obvious reasons, investors are much less concerned about positive surprises. Surely no one is likely to get too upset if a company produces exceptionally good results (an 'upside surprise') and the share price goes up 10 per cent. Yet, even in this instance, the underlying desire of the institutions for a more certain future means that they would prefer to have known.

As part of their continuing crusade to push back the boundaries of uncertainty, fund managers not only prefer to know good news before it happens but place a value on the continuing predictability of such news. Consistency of earnings growth is highly prized, attracting a high P/E. The phrase used in the City is 'quality of earnings', referring to the extent to which investors can rely on regular EPS growth. On Wall Street they talk of 'earnings visibility'. A company that is expected to produce, say, 15 per cent EPS growth annually for several years ahead – with a low risk of that figure not being met – is said to have high-quality earnings (or high earnings visibility). Institutional investors would rather invest in a business that generates a steady 10 per cent earnings growth a year for five years than one that produces 15 per cent in Year 1, 5 per cent in Year 2, 10 per cent in Year 3 and so on – even if the absolute EPS at the end of Year 5 turns out to be higher.

Pension funds and insurance companies have a particularly strong incentive to make the future more predictable, as their own performance depends on meeting known long-term obligations at the lowest possible cost. Variability of future returns leads to extra costs. Unlike the private investor, who has to accept uncertainty as an unfortunate fact of life, institutional investors have the resources at their disposal to do something about it.

Interestingly, the earliest large-scale, systematic attempt to 'tame the future' took place in an industrial context during the 1960s, predating the rise of the investment institutions. In 1959 ITT, a huge, sprawling New York-based conglomerate, with most of its assets outside the US, appointed Harold Geneen as President. Geneen was an accountant to his fingertips, a despot, a workaholic, a loner who came into the ailing company with a fearsome reputation as a profit maker. He could not have been more of a contrast to the flamboyant founder of ITT. Geneen believed fervently that, through the ruthless application of logic, he could create an ordered future. In 1961 he moved the headquarters of ITT into:

> A shapeless grey skyscraper in Park Avenue with no mosaics, no Louis XIV furniture, no French chef: only floor upon floor of manager's offices. Geneen gradually set up the most intricate and rigorous system of financial controls the world has ever seen ... He made it clear that he had to know about everything, to be warned of any likely disaster ... and to all his managers he repeated his ominous warning 'I want no surprises'.

> (Sampson, 1973, p. 68. Reproduced by permission of Hodder & Stoughton Limited)

Today's investment institutions are the natural inheritors of Geneen's mantra: 'I want no surprises.' They too are crusaders for an ordered future. Every institution has to have a view of the future – they need it to function, and clients expect and demand it. In equities, these expectations relate primarily to the earnings and dividends of individual companies, for one, two or more years ahead. When a share price adjusts to reflect expectations it is said to 'discount' the future or – to put it another way – the forecast is 'in the price'. Through this process, the institutions create a framework of what the future corporate world should look like. Companies are judged against these projections (whether, to use the City vernacular, the results are 'in line'). Of course, expectations are sometimes wrong. But that does not detract from the value of creating this framework of expectations in the first place.

Expectations are big business in the City (and, of course, on Wall Street). Generating these expectations on an ongoing basis is a massive operation involving many thousands of participants: analysts (both sell-side and buy-side), equity salespersons, corporate executives, financial public relations firms and others. Together, they collaborate to provide the fund managers with the expectations they demand. Expectations are 'manufactured' by the equity part of the City in the same way that Detroit makes cars or Paris produces haute couture. The process resembles a sophisticated machine, 'the Great Expectation Machine', working constantly to satisfy the institutional craving for greater certainty.

> Senior managers have no choice but to spend a significant proportion of their time on investor relations activities.

However, what appears to happen inside the Great Expectation Machine and what actually happens are two different things. Traditionally, analysts in the securities houses made forecasts of corporate earnings based on their independent judgement. In doing so, they received considerable co-operation from the company concerned – although inevitably some were more helpful than others! Most companies realized that it was in their interest to try to guide these forecasts towards their own internal view of the future, so that actual results did not differ too widely from City expectations. The whole process was a pretty informal one.

Today, under constant pressure from institutional investors for transparency, predictability and share price performance, companies have seized control of this process. The management of expectations is now a fully fledged industry. In large companies, it is highly organized, involving investor relations executives ('IR' in the jargon) and consultancies specializing in promoting companies to analysts and investors ('financial PR' or 'investor relations' agencies). Senior managers have no choice but to spend a significant proportion of their time on investor relations activities.

In large companies, especially, informal guidance has been replaced by public statements and comments in orchestrated meetings providing 'clues' that are sometimes so deliberate and so obvious that an analyst could virtually work out the company's forecast in his sleep! Increasingly, in response to regulatory pressure, companies are publishing more frequent and precise 'earnings guidance' (to use terminology that became standard on Wall Street during 2001). Of course, there is still scope for independent judgment – if only in terms of management's ability to forecast and its optimism or pessimism about these forecasts – but it is severely reduced. The notion – which is beginning to erode – that analysts make independent estimates is a convenient fiction that suits all parties. One consequence is that analysts' estimates are now frequently clustered within a narrow range – where they bunch is the 'consensus' estimate. Frequently 'consensus' is synonymous with 'company'.

In short, as part of their need to manage institutional investors' expectations as best they can, companies make estimates that they feed via analysts (or increasingly directly) to fund managers. These 'analysts' estimates' are also used extensively elsewhere in the City, in investment banking, in venture capital and by financial journalists. We explore the detailed workings of the Great Expectation Machine in Chapters 6 and 7, after we have taken a closer look at fund managers and what drives them.

Defining words

Your guide to the confusing terminology of CitySpeak

- How CitySpeak absorbed StreetSpeak

- The abuse of liquidity and other stories

- A journey from sector to sympathy

- Why investment banks and investment banking are the same but different

- Equity capital markets – riding the rollercoaster

- Make my day with M&A

- The battle of the bulge

The special vocabulary of hackers helps hold their culture together ... Not knowing the jargon (or using it inappropriately) defines one as an outsider, a mundane, or (worst of all in hackish vocabulary) possibly even a suit.* All human cultures use jargon in this threefold way – as a tool of communication, and of inclusion, and of exclusion.

(The Jargon File, a comprehensive compendium of hacker slang at www.fwi.uva.nl)

*Ugly and uncomfortable 'business clothing' often worn by non-hackers. Invariably worn with a 'tie', a strangulation device that partially cuts off the blood supply to the brain.

How CitySpeak absorbed StreetSpeak

In comparison with the arcane vocabulary of the computer world, financial jargon is much less voluminous and relatively transparent. Even so, there are many words in common usage in the City whose definition is not at all clear and whose meaning changes according to the context. Insiders instinctively know this – but it is far from obvious to outsiders. This chapter explains the meaning of certain essential-to-know words and concepts.

Twenty years ago CitySpeak was a pure tongue, rooted in the robust broking and jobbing tradition of the pre-Big Bang stock exchange. It has since been heavily penetrated by StreetSpeak, the language of the New York fund management, securities and investment banking community. Despite this, some parts survive.

> In today's City there is no longer any presumption of objectivity – it is assumed that everyone is 'talking his own book'.

The most interesting – and significant – of these is the phrase 'talking your own book'. This dates from before Big Bang, when jobbers who were holding stock (literally recorded in their book) would tell everyone what a wonderful company it was in an effort to offload it at a higher price. Stockbrokers, by contrast, were free to give a client impartial advice, uninfluenced by direct financial advantage (commission rates make no distinction between buying or selling). In practice, they were frequently influenced by other factors, as when a client was encouraged to buy a share at, say, 140p to secure a (paper) profit for another client who, a few days before, had been persuaded to buy the stock at 130p. A stockbroker who did this was giving non-objective advice under the guise of giving objective advice. In today's City there is no longer any presumption of objectivity – it is assumed that everyone is 'talking his own book'.

A more significant development in the vocabulary of finance is that certain words that were once confined to the financial community have entered the linguistic mainstream. CitySpeak has come out of the closet. This is essentially due to the victory of the 'US model', and also to the huge surge in numbers employed by the City. 'Bull', 'bear', 'upside', 'downside', 'outperform', 'underperform' and many other terms are now an integral part of English as spoken whereas 20 years ago they would have been completely unknown to those outside the closed world of the City. Modern politicians talk freely of 'risk–reward ratios' and 'exit strategies' on the basis that their (non-financial) audience will know what they mean.

Easily the most articulate exponent of CitySpeak is the highly influential daily Lex Column on the back of the *Financial Times*. It is written anonymously in a particularly dense form of CitySpeak (Lexicon?) and directed unswervingly at the institutional cognoscenti. In practice, Lex is talking directly and exclusively to a few thousand senior fund managers in the UK and continental Europe – those whose daily fare includes buying, say, £50 million of BP or selling £20 million of France Telecom. Over half the circulation of the FT is now outside the UK. Comment is focused on large, liquid companies with international appeal because these are the ones that matter to this audience. Little space is given to smaller stocks, unless they are of exceptional interest. Of course, many others in the Institutional Equity Nexus read Lex: analysts, investment bankers, venture capital executives and so on. Indeed, analysts provide much of the input to the group of journalists who write it. Additionally, it is widely read by business executives and private investors. Reading Lex is rather like attending a conference where the speaker on the platform is concentrating his gaze on a small group of senior – and attentive – people at the front while the rest of the audience listens with varying degrees of understanding and interest.

The abuse of liquidity and other stories

No concept in CitySpeak has suffered more grievously from abuse than **liquidity**. It has several meanings, depending on the context. To institutional investors, it usually means the ability to trade in and out of shares in large volume without any significant impact on the price paid. The importance of liquidity in this sense to professional fund managers cannot be overstated. A fund manager can make brilliant buy and sell decisions but, if he cannot actually deal in the size he needs to deal in, at the price he has identified as the 'right' price, it is a sterile exercise. A £500 million fund may have identified a share that is cheap. To make any measurable impact on the performance of the fund the manager needs to buy at least £10 million worth of stock. But if the company he wants to buy has poor liquidity – say it typically trades £250,000 worth of stock a day – he will find it difficult to buy the amount he needs in any reasonable timescale. On top of this, if he is too aggressive, he risks alerting the market and pushing the price up against himself. This is the nub of the liquidity problem.

Liquidity has always been a significant issue for equity fund managers because, in contrast to bonds, there are many more stocks and the average size is much smaller. Eurobond issuers have responded to demands for greater liquidity by creating so-called 'jumbo' issues, worth $4–5 billion a time. Unfortunately, equity issuance is not quite so simple. Liquidity – or rather the lack of it – is probably responsible for more frustration than any other single issue confronting the institutional equity investor. The massive growth in institutional funds, together with the concentration of fund management 'firepower' into ever larger units, the spate of corporate takeovers and the reduction in the supply of equity as companies buy back their shares, has greatly exacerbated the liquidity problem in the past 10 years. From a trading perspective, big fund managers are, as a consequence, driven by access to pools of liquidity. To them, it matters little where these are to be found, whether on traditional stock exchanges or alternative electronic trading networks.

Confusingly, in recent years, liquidity has come to mean four different but interrelated things. (Lex actually uses the term in all four senses – although fortunately not simultaneously!)

■ It is used to mean ease of buying and selling, as defined earlier. The concept can refer to a whole market, such as the gilt market, as well as an individual share. Before Big Bang two other terms were used to describe the same concept in the context of individual equities – 'marketability' and 'dealability'. Gradually, liquidity – an American import – has taken over from these.

■ Liquidity can also mean cash itself, as when a fund manager is asked, 'What is your liquidity?' In reply he will say something like '5 per cent'.

■ It is also extensively used to refer to the quantities of cash flowing into and out of markets – the weight of money going into and out of unit trusts, pension funds etc. and its effect on equity and bond supply and demand, and prices.

■ On a macroeconomic level, liquidity can refer to the measurement of monetary variables in the global economic system. The withdrawal of credit by banks from the system is called a 'liquidity crunch'.

We will continue to refer to liquidity only in the first sense, even though there is powerful evidence that this definition has the weakest claim to be the real thing. 'Marketability', had it survived, would have been a much more accurate and helpful description.

Liquidity is broadly related to company size. Bigger companies generally have better liquidity than smaller companies. Only one corporate size dimension matters to stock market participants: not sales, or profits, or assets, or number of employees but **market capitalization**. Whenever fund managers, analysts or investment bankers ask each other, 'How big is that company?', the answer is always the 'market cap'. Market capitalization is simply the number

Unfortunately, equity issuance is not quite so simple. Liquidity – or rather the lack of it – is probably responsible for more frustration than any other single issue confronting the institutional equity investor.

of shares in a company multiplied by the current share price, so that it reflects on a daily basis the market's view of any particular company. It is also simple to work out if you know the figure for earnings and the P/E (either historic or forward). A company that reported an after-tax profit last year of £100 million and is on a historic P/E of 20 would have a market capitalization of £2 billion. The £2 billion figure also reflects expectations for the current year: forecast earnings of £125 million would imply a forward P/E of 16.

From an investment point of view, market capitalization is a critical component in the way the fund management business operates. Institutional investors divide companies – following StreetSpeak – into 'largecap', 'midcap', 'smallcap' and (in the US) 'microcap'. The levels at which the categories begin and end are subjective, though, at any one point, there tends to be a broad consensus between fund managers. Equating market capitalization with size does, from an outside perspective, look bizarre on occasions, as when an old-line company, employing many thousands and fallen on hard times, is worth a fraction of a company with a handful of employees, no profits and a truckload of expectations! However, as we explain in Chapter 5, market capitalization is really the only yardstick institutional investors can use because that is how *they* are judged. The performance of most fund managers is assessed against an index of some kind, invariably weighted by market capitalization. In the UK this is commonly the Financial Times Stock Exchange (FTSE) Actuaries All-Share Index (often referred to simply as 'the All-Share') which is considered to be synonymous with the UK equity market.

In broad terms, market capitalization and liquidity go hand in hand. But the relationship is not one to one. Liquidity can often differ between two firms with the same 'market cap'. Some companies are easier to trade in than others. There could be several reasons for this. There may be a single large holder, such as a family, or a few large holders. A good example is Associated British Foods, a member of the FTSE 100 Index. The Weston family controls 54.5 per cent of the equity, which considerably restricts the 'free float' (the percentage of the equity that is theoretically available to be traded). Sometimes the stock suffers from an illiquid (or 'thin') market because its shareholder register is dominated by a few institutions which choose to sit on their holdings. This may be because there is general unanimity in the City on the company's prospects – and no one wants to sell given the risk of not being able to get back in.

Conversely, certain shares are the subject of a permanent debate about their prospects, which leads to higher levels of activity as the balance of power switches between the bull and bear camps. BAE Systems (the old British Aerospace) is a good example of what market makers call 'a good two-way market'. There are always opposing views and, as a result, good liquidity for its size. As a consequence, the share price swings around a lot and institutions treat it as a 'trading stock'. In other words, they will buy and sell a proportion of their holding, hoping to ride the short-term price movements. This, of course, further reinforces liquidity.

Also liquidity is not linear. What this means is that a company with £100 million market capitalization does not have one-tenth of the liquidity of a company valued at £1 billion, or indeed one-hundredth of the liquidity of a company valued at £10 billion. It is much worse than that. Our £100 million company will probably not trade at all on some days, and when it does it will only be in a few thousand shares. Contrast this with Rio Tinto, one of the world's largest mining companies, quoted in London (and Sydney) and valued at around £14 billion. On average, Rio's daily trading volume is four million shares, worth around £50 million. At any given moment, a professional investor can buy or sell 50,000 shares (equivalent to £650,000) without difficulty.

> They will buy and sell a proportion of their holding, hoping to ride the short-term price movements. This, of course, further reinforces liquidity.

The reasons for this disparity are essentially similar to those we have already considered. Institutional investors, once they have made a decision to invest in a £100 million company, tend to adopt a 'buy and hold' strategy, due to the difficulty and expense of securing a holding. Clearly, if everyone adopts this view there is no liquidity. As a company grows, there must come a point when liquidity improves. That point is reached when institutions become confident that if they sell, say, 25,000 shares, it will be possible to buy them back – should they so wish – with relative ease. Once everyone begins to believe this, the dam bursts and the stock suddenly becomes more liquid. The relationship between institutions and liquidity is similar to the relationship between elephants and their habitat. Given the choice between an open plain and a dense, difficult-to-penetrate forest, elephants would always vote for more plain and less forest.

The concept of the **cycle** is deeply ingrained in the psyche of the professional investor (and, as a consequence, in the City as a whole). In a capitalist environment, it is a well-recognized phenomenon, applying to economies, industries and markets. Most professional investors still believe that bull markets are inevitably followed by bear markets. Some industries – chemicals, paper, mining, general insurance for example – are inherently cyclical, often because they are capital intensive and sell commodity products. In good times, too much new capacity goes in, provoking a collapse in prices, a profit downturn and (quite possibly) a dividend cut. Institutional investors place these industries in a separate category called 'cyclicals' and frequently treat them as shares to buy at the bottom and sell at the top – if liquidity permits. For obvious reasons, they are less attractive than growth companies, and the stock market usually accords them a low valuation.

But the institutional perception of cyclicality runs deeper than this. Even growth businesses are seen as subject to cycles, in terms of products, in terms of management, in terms of the share-price. A successful product or market formula is bound to tarnish at some point, the management that grew the company in its early days may not be right for the next phase of development and so on. Investors are acutely conscious that 'nothing is forever', which is one of the reasons why, even in a company that produces consistent EPS growth, the share price often swings around dramatically. This transient view of the world is reflected in a widely used City phrase: 'Timing is everything!' Everything has its moment – the difficulty is capturing that moment. Investment bankers look at the marketing effort put in to create an M&A deal in a similar way. Persuading a company to sell one of its subsidiaries is often a matter of hitting the parent with a sensible proposition at the right time.

> When, in November 2001, the British Airways share-price jumped 17 per cent in a day on the back of a fall in the oil price, less than 2 per cent of the shares were traded.

This deep-rooted sense of cyclicality – or perhaps impermanence – helps to explain why share prices always overreact. When the news is disappointing the price goes down too far, and when the news is good it rides too far ahead on a wave of enthusiasm. It is not difficult for an equity salesperson in a securities firm to persuade a fund manager to sell a small proportion of his holding when a share price starts to slide. Equally, when a share price is going up the desire not to miss the bandwagon is a powerful motivation. Stockbrokers make their living from turnover, so they have every incentive to encourage activity. Additionally, it is important not to forget that (in economists' language) share prices are made at the margin. It takes little buying or selling – in relation to number of shares outstanding – to move a share price. When, in November 2001, the British Airways share-price jumped 17 per cent in a day on the back of a fall in the oil price, less than 2 per cent of the shares were traded. A share price reflects the views of those few holders who decided to do something – not the 'silent majority' who have chosen (or decided for reasons of liquidity) to do nothing.

The fact that prices are struck at the margin is one reason why what appear to be mild negative earnings surprises are often accompanied by seemingly disproportionate falls in share prices. However, the key reason is not the actual shortfall against expectations. What worries investors are the implications of that shortfall for future earnings. The results, coupled with any associated statement, cause analysts and investors to rachet their model of projected earnings downwards. Just like puncturing a balloon, a small incursion serves to undermine the carefully constructed edifice in an instant.

Leverage is pure StreetSpeak. The British equivalent is 'gearing', which refers to the debt that a company has in its balance sheet as a percentage of its equity base. The Americans have always referred to this figure as leverage (rhyming with 'beverage'). In the City both terms are used but leverage is increasingly taking over. Leverage is an important calculation for the current generation of institutional investors. It is also a vital calculation in the private equity industry as investors in mature unquoted companies basically make money by leveraging their investments to the hilt (or, more accurately, as far as the banks will allow).

Modern investment fashion says that debt is good, because debt costs a company less than equity. (Apart from anything else, interest payments are tax deductible while dividends have to be paid out of after-tax profits.) A leveraged balance sheet is therefore an efficient balance sheet. It lowers a company's cost of capital, leading to higher earnings for shareholders. The trend on the part of corporations to hand back cash to their shareholders via share buybacks and special dividends is directly related to this change in thinking, as is the surge in corporate bond issuance. With the onset of more difficult trading conditions the mood has shifted. Investors may not subscribe to the 'cash is king' philosophy that held sway more than a decade ago but they are scrutinizing balance sheets with increased rigour.

Leverage is also used in a different sense, both in the financial community and outside. It can also refer to 'a means of accomplishing a purpose, power, influence'. It has been widely used in American business and finance in this sense for at least a generation. US high-tech companies in the early 1980s talked constantly of 'leveraging our internal capability'. What this basically means is doing more with the resources you already have, taking advantage of existing skills to enhance revenues and profits (perhaps by putting an existing product into a new market). A more picturesque way of putting it would be 'getting more bang for your buck' – yet another Americanism as it happens! As the StreetSpeak component in CitySpeak rises, so the usage of leverage in this second sense is increasing.

A journey from sector to sympathy

As we explained earlier, equity investors look for comparisons whenever they can to try to gain a sense of value, although this is much more difficult than in the bond environment. Companies that share the same industry dynamics are an obvious starting point. So, early on, institutional investors grouped companies with similar characteristics into an industry sector and securities firms employed analysts to specialize in particular sectors. 'Sector' is now widely used beyond the City to mean industry, as in 'the energy sector'. Shares that are considered to have the same or similar dynamics are, in CitySpeak, called 'comparables' ('comps' for short). These shares are constantly compared with each other in terms of P/Es and other ratios and with sector averages. Is Tesco expensive compared with Sainsbury's and the rest of the food retailing sector, making due allowance for the differences between them?

Between stock market sectors, however, there is an enormous variation in the degree of comparability. Some, like the oil sector, can be viewed as 'macro' sectors – the biggest single factor in the earnings performance of the constituent companies is the oil price. Similarly, non-food retailers are all affected by changes in interest rates, through the effect on consumer credit. But many other sectors are heterogeneous, containing companies that are not, in fact, very comparable at all in terms of the factors that drive their earnings. At one end of the spectrum is the mishmash of companies grouped by the London Stock Exchange into something called support services which contains an extraordinarily diverse range of companies ranging from De La Rue (currency printing for developing countries) to Shanks (UK and Benelux waste management) and Bunzl (disposables distribution in the US). Who could possibly argue that there is any commonality in the profit dynamics of these three companies? Other sectors, such as engineering and machinery, are also intrinsically varied and difficult to compress into a mould.

> Better an inadequate comparable than no comparable at all. The key point is that, while this reliance on comparisons is clearly helpful in some sectors, it is much more difficult to apply in others.

Investors, in their constant search for a 'value' reference point, have a tendency to downplay the differences between 'comparable' companies, although instinctively some adjustment is made. It is a rough and ready approach to valuation in the absence of anything more scientific. Better an inadequate comparable than no comparable at all. The key point is that, while this reliance on comparisons is clearly helpful in some sectors, it is much more difficult to apply in others. Some sectors are highly artificial constructions.

Sector constituents are always weighted by market capitalization. What this means is that, quite often, a few stocks predominate, perhaps accounting for 70 per cent or 80 per cent or more of the sector value. In market capitalization terms, the UK oil and gas sector consists of BP and Shell and little else. Food producers and processors include Unilever, Cadbury

Schweppes and AB Foods, and a long tail of much smaller companies. Others, such as construction and building materials, have a more even spread. Concentration within sectors is directly related to the size of an economy, and the incidence of quoted companies in that economy. In the US, the size of the economy and the large number of quoted companies – probably 15,000 compared with 2,400 in the UK – means that sectors tend to have more constituents, more equal constituents and more readily comparable constituents. At the other end of the scale, the concept of sectors has limited value in a country as small as Finland, with 150 listed companies. Nokia not only accounts for virtually the whole of the telecommunications and electronics sector, it is responsible for more than half of the capitalization of the entire market!

The institutional stock market is a stock market of sectors. Much professional investment activity is sector driven. From a fund management perspective, being in the right sector is often a more important influence on performance than stock selection. Sectors, and the major stocks contained within them, are critically important in the construction of investment portfolios. The 'mind map' of a typical UK fund manager is shown in Table 3.1.

Table 3.1 UK stock market sectors and key constituent companies

Industry sector	Sector market capitalization as a percentage of the All-Share Index capitalization	Major constituent companies (market capitalization as a percentage of the All-Share Index capitalization)	
Banks	19%	HSBC	5%
		Royal Bank of Scotland	4%
		Lloyds TSB	3%
		Barclays	3%
		HBOS	2%
Oil and gas	13%	BP	9%
		Shell	3%
Pharmaceuticals and biotech	12%	GlaxoSmithKline	7%
		AstraZeneca	4%
Telecommunications services	7%	Vodafone	5%
Subtotals	**51%**		**45%**
The rest (31 sectors)	49%		55%

Source: FTSE Actuaries All-Share Index, April 2002

While market capitalizations of sectors and stocks swing around significantly as share prices go up and down, from the perspective of a fund
manager the focus on a few dominant sectors and stocks is a permanent
feature of modern stock markets. The degree of concentration in both sectors
and stocks reached in early 2000 is unprecedented in recent history. Just 10
stocks accounted for close to 50 per cent of the All-Share Index. In 1990
25 stocks accounted for 40 per cent of the All-Share. The glamour sectors of
telecommunications, media and technology (TMT) were alone responsible for
over one-third of the market. With the bursting of the TMT bubble, the
degree of stock market concentration has been restored to the more 'normal'
levels shown in Table 3.1 (in which four sectors are still dominant).

Investment managers look closely at the percentage of the total market
that a sector represents and make a conscious decision whether or not to
match that 'weighting'. For them (as we explain in Chapter 5) it is crucial to
make a correct judgment on these major sectors and stocks. The inevitable
corollary is that smaller sectors and stocks fall (in CitySpeak) 'below the
radar screen' and attract little attention. Fund managers and analysts also
endeavour to compare stocks in the same sector across national boundaries. This obviously makes more sense in a sector that is genuinely international, like pharmaceuticals or oil and gas, than one that is essentially
domestic, such as retailing.

Sectors are also important to companies. In theory, each share is evalu-
ated on its individual merits but, in reality, it is at least partially judged by
the company it keeps. A good company in a poorly regarded sector will suffer, or vice versa. To try to benefit from this effect, companies are constantly
seeking to convince the committee that controls these things that they are
more suited to another sector – which, as it happens, stands on a higher
average P/E. Sometimes, companies change the composition of their business to accomplish this. It is, in effect, a form of arbitrage. Since the late
1990s the magnet for many service-oriented companies has been the –
seemingly – all-embracing support services sector. Several companies in the
sector, such as Capita and Serco, have long enjoyed high P/Es, reflecting
their involvement in the fast-growing and fashionable business of outsourcing. Former construction companies, like Amey and Jarvis, switched to
support services in a bid to capture the positive image the sector has in the
minds of investors.

The creation of new sectors, a change in the composition of an existing
sector, or the addition or removal of individual companies from a sector has
important investment and share price implications. In January 1998 the
London Stock Exchange carved out an information technology sub-index,
and investors piled into the new sector, sending it up 88 per cent in seven

months. The rise was driven largely by sentiment – the underlying earnings growth was good but not generally considered sufficient to justify this kind of share price performance.

Sentiment is an elusive concept. It is a way of describing the collective mood that drives individual share prices, sectors and the equity market as a whole. Basically, it is an emotional reaction to a piece of corporate or other stock market-related news. Individual shares and whole sectors move in and out of favour. Investors may become positive on the electronics sector while 'negative sentiment' affects food retailers. 'Sector rotation' – over a period of weeks or months – is a well-established investment phenomenon.

Quite often, this rotation occurs between groups of sectors. The major swings tend to be between 'growth stocks' and 'cyclicals' (or, as one American magazine put it, 'from glamour to grit'). Sometimes 'sector' is used more loosely to refer to such a grouping, as in 'the growth stock sector'. In reality, there is no hard and fast line between the two groups: many companies are, in fact, 'growth cyclical'.

Cyclicals fall into a much larger category called 'value stocks' – companies that are, by measures such as a low P/E relative to the market, above-average yield or low price-to-cash-flow ratio, undervalued at the current share price. A 'value stock' is any share that is perceived to be priced at a discount to its true worth. The value investor is a bargain hunter. Like the pawnbroker he is convinced that what he is buying can be sold, in short order, for significantly more than he paid. 'Value analysis' has its origins in 1930s' America, in a seminal book called simply Security Analysis by Benjamin Graham and David L. Dodd (1996). A disciple of Graham, a young man called Warren Buffett, picked up these ideas in the 1950s and applied them so successfully to the US equity market from his base in the Midwest that he became known as 'the Sage of Omaha'. Through his investment vehicle, Berkshire Hathaway, Warren Buffett purchased value stocks, avoiding technology shares, a strategy that has produced sustained long-term performance.

> The rise was driven largely by sentiment – the underlying earnings growth was good but not generally considered sufficient to justify this kind of share price performance.

The growth stock investor buys a share that he knows to be highly priced because he believes its revenues and earnings will continue to grow – and that the share price will follow. He is like the house purchaser who consciously pays over the odds to buy a house in an area that has already 'come up', on the basis that, having become fashionable, houses in the area will always remain in strong demand. Growth stocks can come from any industry but, in practice, high-tech companies predominate. The growth school of investment also originated in 1930s' America. It is particularly associated with T. Rowe Price, who went on to found the company that bears his name, now one of the leading US asset managers.

For professional investors, the difference between the growth stock approach and the value stock approach to investing represents a genuine philosophical divide. In the US, the terms 'value' and 'growth' are just as familiar to retail investors. Mutual funds (the American equivalent of unit trusts) are categorized on this basis and their managers proudly proclaim themselves as either committed value investors or committed growth investors. In reality, the distinction between these two approaches is not as clear cut as it appears. Professional investors will often employ elements of both. Nevertheless, fund managers tend to ally themselves with one camp or the other. During the nineties the growth camp was in the ascendant but, since the middle of 2000, value managers have been back in the driving seat.

> If, say, a computer company produces unexpectedly poor results, the immediate reaction of analysts, traders, equity salespeople and investors is to sell the shares.

There is invariably a rational basis for a stock market reaction but sentiment implies that the share price move has been overdone in terms of what are called the **fundamentals** – the things that actually affect a company and its prospects. (Fundamentals are contrasted with the purely 'technical' factors that affect a share price, such as patterns in trading volume.) When, in the late 1980s, Britain suffered a postal strike, the share prices of the quoted mail order companies fell sharply, despite the fact that they hardly relied on the mail for deliveries. In essence, sentiment is a residual – the element in a share price move that cannot be explained by reference to the fundamentals. There can, of course, be no hard and fast division between these two elements in a share price move. Rather like an English essay, the allocation of marks is inherently subjective!

Sentiment is definitely not sentimental. The death or resignation of a company chairman or CEO can provoke a rise in the share price, if it was felt he was holding the company back or that it might now attract the attention of a bidder. Just as sentiment is not sentimental, **sympathy** is not sympathetic. In CitySpeak it refers to the share price changes that occur in other companies – usually in the same sector – as a consequence of news affecting one company. If, say, a computer company produces unexpectedly poor results, the immediate reaction of analysts, traders, equity salespeople and investors is to sell the shares. The next reaction is to cast around for other computer companies whose earnings might be similarly affected and sell them. Once this has happened, these other companies' share prices are said to have moved 'in sympathy'. A bid for a company will trigger upward moves in other companies in the same sector. Sympathetic moves are a gut reaction and have much to do with sentiment. It is obviously a matter of judgment on the part of analysts and investors as to whether the news is specific to the company or actually indicates something about the industry as a whole.

Why investment banks and investment banking are the same but different

While most financial market participants would have little difficulty in coming up with an agreed definition of 'investment banking', everyone has a different conception of what an 'investment bank' is and what it does. One thing is clear – an investment bank always includes investment banking. It may have started there or moved into it from other activities. The problem arises over the myriad other activities in which investment banks are now involved (which are often referred to loosely as 'investment banking'). A reasonable working definition of what an investment bank does is that it covers those banking activities whose earnings are affected by the vagaries of the securities markets. Confusingly, investment banks and commercial banks – now entirely freed from the restrictions of Glass–Steagall – are busy trampling over each other's patches and the line between them is becoming increasingly blurred. It has got to the point where anyone who does a modicum of investment banking and a bunch of other banking activities can get away with calling themselves an investment bank – if that is what they want to be!

Investment banking, as we saw earlier, involves raising money via the issue of securities for 'corporates' (CitySpeak for any kind of organization capable of using the capital markets). Investment banking and securities trading are closely related although, strictly, stockbroking is not part of investment banking. It is a mutually beneficial relationship. Investment bankers rely on securities analysts and salespeople to sell the issues that their marketing efforts have generated. These people are the essential link with the institutions and individuals who buy new issues, a relationship that prevails because there is a continuing dialogue between them on shares already being traded. Long ago, all the American investment banks set up securities arms rather than depend on an outside party. Some were later than others to grasp the importance of control over selling and trading. Morgan Stanley, formed in 1935 when the all-powerful J.P. Morgan bank was obliged to divest its securities-related activities, disdained the grubby business of dealing in securities until, in the 1970s, upstarts like Goldman Sachs and Salomon Brothers forced them to follow suit. The securities business has also benefited from this connection. As profits on trading in existing stocks have come under increasing pressure, investment banking has come to represent a highly important source of income.

It is a pity that British merchant banks were prevented by the rules of the stock exchange from treading the same path. After Big Bang in 1986, some of the merchant banks acquired securities operations, which brought their activity profile more into line with that of a US investment bank. Commercial lending had always been a part of traditional UK merchant banking but, for the majority, it had become a minor activity. By the 1980s the mainstays of merchant banking were advisory and equity-raising work for corporate clients, and fund management. The Accepting Houses Committee, the elite club of 16 British merchant banks, was disbanded in 1988 and replaced by a rather less select grouping, the British Merchant Banking and Securities Houses Association (BMBA), including – perhaps regrettably but almost certainly inevitably – foreigners. Confronted with the increasing presence of the US investment banks in London and in international markets – and the need to convince clients that they could do all the things that these sleek new competitors claimed to be able to do – the merchant banks reluctantly began to call themselves investment banks. In 1994, the BMBA changed its name to the London Investment Banking Association (which is considering dropping 'London' from its name, to reflect the fact that almost all investment banks based in the UK are now foreign-owned).

Using a syndicate of banks to help companies raise funds in the securities markets is a well-established practice in the US. It was first used in the 1890s by J.P. Morgan, the leading banker of his time. The classic US-style investment banking model that has become the preferred way of raising capital worldwide, whether debt or equity, is a three-step process.

1 *Origination.* This covers the process of winning the mandate for the deal, structuring and arranging it, including writing the prospectus which, in the US, needs to be registered with and approved by the Securities and Exchange Commission (SEC).

2 *Underwriting.* Essentially, underwriting is a guarantee that the issuer receives the amount of money agreed with the investment bank, whatever happens in the marketplace. It involves the investment bank in risk – as it is obliged to make up any shortfall itself – but the degree of risk can in practice be very substantially reduced (as we explain in the following section). Every deal of any size is underwritten by a syndicate of investment banks, with the mandated bank acting as the lead underwriter and manager.

3 *Distribution.* New issues of securities are sold through what is known as a distribution syndicate. To sell the issue, the lead underwriter

organizes a 'roadshow' in which management takes its case directly to institutional investors. A distribution syndicate includes all the members of the underwriting syndicate – or their securities arms to be exact – and a 'selling group' of securities firms who bear no risk. Sometimes the underwriters decide to do all the selling themselves and the two syndicates are one and the same. The underwriters are always responsible for the bulk of the distribution: those in the selling group receive only small allocations to sell on to their clients.

The generic term for any kind of security issuance is an **offering** or **offer**. This is StreetSpeak but is increasingly used in CitySpeak. In its purest sense, investment banking is all about underwriting new issues, about making offerings. The London Stock Exchange has its own traditional system of equity issuance but, increasingly, UK and continental European issuers of any size are opting for a US-style offering in the international equity market, the equity version of the Eurobond market.

There are a variety of offerings that a company can make, once it has decided (with advice from investment bankers) on the most appropriate type of security. The security could be a bond or equity, or something in between, such as a convertible bond (one that can be converted into equity at some point in the future). An important distinction exists between primary and secondary markets. 'Primary' and 'secondary' are terms that are used widely in the City.

> In its purest sense, investment banking is all about underwriting new issues, about making offerings.

The **primary market** for securities is the market in which securities are first issued. In other words, this company has not issued this type of security before. The key point is that the company is selling securities to raise fresh money from investors to finance the company or repay the founders or backers. It is not a matter of investors buying shares or bonds from other investors. Within investment banks, the division that is responsible for this business is often called 'capital markets'. In the equity market, a capital markets issue is called a flotation or, in StreetSpeak, an initial public offering (IPO). Increasingly, in London, the terminology used is IPO – it is actually more self-explanatory as it emphasizes the first-time nature of the offering.

The **secondary market** is the market in which already existing securities are traded by investors. This is what securities firms do on the stock market on a daily basis (except when helping to distribute a primary market offering). Offerings can also be made on the secondary market: in StreetSpeak these are called 'follow-on' offerings.

What, then, does an investment bank do? Clearly, it is engaged in investment banking and securities operations. But nowadays it can also do a whole range of other things. Corporate advisory work is a logical extension of investment banking and has always been regarded as part of the service. The larger investment banks leverage their balance sheet and trading skills by offering derivatives and engaging in proprietary trading (taking big bets on securities using the firm's own money). When investment banks choose to put the firm's balance sheet on the line in pursuit of profits from 'prop trading', or indeed in the normal course of trading securities, they are said to be acting as a 'principal' rather than as an 'agent'. Corporate advisory is an agency business – there is no risk to the firm other than the loss of an expected fee. Proprietary trading and market making, on the other hand, are principal businesses involving a serious risk of loss to the firm. Even when trading in the secondary market for institutional clients, traders may use the firm's own 'book' to facilitate a client deal. It is this willingness to take risk that secures large institutional trades for market makers. Effectively, the investment bank is creating liquidity for the institution that wants to, say, sell £100 million of Unilever immediately by using the bank's own balance sheet.

Most investment banks are also active in fund management. It is now regarded as a major activity and one that they wish to expand. This was not always so. As recently as the early 1990s several investment banks were ambivalent about fund management, on the basis that they might be perceived to be competing with their clients. Goldman Sachs, in particular, was a late convert to the benefits of an in-house fund management operation. Others, such as Merrill Lynch, acquired funds through their vast retail network that sells directly to the US public and the takeover at the end of 1997 of Mercury Asset Management, the largest institutional fund manager in the UK. Deutsche Bank and UBS started down the investment bank road with large, captive domestic fund management operations and then added to them by buying Morgan Grenfell and Phillips & Drew respectively, although in neither case was fund management the primary motivation for the deal.

In the 1980s the Wall Street investment banks entered the business of investing directly in unquoted companies, predominately the leveraged buyouts (LBOs) that were all the rage at the time. These were generally deals they had arranged, taking the view that if they thought it was a good deal, they should put some of their own money in. This is a form of private equity activity that, like trading, exposes the firm to risk. The basic idea is to leverage existing knowledge and contacts – and generate further investment banking opportunities. Morgan Stanley, Merrill Lynch and a host of others set up funds for this purpose, inviting investment institutions to participate. For a time in the nineties, the Wall Street term for this business was – confusingly – 'merchant banking'. It is now more commonly referred to as private equity. US investment banks were in the forefront of the race to invest in unquoted TMT opportunities during the dotcom boom. Then, in 2001, with values sharply down and the IPO market virtually closed, these bold new ventures turned swiftly from (potential) benefit into burden. Almost every investment bank has since reported significant write-downs on its private equity portfolio.

Lending was once a commercial bank preserve but, in 1994, three leading Wall Street investment banks signalled their intention to move into this business by hiring bankers to create commercial loans units. By 1997 nearly all the others had followed suit. (This makes the definition of an investment bank even more elastic, as many would argue that an investment bank is a bank that does *not* make loans!) The object of the exercise is primarily to act in support of a major takeover or merger by adding to the range of financing options available to a corporate client. The popular name for this strategy is the 'one-stop shop'. Its application in practice was well illustrated in 1998. In the bid battle between Texas Utilities and PacifiCorp for the UK-based Energy Group, Merrill Lynch and Goldman Sachs agreed to lend £2 billion and £1.8 billion from their own resources to their respective clients.

> For a time in the nineties, the Wall Street term for this business was – confusingly – 'merchant banking'. It is now more commonly referred to as private equity.

It should be obvious by now that the only true definition of an investment bank lies in the eye of the beholder. Through their involvement in IPOs, securities broking and trading, fund management and private equity, investment banks straddle the equity world (and a great deal more besides, especially debt). Table 3.2 summarizes the key activities of a representative investment bank, based on the categories that the leading investment banks use in their public financial statements.

Table 3.2 Key activities of an investment bank

Investment banking
Primary market activities
Corporate advisory

Trading and principal investments
Secondary market activities
Private equity investments

Asset management
Fund management and private client services

From the perspective of the stock market – and nearly all the major investment banks are now quoted – the earnings stream from trading and principal investments is both risky and volatile. Earnings from investment banking are also variable but considerably less risky. However, both activities can be extremely profitable. Asset management does not offer the same potential for profitability but has much more predictable earnings. (Chapter 5 explains why this is so.) This higher-quality earnings stream is one reason why the investment banks overcame their concerns and are busy expanding their presence in this area.

As, during the 1990s, the Federal Reserve Bank gradually dismantled the restrictions imposed by Glass–Steagall, many US commercial banks flirted with the idea of becoming a significant force in investment banking. Few have succeeded. Tensions inevitably arise between the two cultures – between the high-bonus, free-wheeling investment banking approach and the structured, risk-averse ethos of the commercial banker. Bankers Trust and J.P. Morgan both failed to transform themselves from organizations dependent on the interest margin, succumbing to bids from Deutsche Bank and Chase Manhattan respectively. For Chase (which immediately rebranded itself J.P.Morgan Chase & Co.) the acquisition in December 2000 marked the culmination of a spending spree involving several smaller investment banks, including Flemings, the London-based private bank with large interests in Asia. Melding these separate operations into a coherent (investment banking) whole has proved to be a demanding task, particularly in the context of weaker business conditions. The one commercial bank that has succeeded – at least on the evidence so far – in grafting an effective investment banking business on to its original core is Citigroup, created in 1998 via Citicorp's purchase of Travelers Corporation (a major insurance company, that owned Salomon Smith Barney).

> Many view investment bank-type activities as a useful adjunct to their core activity but have no desire to let them grow to the point where they unbalance the business.

Commercial bank attitudes vary. Many view investment bank-type activities as a useful adjunct to their core activity but have no desire to let them grow to the point where they unbalance the business. European banks have always espoused the multi-product 'universal banking' approach. Now, released from Glass-Steagall, some US commercial banks are pursuing a similar philosophy. Others have turned their back on investment banking entirely. Lloyds TSB is totally focused on retail banking while the Bank of New York has become the worldwide leader in the 'back office' business of custody (the task of processing trades for institutions, and holding and reconciling investments for them).

American investment banks, as we noted in Chapter 1, enjoy very substantial advantages by virtue of their history and their home base in the largest, most lucrative, most innovative market for investment banking services. Non-American investment banks suffer from a permanent handicap – rather like the boxer who has difficulty reaching his opponent, let alone being able to land a telling punch. For an investment bank based outside the US with global ambitions, a genuine and substantial presence in New York is therefore a sine qua non. In Europe, only three commercial banks with such aspirations can lay claim to a seat at the top table: Crédit Suisse of Switzerland, through its prescient initial investment in First Boston as far back as 1978; UBS, also Swiss, through UBS Warburg; and Deutsche Bank through the acquisition, in 1999, of Bankers Trust.

Equity capital markets – riding the rollercoaster

The Euroequities (or international equities) market is a natural extension of the Eurobond market. Like the Eurobond market it is European based and centred on London. **Equity capital markets** (often abbreviated to ECM) is the term given to the primary markets business of securing new equity from multiple international sources. It operates on the basis of the US-style offering system (origination, underwriting, distribution) we described in the last section. During the 1980s the approach that had proved so successful for Eurobonds was adopted by many large companies wanting to access equity from institutions located outside their domestic market – so enlarging the investor base and improving the issue terms (higher price, lower yield).

Promoted by the City-based Eurobond investment banks, the Euroequities business really took off in the 1990s, fuelled by several large-scale continental European privatizations. More than $300 billion of state assets were sold via the marketplace between 1987 and 1997, accounting for 55 per cent of all European ECM business. More recently, corporate deals, mostly as a consequence of European industrial restructuring due to the influence of the 'US model', have taken over the running from government-initiated offerings.

ECM is a notoriously lumpy business, often giving issuers and investors a rollercoaster ride. Continually shifting investment sentiment means that countries, currencies and sectors move in and out of favour, rather like sector rotation in the secondary market. In fact, investment bankers involved in capital markets operations will, when talking about current business trends in particular areas, such as Asia or utilities, describe the market as being either 'open' or 'closed'.

The way a US-style primary market offering works is very different from the traditional European domestic stock market mechanisms for raising equity, like the UK offer for sale and rights issue approaches, which it has largely supplanted. IPOs are invariably conducted the American way but, in several European countries, the legal obligation companies have to offer new shares to existing investors (known as 'pre-emption' rights) means that, in secondary market offerings, domestic mechanisms are still used. At the heart of the US-style offering lies a process of 'bookbuilding', which allows the investment bank running the deal to assess institutional demand and adjust the price and size of the issue accordingly. In the UK, the most common way of selling new equity today is via a 'placing', which is normally conducted using bookbuilding techniques.

ECM origination starts with a 'beauty contest'. A company contemplating an equity issue interviews the investment bankers competing for the underwriting mandate and selects one to act as its lead manager. The lead manager is very much in the driving seat, being responsible for managing the whole offer process. The lead manager is also the bookrunner – it is his job to keep the 'book' which contains the shares to be sold and the orders received for those shares. In a small corporate issue there is usually only one bookrunner. But in a large issue, with tranches of stock sold on a regional basis, there may be regional bookrunning lead managers reporting to a global co-ordinator, who ultimately merges these books into a single global book. The lead manager is responsible for writing the prospectus, having satisfied himself through a 'due diligence' investigation that the company has represented itself truthfully and accurately to potential investors. The issuing company appoints a syndicate of underwriters, controlled by the lead manager through a hierarchy of co-lead managers and co-managers. The key to a US-style equity offering is the pre-marketing phase. This is the stage at which, via their securities arm, capital markets executives contact fund managers to assess their reaction to the company as an investment. This stage is actually preceded by a pre-screening operation in which the concept of the proposed issue is tested in conversations with a few selected fund managers. It is a classic 'what if?' exercise. In the pre-marketing phase investors provide feedback on the attractiveness of the issue and, especially, their views on valuation.

> The lead manager is very much in the driving seat, being responsible for managing the whole offer process. The lead manager is also the bookrunner.

Once all this information is in, the investment bankers can make a decision on the upper and lower price limits likely to be acceptable to investors and the number of shares that the market might be prepared to absorb.

The indicative price range and size of offer is then published in a preliminary prospectus, which contains basic business and financial information
on the issuer and the offer itself. In America, this document is known as the
'red herring'. (The name comes from the warning, printed in red, that the
information is still being reviewed by the SEC and is subject to change.) The
UK equivalent is the so-called 'pathfinder' prospectus (which – perhaps
intentionally – sounds like an interplanetary space probe!). It was first used
in 1984 for the British Telecom IPO.

Interest in the marketing phase is generated by the company roadshow
– a large issue will involve two teams of top managers putting the case to
investors in cities across the globe. A roadshow involves both group presentations and, for larger institutions, one-on-one meetings. It normally
lasts one to two weeks, during which time the capital markets team is building the book by soliciting and receiving indicative orders from investors.
Securities sales and research personnel are an integral part of this process.

Outside the US, sector analysts employed by syndicate members write
and circulate research on the company to investors before the roadshow.
The lead manager co-ordinates this process to ensure that these reports are
all fundamentally telling the same story. Interestingly, no such research can
be issued in the US during an offer period. The SEC works on the principle
that the preliminary prospectus, which must be a comprehensive assessment of the company, its prospects and the risks involved, should be the
sole source of written information in front of investors when they make
their decision.

At the end of the marketing phase the investment bank fixes the price,
the prospectus is finalized, shares are allocated to investors and trading
begins. Bookbuilding allows the bookrunner to construct a comprehensive
picture of the strength of institutional demand for the shares. Bookrunners
use it to create 'price tension' between investors, rather in the way that an
auctioneer uses competition to force up the price in a sale room. It also
enables the bank to pinpoint longer-term investors and push more shares
in their direction – not always an easy task.

The period immediately after a stock is listed is called the 'after-market'.
The lead manager has an obligation to create liquidity and provide research
coverage in the after-market. Investment banks deliberately price new
issues below what they really think the market will pay to ensure a premium
in the after-market. This discount (usually of the order of 10–15 per cent) is
needed to grease the distribution channel, ensuring a positive reception
from syndicate members and the selling group. Achieving the right after-
market price is a balancing act. The investment bank tries to maximize
the value for the vendor while leaving just enough on the plate to keep the

buyers happy. In effect, the lead manager has two 'customers' – the company that pays his fee and the investors who buy the issue.

Underwriting involves risk, at least in theory. The risk is that the investors are not prepared to put up the money the company requires. In a US-style offering this risk is borne by the investment bank plus its syndicate of underwriters. By contrast, the traditional UK method of raising equity involves a fixed price offer underwritten by a merchant (now investment) bank backed up by a horde of sub-underwriters, who are actually institutions, not fellow investment banks or securities firms. The big drawback is the need to take a stab at the 'right' price several weeks before trading begins. Making the right decision depends on fine judgment and is reliant on there being no material change in market sentiment or conditions over the period. There is, however, one major plus – the company is guaranteed a specific sum of money at an early stage in the process. A traditional UK offer for sale or rights issue is also cheaper. An offer for sale allows ample opportunity for the individual investor to obtain a holding. A US-style offering, in the UK at least, effectively shuts out the private investor unless, as in privatizations, a tranche of equity has been specifically set aside for the retail market.

From the perspective of an investment bank, the beauty of a US-style offering is that it removes nearly all the underwriting risk. By the time bookbuilding is complete the lead manager knows, barring a sudden change in corporate or market circumstances, what the demand will be and at what prices. Shares are then allocated and fund managers asked to confirm their commitments. Trading takes place a day or a few days afterwards. At this point, the only risk to which the investment bank is exposed is the risk that the institutions that have committed to buy fail to come up with the money. In the capital markets business, a US-style offering is often described as 'soft' underwriting. The lead manager is really being paid for the skilled and arduous task of procuring buyers, not for taking underwriting risk.

> Making the right decision depends on fine judgement and is reliant on there being no material change in market sentiment or conditions over the period. There is, however, one major plus – the company is guaranteed a specific sum of money at an early stage in the process.

The pros and cons of the US-style offering process versus the fixed price approach are the subject of a complex and convoluted debate in financial circles. For our purposes it is sufficient to note that, whatever its merits or demerits, the US-style offering process has in practice swept all before it. Even smaller UK IPOs are done this way. The syndication approach to new equity does, in fact, have some very significant positives. It is generally more flexible and responsive. A key point is that every issue is actively marketed. In a secondary market offering the roadshow goes to both exist-ing and new institutional investors, so extending the shareholder base. European-style equity-raising mechanisms have much less of the 'Go forth and deliver the message' about them. The existence of a syndicate means that firms other than the lead manager feel obligated to make a market in the stock and write research on the company after the issue. Bookbuilding is an iterative process and is bound to produce a more accurate result because it reflects investors' up-to-date views on valuation.

ECM is a substantially profitable business, unlike secondary market trad-ing which makes little or no money (for reasons explained in Chapter 7). Fees are typically 2–4 per cent of the sum raised, the bulk of which go to the lead manager. Fee levels are considerably lower for privatizations. US domestic equity underwriting fees are significantly higher than those pre-vailing in Europe. Despite difficult market conditions in 2001 domestic fee levels fell only slightly (to 3–4 per cent for secondary market transactions and a remarkable 6.5 per cent for IPOs). The US IPO business is effectively controlled by a small group of US investment banks, prompting the Depart-ment of Justice to announce an investigation into 'the possibility of anti-competitive practices' in May 1999. (It was quietly dropped in mid 2001.) The leading US banks remain a powerful force in European equity capital markets, based on their ability to convince European corporates of the reach of their distribution machines, particularly the level of access they offer to the 50 or so largest (predominately American) global institutional investors who effectively decide whether an offering succeeds or fails.

Make my day with M&A

From an investment banking perspective the **merger and acquisition** (or corporate advisory) business has several features that make it attractive.

■ First and foremost, it can be extremely profitable. Fees are related to the value of the transaction. Consequently a great deal of money is made when companies are busy buying and selling themselves (or bits of themselves) and the deals are big, as happened in the long bull market of the 1990s. And, unlike secondary or primary market activity, M&A is an agency business: it does not normally require the firm to commit capital, with its attendant risks.

■ The decision to do an M&A deal – and therefore the decision on who to appoint to the advisory role – will invariably be made by the chief executive of a company, perhaps by the board of directors as a whole. Compare this with a fund-raising exercise. The selection of a bank to lead or participate in an equity issue will probably be made by the finance director. For a bond issue it is likely to be the corporate treasurer. M&A is a 'company critical' decision and, because it involves corporate strategy and bid tactics, represents a golden opportunity to build a relationship with the prime mover and shaker in an organization (and key potential provider of further business). Some banks therefore – in investment banking terminology – accord lead 'coverage' responsibility to an M&A executive. It is the job of the coverage executive to deliver fees on *all* of the bank's products.

■ M&A also appeals to investment banks because corporate deals frequently have financing consequences. Often a company focuses on an acquisition and then finds itself casting around for the most effective way of paying for it – creating a good opportunity for the bank that has been appointed to advise on the deal to sell its expertise in bond or equity-raising or other financing techniques. In a perfect (investment banking) world, the bank ends up with two fees: one for advice and another for finance. Sometimes, as in the case of a high-yield bond issue, the fee earned from doing the financing can be several times the advice fee.

■ For an investment bank, M&A is a high-profile business. Large, headline-grabbing deals penetrate public consciousness in a way that the other activities of an investment bank do not. As the next section explains, in the absence of any acceptable overall ranking system, investment banks tend to be judged by their M&A prowess.

Reading the business pages of the newspapers it is easy to get the impression that most M&A deals are large, noisy affairs involving reams of rhetoric. In truth, the majority of transactions are small and agreed, attracting little attention outside the City. Most activity consists of Big Company A selling a subsidiary to Big Company B, or Big Company A buying a smaller, private competitor.

In the UK and the US, a bank advising on a deal must act for one side or the other, just like a barrister representing a client. It cannot act for both. No doubt this rule reflects the adversarial nature of the Anglo-American legal system, in which it is assumed that each and every party has separate and identifiable interests that must be protected. On the Continent of Europe they see things differently and it is not unknown for two companies involved in a friendly deal to use a single adviser.

Contrary to what some outside the City suppose, retaining the services of an adviser in an M&A deal is not compulsory. Large companies, with the appropriate internal resources, can do without. Cable & Wireless has a history of doing its own deals. When, in January 2002, AOL Time Warner acquired the 49.5 per cent of AOL Europe it did not own from Bertelsmann for $6.8 billion it did so without an adviser. However, a do-it-yourself approach is not feasible if the company being bid for – or possibly the buying company – is a quoted entity. An investment bank is needed to ensure compliance with stock exchange regulations.

Investment banks compete to obtain a contract (referred to as a 'mandate', as in fund management) to advise on a particular proposed deal: principally acquisition or sale. The mandate specifies the fee the bank will receive if – and only if – the deal goes through. A key point is that fees are heavily success-weighted. True, this is the norm in the City but the risk that the bank will not receive the agreed fee is generally higher in the corporate advisory field. Particularly when a bank is appointed to advise on an acquisition. There are several reasons why a deal may not complete – most often when another firm wins the day by paying more or moving faster. Or when, on further inspection (called in the trade the 'due diligence' investigation), the bidder pulls out because it does not like what it finds.

A bank holding a sale mandate is generally better positioned. Once a client has decided to sell a company the chances are that it will actually go through with it, perhaps at a lower price. It may be withdrawn from what is known as 'the sale process' (usually involving an auction to try to flush out a high price) but tends not to be once the process has been set in motion. One reason is that, almost inevitably, news about the proposed sale leaks out, with potentially adverse consequences for employee morale and customer attitudes. Bidders in a sale process are asked to sign a Confidentiality Agreement to try to prevent this happening but, in practice, the industry gossip machine is invariably too effective.

A typical buy or sale mandate takes several months to complete. If it falls at any fence before the final one the fee received by the bank will typically be 15 per cent of the figure in the mandate letter. As a rule-of-thumb fee levels for completed (agreed) deals are around 0.75 per cent – 1 per cent of the value of the deal. Above $1 billion the percentage 'take' falls to 0.5 per cent or lower. Conversely, fees on small transactions can be as high as 2 per cent. This sliding scale goes some way towards compensating for the fact that the amount of work involved in a deal is not intrinsically related to size – but not enough! Making real money in M&A is essentially a matter of doing – and completing – big deals.

How do investment banks go about getting M&A business? Senior-level corporate advisory bankers, backed up by an army of 'foot soldier' researchers,

> Almost inevitably, news about the proposed sale leaks out, with potentially adverse consequences for employee morale and customer attitudes.

maintain a relentless pursuit of corporates, particularly large international corporations with a perceived appetite for M&A activity. They do this by offering a continual flow – some would say barrage – of 'free' information and ideas on possible acquisitions ('targets' in the jargon) and disposals. For M&A bankers, life is a constant round of presentations to senior corporate management, aimed at securing that key advisory role. In a competitive business, with not a lot of difference between suppliers in terms of product or capability, keeping 'in front of the client' is seen as crucial. Which is why executives in M&A tend to work longer hours than their counterparts elsewhere in investment banking.

Most UK companies of any size employ someone, usually called the 'corporate development director' or something similar, specifically to handle the stream of investment banking M&A presentations. Their function is to protect the chief executive and, especially, the finance director from spending too much time looking at potential deals, at least at an early stage. Of course, direct connections exist at the more senior levels and senior bankers spend considerable time cultivating – and cementing – these contacts through corporate entertainment. Without the dedication shown by investment bankers and their guests, Covent Garden, Wimbledon and the like would have a much harder time making ends meet.

Despite all this effort, the fact is that most corporate deals are initiated by companies and not by banks. For companies, the great majority of deals they might wish to do are obvious – it is more a matter of availability, timing, price and so on. However, more often than might be supposed, there are instances when a banker spots an opportunity that an executive heavily involved in a sector has missed.

Companies nowadays, and especially large international corporations whose business banks are extremely keen to obtain, have substantially relaxed the traditional UK concept of the 'retained' adviser, who acted on their behalf in all circumstances. Under pressure from the Americans, the gentlemanly merchant bank-corporate client relationship broke down during the 1980s. Companies may have 'nominated' advisers – sometimes a veritable raft of them – but this indicates a bias rather than any degree of exclusivity. Indeed, there is evidence that large companies deliberately spread their investment banking business around, in an effort to keep the leading banks 'onside'. Such is the power of the leading investment banks that firms seek to avoid giving a bank cause for adopting negative stance on the company (which might have share-price and/or M&A implications).

Today it is much more a matter of 'horses for courses'. Investment banks are generally awarded mandates for specific projects, often on the basis of their contribution to the development of an M&A idea or special expertise relevant to a particular deal. As a rule, companies will reward a good idea with a mandate to execute that deal. Apart from coming up with original M&A ideas – no easy task – how do investment banks compete? By being helpful, by providing extra insight into the industry or the proposed deal, by being alert at the right time and by being creative on the financing front. And by demonstrating a track record of deals, preferably in the client's sector or in the type of deal under consideration.

During the 1990s specialization by sector became virtually de rigeur in the leading US investment banks. Under this structure M&A bankers work in industry teams – energy and utilities, financial institutions, technology, general industrial and so on. Client responsibility – from marketing through transacting a deal – lies exclusively within the sector coverage group. In part, the impetus for this approach came from a desire to align M&A marketing with sector research in the securities division, better to leverage the knowledge and contacts that exist there (as explained in Chapter 7).

> As a rule, companies will reward a good idea with a mandate to execute that deal.

Sector specialization has been adopted by the European-based investment banks, though not quite as enthusiastically. One drawback is that, when a banker leaves or a sector goes through a bad patch, it is not easy to transfer people from elsewhere. Even so, there is no doubt that it can be an effective strategy. A good example is the purchase of the UK company, PowerGen, by the German utility company, EON, in April 2001. Goldman Sachs was in the advisory driving seat, the result of an established relationship. Yet, despite Goldman's evident all-round capability, EON was persuaded by Rothschilds it needed the bank's expertise in navigating the US utility regulatory minefield (PowerGen owned a US utility). Rothschilds had previously advised National Grid on the purchase of three American utilities. Goldman Sachs retained the lead role but Rothschilds was brought in alongside to advise on the US aspects of the transaction.

It is sometimes assumed by City outsiders that falling share prices, because they make everything cheaper, are good for M&A activity. In fact, the reverse is true. M&A activity turned down sharply in 2000, after the boom years of 1998 and 1999, and continued at lower levels through 2001. Buyers have more difficulty in financing an acquisition when their own share price is falling. In a bear market, investors become nervous and may withdraw their support for M&A activity. Management hesitates because next month the target could become cheaper still. Borrowing becomes less of an option as banks draw in their (lending) horns. All in all, when the stock market goes down or has no discernible trend, M&A activity generally declines.

The battle of the bulge

For a long time in the US, investment banking and securities trading have generally been carried out by a single entity. Investment banks originated in one of two ways – and the difference in background continues to have a significant influence on their current operations and strategy.

■ Wholesale investment banks, with strong corporate connections, specializing in selling securities to the institutional investors who came to dominate the stock market in the 1970s. The prominent names in this group are Morgan Stanley, Goldman Sachs, Salomon Brothers and First Boston.

■ Retail securities firms, selling securities to individual investors via thousands of salesmen located in offices across the country, a business that really came into its own in the 1920s. Known as 'wireline' houses – reflecting the use of the telegraph to convey news of the latest hot stock to a waiting audience – the names associated with this group are Merrill Lynch, Dean Witter, Smith Barney, PaineWebber, Shearson, L.F. Hutton and Bache.

> In the 1920s, brokerages and the securities affiliates of banks began to pursue the individual investor, promoting stocks as a safe bet for the middle classes.

While the concept of an investment bank has some parallels in Europe, the retail securities firm-cum-investment bank is an exclusively American phenomenon. To an extent, the history of the retail securities business is the history of that quintessentially American practice – the 'hard sell'. Mass stock market investment originated during World War I with Liberty Bonds, sold to a patriotic public to pay for the war. In the 1920s, brokerages and the securities affiliates of banks began to pursue the individual investor, promoting stocks as a safe bet for the middle classes. Thousands of salesmen were recruited and offices opened on every main street. That indispensable American marketing tool, the 'cold call', was invented. Broking firms encouraged investors to trade in the secondary market and also played a key role in pushing new issues, as few investment banks at the time controlled their own distribution. The hothouse atmosphere of the time is brilliantly captured by a quote from Ron Chernow from his essay on the constantly shifting relationship between investment and commercial banking:

> *Buying stocks … was invested with new respectability and the public rejoiced in a New Era of blue skies and perpetual prosperity,*

as if the business cycle had been repealed forever. In this giddy environment, Wall Street discovered it could move stocks, like soap suds or cereal, through high-pressure salesmanship.

(Chernow, 1997, p. 41)

It is interesting to contrast the emergence of these networks – with a brief to go out and sell stocks and bonds – with the development of the equivalent business in Europe. Private client business conducted by stockbrokers or merchant banks remained discreet, low key and essentially passive, targeted at the wealthy rather than the middle classes. The concept of setting up a network of offices close to the customer to access a larger market was totally alien. Far better the client came to see them in London (or Edinburgh, or Geneva, or Luxembourg). When public interest in the stock market did develop in Europe, it was promoted by collective investment vehicles like unit trusts. Or it occurred as a result of privatization coupled with a government commitment to creating a new breed of individual shareholder. The key point is that, in the US, there exists a well-established, comprehensive, proactive system for selling securities to private individuals on a person-to-person basis. It is this tradition that forms the basis for the high level of private shareholder participation in the US stock market. No equivalent exists anywhere in Europe.

Inevitably, the wholesale banks looked down on the retail houses, regarding them as useful for additional distribution but little more. Morgan Stanley, in particular, regarded itself as the social pinnacle of Wall Street. It was staffed by legions of young men who had been to the right schools and belonged to the right clubs. They were known as 'white-shoe' bankers (a description that presumably reflects the ready availability of shoeshine boys in the New York of the 1930s). By contrast, the lowly securities houses lacked corporate contacts and were not in a position to capture a part of the prestigious and lucrative investment banking business. These two groups maintained an uneasy alliance until things changed in the 1980s. Before then, corporate client relationships were sacrosanct. If Morgan Stanley was your underwriter, Morgan Stanley was always your underwriter. Corporations did not move around. The cartel broke down in 1979 when IBM, a Morgan Stanley client, brought in Salomon Brothers, an upstart wholesale bank, to co-manage a billion-dollar debt issue. Morgan Stanley reacted in horror but from then on no client was safe from a predatory competitor, wholesale or retail.

When the floodgates burst open nearly all the securities houses tried to turn themselves into multi-capability investment banks. How have they fared? In general, not well. Despite the loosening up of the corporate market and the emergence of a whole new range of opportunities, most of the old wireline houses have been subsumed into someone else. Only Merrill Lynch, the largest US retail brokerage, still exists as an independent entity. PaineWebber sold out to UBS in July 2000. Merrill Lynch is the one unequivocal success story. Even so, as little as 10 years ago, it was far from clear that it would succeed in competing with – let alone beating – Goldman Sachs and Morgan Stanley in the wholesale markets. In 1989 Merrill Lynch reported a record loss. A respected industry journal summed up its strengths and weaknesses at that time:

> A factor in most major business lines in the US, simply too big and powerful to ignore. Also has a strong presence in the Euromarkets. Downside: heavy exposure to shaky bridge loans and sour merchant banking deals; terrible at cost control; frequent shifts in strategic focus; huge and expensive retail network isn't yet paying its way.

(*Institutional Investor*, January 1990)

One thing the success of Merrill Lynch has done is demonstrate the power of an effective retail–wholesale combination in investment banking. Suddenly, in the 1990s, retail broking no longer had the status of a poor relation but became where investment banks wanted to be, with Merrill as the model. In 1997 Morgan Stanley acquired Dean Witter, with its 370 offices and three million customers. Smith Barney became part of Citigroup.

The immediate rationale for being in retail is to strengthen the firm's ability to distribute the offerings that it leads or participates in as a syndicate member. But, to a greater extent, the new-found enthusiasm for retail reflects the rise in the importance of the private investor. Private investors are not simply buyers of securities – they can also be sold mutual funds or other similar products and encouraged to leave spare cash on deposit with the firm (pioneered in 1977 by Merrill Lynch as its Cash Management Account). In short, the real object of the exercise is the accumulation of customer assets, on which interest and fees can be earned, a relatively stable source of income. For a brief period, the 'Merrill model' faced a challenge from the internet, which fizzled out as online dealing activity declined. Although under pressure, US retail broking remains solidly profitable. The retail–wholesale combination retains its validity.

Which are the leading investment banks? Banks nowadays live (and die) by league tables, ranking each competitor in terms of business done. Tables are compiled by outside parties, such as information vendors and specialist publications, for every conceivable segment of the business. League table credits are seen as a vital marketing tool – conferring so-called 'bragging rights' – in the race to capture the next deal. There is, however, no generally accepted table covering *all aspects* of investment banking. In practice, as we noted in the previous section, investment banks tend to be judged mostly by their position in the M&A rankings.

The top firms in the investment banking industry have long been known in StreetSpeak as the 'bulge bracket'. The term dates from the 1940s and 1950s when a few banks on Wall Street ran a near-cartel of securities underwriting. Every issue they handled was recorded in a 'tombstone' advertisement in the financial press. (A page of tombstones is, of course, 'a cemetery'!) The names of these select few firms were printed in larger and bolder type than the others and consequently 'bulged out'. Membership of the bulge bracket is a matter of general consensus within the industry. One thing is clear. To qualify for bulge bracket status it is not enough to have a presence on Wall Street – it needs to be a major presence on Wall Street. Table 3.3 lists those firms that are generally considered to qualify.

The top tier includes the three 'pure' investment banks, together with Citigroup, reflecting the huge progress made by the bank during 2001. The composition of the second tier is more problematic. Some would argue that, although Deutsche and UBS have made great strides, they do not yet qualify for membership.

In the 1990s the pure investment banking model – exemplified by Merrill Lynch, Goldman Sachs and Morgan Stanley – appeared to be unassailable. But the onset of a bear market in equities has raised some serious questions. Fortunately for the commercial banks, the repeal of Glass-Steagall came just at the right time. Once the Cinderellas of the investment

Table 3.3 Investment banks: the 'bulge bracket'

First tier
Merrill Lynch
Morgan Stanley
Goldman Sachs
Citigroup
Second tier
Crédit Suisse First Boston
Lehman Brothers
J.P. Morgan Chase
Deutsche Bank
UBS Warburg

banking business, in the absence of easy access to equity, their ability to advance credit cheaply and in large amounts has become a source of leverage. It can be as simple and as crude as saying to corporate clients 'We will lend money – or extend credit – only if we receive a share of your investment banking business'. Equally, companies are linking the award of mandates to the provision of debt. This has had the effect of reinforcing the already strong linkage between lending and bond issuance. Surveys suggest that the link between lending and ECM or M&A work, while higher than it was, is markedly less strong. The extent to which balance sheet has come to influence the ability to secure investment banking business is the subject of a vigorous debate. For the moment the balance of advantage lies with the universal banking model. But will it last? What happens when equity issuance once more becomes a realistic option?

In the 1990s the pure investment banking model – exemplified by Merrill Lynch, Goldman Sachs and Morgan Stanley – appeared to be unassailable. But the onset of a bear market in equities has raised some serious questions.

Institutional flows and institutional power

How source signifies behaviour

- The rise and rise of the institutions

- All change in pensions

- Rather surprisingly, for a long time British pension funds kept their balance

- An American runaway called 401(k)

- When life does not mean life

- The appeal of the collective

- Overseas investors learn to love London

Pensions ground planes. How occupational pension funds are constructed can have a dramatic impact on the company setting them up. In the final quarter of 1998, just after the stock market crashed, American Airlines was forced to cut its flight schedules as pilots retired in droves, taking advantage of a quirk in their pension plan that allowed them to cash in their pension at the value it had three months earlier.

Cockpit captains opted for retirement at three times the normal rate – with a pension worth 10 per cent more than current values!

The rise and rise of the institutions

Throughout the Western world, money flows into investment institutions continue to be very strong. In its 2001 annual report, the International Monetary Fund calculated that, between 1990 and 1998, assets managed by mature market institutional investors more than doubled, to over $30 trillion. Tax incentives, heavy marketing, ignorance, and the difficulty and cost of doing it yourself conspire to push individuals into the welcoming arms of the institutions. Only in the US has the siren call been resisted to any significant degree, partly because certain popular pension plans sometimes allow individuals to manage their own securities portfolio if they so choose. This chapter looks at the sources of institutional funding, concentrating on the key role played by pension funds.

In terms of the absolute value of aggregate institutional investor assets held globally, the US is overwhelmingly dominant. Figures produced by the Bank for International Settlements in 1998 (relating to 1995) show the US accounting for 50 per cent of all institutional assets, with Japan second at 14 per cent and the UK third at 9 per cent. France and Germany are both at the 5–6 per cent level. After that, the asset proportions fall away rapidly to 2–3 per cent (the Netherlands, Switzerland and Canada) and a string of 1 per cents or lower (Australia, Spain, Italy, Sweden, Denmark, etc.).

Much more interesting than the absolute figures are the kinds of funds that contribute to each country's total. Here we see a big variation in the mix. Institutional funds can be divided into three broad types according to the source of those funds:

- pension funds
- insurance companies
- investment companies.

The first category relates largely to occupational pension schemes run by corporations and other organizations for their employees (which must, of course, by definition be funded). Insurance companies have moved a long way from their roots and nowadays run a whole variety of funds, including pension funds for groups and individuals. Investment companies (covering mutual funds – the generic term for unit trusts outside the UK – and investment trusts, a peculiarly UK phenomenon) are inherently different from the first two categories. They are retail collective investment vehicles. The private investor selects a fund – Asian equities or European corporate bonds, for example –

> Only in the US has the siren call been resisted to any significant degree, partly because certain popular pension plans sometimes allow individuals to manage their own securities portfolio if they so choose.

from a range of options. In a standard occupational pension scheme or a traditional insurance policy, the individual has no influence at all on the investment decision. Other types of fund exist but they are not significant. The one exception is the US, where charitable endowment funds, often university-based, are a major factor. (The Americans lump pension funds and endowment funds together into a category called 'tax-exempt' funds.)

In practice, the three types of funds are becoming increasingly intermingled, both at a product and corporate level. Insurance funds now offer a degree of choice. Most professional fund management organizations of any size have a stake in all three fund types. For example, Lloyds TSB runs corporate pension funds, unit trusts and, through Scottish Widows, insurance funds. Figure 4.1 compares the relative importance of the different types of institutional investor geographically.

Figure 4.1 International comparison of institutional investor financial assets by type, 1999

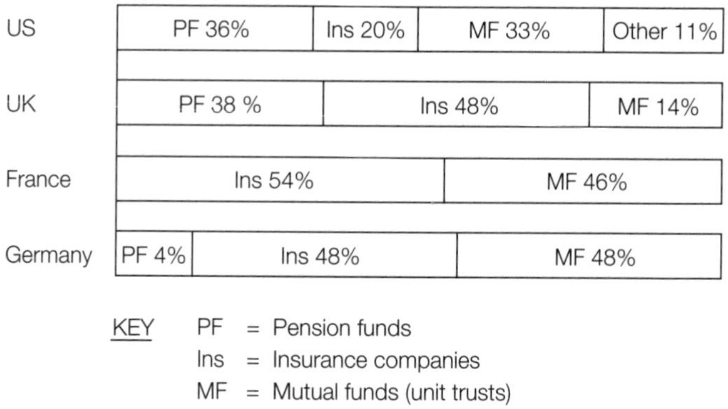

US	PF 36%	Ins 20%	MF 33%	Other 11%
UK	PF 38 %	Ins 48%	MF 14%	
France	Ins 54%	MF 46%		
Germany	PF 4%	Ins 48%	MF 48%	

KEY PF = Pension funds
Ins = Insurance companies
MF = Mutual funds (unit trusts)

Source: The Conference Board, Institutional Investor Report, April 2002

> The mutual fund business in France is at least twice the size of the unit trust business in the UK. Neither, however, approaches the sheer scale of the US mutual fund industry.

Funded pension schemes are very important in the US and the UK, play a minor role in Germany but are non-existent in France. Some smaller European countries, notably the Netherlands, Switzerland, Sweden, Denmark and Ireland, have an established funded pensions industry. Canada and Australia, not surprisingly, also follow the Anglo-Saxon pension model. France, on the other hand, has the highest proportion of mutual fund assets, followed by Germany. The mutual fund business in France is at least twice the size of the unit trust business in the UK.

Neither, however, approaches the sheer scale of the US mutual fund industry. Relative to the UK and continental Europe, the insurance industry in the US grew rather slowly in the 1990s. In France, insurance company funds have been the fastest growing type of asset by a wide margin but the industry has also shown good growth elsewhere, especially Italy but also in the UK.

Looking specifically at the UK – and making full use of the most recent Office for National Statistics survey of share ownership – certain trends are clear:

- Occupational pension funds still form the backbone of the institutional fund management industry and their needs determine much of its practice. However, they have been sellers of UK equities since the early 1990s, partly due to a slowdown in the growth rate of cash flowing in but mostly because of a deliberate move into bonds, especially in recent years. The proportion of the stock market controlled by pension funds has fallen sharply, from 32 per cent in 1992 to 18 per cent in 2000.

- Insurance companies have gradually increased their share of the equity market during the last decade, reflecting their successful promotion of equity-based products. At 21 per cent, their share is now ahead of pension funds. Indeed, in terms of the total assets they have under their control, insurance companies now far exceed pension funds.

- Unit trusts and investment trusts together account for about 9 per cent of stock market capitalization.

These three types of fund influence the UK equity market in different ways. To them must be added a fourth major influence: overseas investment institutions. At 31 December 2000 foreign investors accounted for 32 per cent of the value of London equities. Foreign investment in British companies has been on a strongly rising trend since the mid-1990s, with an increasing impact.

Fund management operates within a context. That context is the source of the money under management. Decisions on asset allocation, stock selection and timescale are heavily influenced by context. In the UK the big picture is: on the back of buoyant cash flows, insurance companies, unit trusts and overseas institutions have been buyers of UK equities as pension funds reduce their holdings. In America, equity buying during the 1990s was fuelled mainly by occupational pension fund money invested by individuals through mutual funds.

All change in pensions

It is important not to confuse pension funds with retirement provision. The term 'pension funds' refers to corporate occupational funds that are separately identifiable and separately managed ('self-administered' in the jargon). In practice, this generally means the larger funds. But the retirement provision industry is much wider than this. Insurance companies and other financial institutions operate pension schemes for smaller companies and for individuals. In addition, much saving through insurance contracts and via unit trusts is for retirement purposes, even though it is not actually labelled as such.

Originally set up between the wars, corporate pension plans were until the 1970s mostly run by insurance companies. Today the corporate pension landscape is dominated by self-administered funds. The investments are managed internally by company executives or by external managers appointed by the fund (or a combination of both). Occupational pension schemes cover around half the workforce. In America, the first modern corporate pension fund was established by General Motors in 1950. Companies that set up funds became known in StreetSpeak as 'plan sponsors' (a more helpful term than 'pension fund' as this can refer to either the sponsoring company or the actual fund). Similarly, the asset management firms that compete for this business are known as 'money managers'.

The Anglo-Saxon funded approach to providing pensions exists to supplement state provision for retirement, which operates on a pay-as-you-go basis (retirees are paid out of taxes levied on the incomes of the current working generation). In most of continental Europe, the reliance on pay-as-you-go is extremely high relative to the UK (and the US). In Germany company schemes are significant but they mostly operate on a 'book reserve' basis (whereby the sponsoring company makes a provision in its balance sheet). Book reserve schemes are not funded – which means that the members are at risk if the company goes bust. France also has occupational pension funds but they are almost entirely pay-as-you-go, relying on the revenues of the sponsoring firm.

> Greater longevity and a decline in fertility mean that the ratio of the population of working age available to support the generation that has retired is in long-term decline. This is a problem for all advanced countries but will clearly have a lesser impact on the Anglo-Saxon nations.

What has been called the 'demographic time-bomb' is placing an increasing strain on the pay-as-you-go system and on pension systems generally, including funded schemes. Greater longevity and a decline in fertility mean that the ratio of the population of working age available to support the generation that has retired is in long-term decline. This is a problem for all advanced countries but will clearly have a lesser impact on the Anglo-Saxon nations. Even though the situation does not become acute until after 2010, all governments are having to think seriously about pension reform. The (further) encouragement of funded schemes – both occupational and personal – is an obvious route, making use of fiscal and other incentives.

Funded occupational pension plans do not all operate on the same basis. A crucial distinction – with major implications for the future of the pensions industry – exists. Depending on the way the scheme is structured, there is a different allocation of risk between the employee member and the corporate sponsor.

■ A 'defined benefit' (DB) scheme provides the employee with a retirement income based on career earnings, normally related to the final year's salary. DB is also often referred to as a 'final salary' scheme. For the sponsor, this represents an open-ended commitment – the company is obligated to pay benefits at the contracted rate even if the fund proves inadequate. DB is 'a promise'. Usually, employee contributions are fixed and employer contributions vary from year to year, in line with the need to keep the fund in balance according to actuarial calculations. The employee has no involvement in investment strategy.

■ In a 'defined contribution' (DC or 'money purchase') plan the individual bears all the investment risk. All contributions are made at a pre-determined rate and the contributing individual has a separately identifiable 'pot' of money. The pension received on retirement is wholly dependent on the value of the investment in the fund at that point in time. Normally, the individual cashes in the fund and buys an annuity from an insurance company to generate his pension income (which, for recent retirees, has turned out to be a poor deal, due to a sharp fall in annuity rates). DC plans can be organized by an individual or sponsored by an employer. When a DC scheme is occupationally based the company usually supplements the contribution made by the employee. The employee has an input into the investment decision but most employers opt for the simple approach of a few investment managers and a restricted choice of funds.

Traditionally, corporate pension plans have been set up on a DB basis. Currently, however, there is a big swing in favour of DC, following the trend in the US. For the employer, DC has the appeal of financial certainty. All types of fund manager have entered the DC market, attracted by the growth prospects. One of the first was Mercury Asset Management (now Merrill Lynch Investment Managers) with its 'Lifestyle' product, which shifts the fund into bonds a few years before retirement, to reduce the asset risk as the due date approaches.

At present, probably 20–25 per cent of UK occupational fund assets operate on a DC basis. Most companies have set up DC schemes in parallel with the existing DB scheme, which is then closed to new entrants. For a time it looked as if the government's low-cost 'stakeholder' pension scheme, aimed squarely at individuals and launched in April 2001, might slow this trend but it does not appear to have done so. Meanwhile, traditional DB pension funds have seen a decline in new cash inflow. This is partly because many of the long-established DB funds are now increasingly 'mature' – the cash flowing in from contributions matches or falls below the sums paid out each year so fund growth is low or non-existent.

What has caused this shift to DC? Probably the single most important reason is the desire of companies to limit their exposure to volatile pension costs, as these have implications for their own accounts. Legislation (the 1995 Pensions Act, which was essentially a reaction to the ease with which Robert Maxwell was able to raid the corporate pension fund to prop up his sinking empire) and changes in accounting standards have exacerbated the position. Specifically, a new accounting standard known as FRS 17 forces companies to recognize the impact of pension liabilities and surpluses on their balance sheet. Although not fully in force, companies are already feeling the impact. It is, unfortunately, being introduced at a time of lower equity prices, which serves to highlight the issue for sponsors of DB schemes. Lower costs are also a highly significant incentive for employers: companies tend to contribute materially less to DC schemes. To an extent, DC reflects a demand from employees for more flexible pension arrangements than those offered by the typical DB scheme. It is particularly suitable for employees who change jobs frequently as it offers total portability between one employer and another.

Rather surprisingly, for a long time British pension funds kept their balance

Pension funds in the UK operate under a legal framework based on the principle of trusteeship. Legal trusts were developed during the Crusades to hold and protect assets. Every trust must be set up using a trust deed, which separates the control of wealth from the right to benefit from it. Effectively, when they were first established, pension funds 'borrowed' the trust concept and adapted it to a different set of circumstances. The prime duty of any group of trustees is towards the beneficiaries – in this case the members of the pension scheme. A key point is that a trust is a distinct legal entity, and is 'ring-fenced' from the sponsoring employer. The 1995 Pensions Act was passed to reinforce the existing trust-based framework.

In the UK there are probably around 200,000 self-administered pension schemes, all with trustees. Three-quarters of these have fewer than six members and two trustees, and are run by an insurance company. Larger schemes have up to 20 trustees. A self-administered fund has two alternative ways of organizing its investment management:

■ Putting the assets into a 'managed' fund (or funds) run by an insurance company or a 'pooled' fund run by a money manager. These are effectively unit trusts for institutions. Smaller pension funds (say, under £50 million of assets) are encouraged to use this route.

■ It can have the money managed by a professional fund management organization (which could be an insurance company) on what is called a 'segregated' basis. The fund is separately managed by an identified fund manager. All larger plan sponsors opt for segregated management.

Trustees need not be investment specialists – their job is to select and oversee the experts. Scheme members are entitled to elect one-third of the trustees. The interests of the sponsor are inextricably bound up with those of the fund and corporate executives will serve as trustees. Usually, the finance or HR director takes the chair.

> The prime duty of any group of trustees is towards the beneficiaries – in this case the members of the pension scheme.

Investment policy is governed by a body of case law. A landmark case in 1984 (the Megarry Judgement) underpins the whole basis of UK pension fund investment. At issue was a difference of opinion between the employer trustees and the employee trustees on the National Union of Mineworkers Pension Fund. Arthur Scargill's union wanted to prevent the fund from investing overseas or in companies involved in the supply of fuels that competed with coal. The judgement made the objectives of the trustees absolutely clear. Their function is to invest to 'yield the best return for the beneficiaries', having regard to the risk involved. In other words, whatever their thoughts or feelings about any particular investment, the trustees must at all times endeavour to maximize the value of the fund. Since July 2000 UK pension funds have been obliged to publish a Statement of Investment Principles, stating the extent to which social, environmental and ethical considerations are taken into account when making investment decisions. In practice, most such statements are vague and have a negligible impact.

Not being experts, trustees need to delegate the management of the fund to others. Originally, many funds were managed in-house by investment managers recruited or trained by the company. But, for several years now, the trend has been for trustees to place funds with professional fund managers, be they investment banks, insurance companies, specialist asset managers or other types of financial organization. For segregated funds, control is exercised via quarterly reports on performance and regular meetings with the fund manager. In selecting the manager or managers to look after the investments, the trustees are strongly encouraged to seek advice from pension fund consultants, actuaries and other pension fund professionals. If they do not, they run the risk – albeit a small one in practice – of being sued by the beneficiaries.

Actuaries occupy an unassailable position in the traditional corporate pension fund business. The actuarial input into DB funds is very substantial. Every DB plan must appoint a 'scheme actuary' whose job is to assess the value of the fund's assets in relation to its liabilities. A DC fund has no such obligations so there is no comparable statutory requirement. Actuarial firms were once solely concerned with valuation work but, during the 1970s, plan sponsors started to ask them for advice on investment strategy and ways of measuring the performance of the managers they had hired. It was entirely logical for trustees to turn to the actuaries already known to them to do this work on a consultancy basis. Once the consultants had identified poorly performing managers, trustees could begin moves to replace them. And who better to advise on the selection of a new manager than the same trusted actuaries? Investment consulting is now the leading-edge activity of the actuarial consulting firms. The valuation and administration of funds has become a commodity business, in much the same way that auditing has become a standard, cash-generative activity for the accountancy profession. Several of the larger firms have extended the range of services they offer beyond pensions and investment, reinventing themselves as 'employee benefits consultants'.

> The valuation and administration of funds has become a commodity business, in much the same way that auditing has become a standard, cash-generative activity for the accountancy profession.

These firms play a key role in the formulation of strategy and in the selection of investment managers. In the pension fund business, the investment consultants are in a uniquely powerful position, occupying the middle ground between trustees who rely heavily on their advice and the professional fund managers who desperately crave their approval. We look more closely at how the system works in the next chapter.

The structure that UK trustees have, until recently, used to manage the pension funds for which they are responsible has changed remarkably little since the early days of the industry. Generally, trustees have appointed managers to look after funds on what is called a 'balanced' or 'discretionary' basis. In the UK, sponsors with large funds often appointed several balanced managers. The fund manager of a balanced fund has the freedom to invest in a range of asset classes, using in-house specialists to manage parts of the portfolio. The key point is that, under balanced management, the asset allocation decision is essentially delegated to the investment manager. In recent years trustees have generally moved to exert some overall control over the Big Decision by imposing asset allocation target percentages, together with ranges within which the manager is asked to operate (known as 'multi-asset management'). In reality, these ranges have tended to be very wide (say, 45–65 per cent for UK equities), effectively leaving the manager with a high degree of discretion.

The alternative approach is the 'specialist' route. Under this structure asset allocation is determined by the trustees, with advice from an in-house expert or an investment consultant hired for this purpose. Specialist managers are appointed to run portions of the fund. Twenty years ago, the view developed in US investment circles that handing the asset allocation decision to someone else represented an abdication of responsibility. This is the way the majority of US plan sponsors structure their manager mandates, having moved away from the balanced approach in the 1970s. Specialist managers are usually set more demanding performance targets: the whole approach tends to be higher risk, higher reward than balanced management. 'Balanced' versus 'specialist' has been the subject of a vigorous debate in UK pension fund circles for at least a decade and continues to be a 'hot' issue, not least because of pressure from US money managers and investment consultants wanting to break into the UK pensions business. Specialist has been replacing balanced for several years but at a slower rate than many expected. Since early 1999, however, the shift to specialist has gained significant momentum. What was a trickle has turned into a tidal flow.

Various criticisms are levelled at the balanced approach. A fundamental point is that trustees are asking others to make the asset allocation decision. Most professional investors agree that this is the single most important determinant of fund performance. Surely, the argument goes, this is a decision the trustees should take? Once a balanced appointment has been made, the trustees are not really involved. Control can only be exercised through the cumbersome mechanism of hiring and firing managers on the basis of their performance numbers.

Balanced management made sense, it is argued, when DB schemes were immature and all pension funds could safely follow a similar investment strategy. Now funds are mature and they need to match their assets to their liabilities in a customized way. The usual starting point is an asset/liability study carried out by an actuarial consultant, resulting in an asset allocation model specific to the scheme. Trustees need to become involved in this process and, in doing so, they often bring the asset allocation decision back in-house. The debate has progressed from, 'Should the strategic framework be set by the trustees or the manager?' to, 'What are the trustees' objectives and how best can they be achieved?' From this point, it is only a short step to specialist management.

What specialist means in practice is that the trustees split the fund into asset classes and hire managers with known skills in that area – domestic equities, foreign equities, bonds and cash. In the US these asset classes are often further divided and handed to managers with an even greater degree of specialization. In addition, there is commonly an allocation to alternative assets that currently amounts to 6–7 per cent of a typical fund (including property). The downside of the specialist approach is that it demands more time and resources and higher levels of expertise on the part of the trustees and those executives in the plan sponsor responsible for management of the pension fund (as opposed to the management of the investments). It is also significantly more expensive than balanced management. Balanced has always had a reputation of being low cost, which is no doubt one reason why it has been able to hang on for so long.

> It is also significantly more expensive than balanced management. Balanced has always had a reputation of being low cost, which is no doubt one reason why it has been able to hang on for so long.

However, none of these changes, while significant, addresses the larger and more fundamental question: does the pension fund industry invest the savings it gathers from the public in a way that is optimal for the British economy? In May 2000 the government concluded that – very probably – it did not. To sort out fact from myth, it initiated an investigation by Paul Myners, chairman of Gartmore, one of the leading UK fund managers, into the structure of institutional investment and its influence on those who make investment decisions. His report was issued in March 2001. In a comprehensive and well-crafted analysis, the 'Myners Review' (or just 'Myners') concluded that much could be done to improve the quality and transparency of investment decision-making, setting out 'a blueprint for change' in the shape of over 50 detailed recommendations. Myners considered that implementation by the pensions industry – which accepted the general thrust of the report – would best be served by a voluntary 'buying into' the suggested code of practice. The government agreed and said it would 'take forward' the great majority of the recommendations on a voluntary basis. But it retained the right to impose reform through legislation if, after a probationary period (that ends in March 2003), the industry showed signs of dragging its feet. In January 2002 (and subsequently) Paul Myners expressed himself less than pleased with the pace of change so far, saying:

> *Parts of the industry remain in denial about the idea of improving their surveillance of investments. Not enough self-improvement is taking place.*

> (*Financial News*, 7 January 2002)

What, then, are the key influences on a manager of a (DB) pension fund in making his investment decisions? In principle, pension fund cash flows are predictable, so the fund manager need keep little in cash and can afford to take a measured approach to investment. In the 1980s, when they were immature, pension funds were natural and consistent buyers of equities. This is no longer true. Mature funds have a requirement for higher and more reliable bond income to meet current and near-term pensions.

Pension funds are therefore moving out of equities into bonds. The phased introduction of FRS 17 has given this process added momentum as, to meet the standard, a fund's liabilities – its obligations to current and future retired employees – must be valued by reference to the yield on AA rated corporate bonds. As we observed in Chapter 2, corporate bonds are now firmly on the pension fund radar screen.

An American runaway called 401(k)

The legal basis for American pension funds is English trust law, modified by legislation in the 1970s. A comprehensive piece of legislation in 1974 called the Employee Income Retirement Security Act (universally known as ERISA) underpins the regulatory framework. It imposes stringent rules on minimum funding levels for DB plans, which is one reason why American funds tend to have a lower equity allocation. ERISA requires fiduciaries to manage funds 'prudently', which has been interpreted as meaning that a fund should be diversified in its investments. Diversification became an article of faith for American pension funds, to an extent that never occurred in the UK. In fact, the principle that a fund should not 'put all its eggs in one basket' underlies much of modern institutional portfolio strategy. The diversification imperative introduced by ERISA provided the backcloth to the steady move by American pension funds into foreign markets during the 1980s.

> The so-called 401(k) pension plan has been a runaway success story since its introduction in 1981 and is now far and away the leading version of DC.

Occupational pension schemes cover 50 per cent of the US private sector workforce. But, unlike the situation in the UK, DC has convincingly overtaken DB as the primary retirement vehicle for American workers. And, within DC, one particular DC option has been substantially responsible for this, snappily named after the number of a paragraph in the Internal Revenue Code! The so-called 401(k) pension plan has been a runaway success story since its introduction in 1981 and is now far and away the leading version of DC (see Table 4.1). 401(k) is an occupationally based plan over which the individual retains full control – offering the best of both worlds. Its phenomenal success has had important implications for Wall Street and for the continued survival of the US private investor.

Table 4.1 Growth of US defined contribution plan participation and assets

Year	401(k) participants	Total DC participants	401(k) as a % of total participants	401(k) assets	Total DC assets	401(k) assets as a % of DC assets
1985	10m	35m	28.6	$144bn	$427bn	33.7
1990	19m	38m	50.0	$385bn	$712bn	54.1
1995	28m	48m	58.3	$860bn	$1.32trn	65.2
2000	35m	58m	60.3	$1.7trn	$2.52trn	67.5

Source: US Department of Labor, Pension and Welfare Benefits Administration, Winter 2001 (2000 results are estimated)

In the meantime, traditional DB plans have stagnated, basically because employers have moved away from them for reasons we explained earlier. DB tends to be less generous than in the UK. Most corporate pension plans in the US are financed by employers' contributions only. In terms of the number of participants – note the use of the word 'participant' rather than the less inclusive British nomenclature 'scheme members' – DC overtook DB in 1992. The common pattern is for plan sponsors to offer DC as a supplement to the existing DB plan. For small firms and new firms DC is without doubt the preferred option.

Why has the 401(k) been taken up so enthusiastically by American corporate employees? And what are the implications for the investment business? Above all else, the 401(k) is designed for employees, unlike another popular type of DC plan called an individual retirement account (IRA) which is aimed at those without an occupational pension. The 401(k) has several attractive features which make it both tax efficient and flexible. Employees' contributions are tax free. The employer normally makes a matching tax-deductible contribution. The employee decides on the amount of saving, up to certain limits. The fund belongs to the employee, is portable and, in contrast to an equivalent DC plan in the UK, it is possible to take money out, or borrow against it, *before* retirement. The whole package is marketed not as a pension plan but as a flexible, tax-deferred savings plan.

The majority of employers restrict the investment options to a range of mutual funds – ten on average – covering equities (domestic and foreign), bonds, money market funds and so on. In practice, participants invest most of their assets in equities (including company stock – an issue highlighted by the collapse of Enron at the end of 2001). Many plans value fund balances daily, offer internet access to accounts and allow participants to shift money between investment funds on a daily basis. With their existing investment in technology and systems, the big mutual fund houses, such as Fidelity and Merrill Lynch, soon emerged as the major 401(k) plan providers to corporations. Providing millions of employees with little or no prior investment knowledge with the means to make sensible asset allocation decisions has involved an enormous education process on the part of employers and financial service companies. In essence, what the 401(k) has done is to take a large chunk of US occupational pension fund assets away from the wholesale institutions, whose modus operandi involves total control over investment policy, handing it to individuals who then decide investment strategy for themselves, either in the form of parameter setting for retail funds or through direct stock market investment.

> Faced with lower stock market values, participants are taking more out of plans than workers and their employers are putting in. (Resorting to black humour, some refer to their plan as a 201(k)!).

There can be no doubt that the rising tide of contributions to 401(k) plans made a significant contribution to the nineties bull market on Wall Street. Since early 2000, however, the 401(k) market has gone into reverse. Faced with lower stock market values, participants are taking more out of plans than workers and their employers are putting in. (Resorting to black humour, some refer to their plan as a 201(k)!). Mutual funds have been the biggest beneficiaries of 401(k) money due to the way most plans are structured. Only a minority of employers allow 401(k) participants to invest in stocks directly (called self-directed 'brokerage accounts') but this facility is growing rapidly from a low base. And those participants who do exercise this option tend to be on higher salaries with bigger pension plans. Most IRA plans, on the other hand, offer a wide range of investment options, including direct investment in stocks. The number of IRA plans has been boosted significantly by the option of allowing an occupationally based DC plan to be rolled over into an IRA, so that IRAs now represent the single largest pool of US retirement assets, eclipsing private sector DC and DB plans.

There is no real British equivalent to the 401(k). In employer-sponsored DC schemes there is less flexibility and individual control over investment policy is more limited. There is apparently no legal or regulatory reason why DC schemes could not offer increased investment choice, including a direct equity investment facility of the kind available through an IRA or, to a lesser extent, a 401(k). The issues are structural and practical. The government is known to be interested in schemes that give the individual greater control over their personal pension 'pot'. In the summer of 2001 the Treasury quietly launched its Individual Pension Account (IPA), claiming that it contained several 401(k)-like features (though not the ability to hold shares directly). The investment management industry reacted unenthusiastically – arguing that the legislation was too complex – and very few have been sold.

When life does not mean life

Insurance products can be divided into two categories: life and general. Some companies offer both but, increasingly, providers are tending to specialize in one or the other. General insurance – more helpfully called property/casualty by the Americans – is a commodity, cyclical business relying on short-term cash flows. Accordingly, the amounts available for investment are relatively small. Life insurance, by contrast, is a business with large, fairly stable cash inflows from contractual savings and long-term pay-out obligations. The life insurance industry is therefore a significant investor and fund management is a core activity.

Life insurance (or 'assurance' for the purists, to distinguish them from their lesser brethren) began 200 years ago when it was realized that it was possible to predict mortality. The original products were all about financial protection against the risk of death. As time went by, however, a savings element crept in and the balance began to swing towards investment. This process accelerated in the 1970s when the industry was forced to come up with new products for individuals to replace the pension fund business they were losing to companies wanting to bring these burgeoning sums of money under their own control. New products were introduced, covering pensions, mortgages, health insurance and so on, based on the traditional 'with-profits' policy model in which the company endeavours to even out variable, long-term investment returns. Additionally, managed funds were set up that allowed a self-administered pension fund or an individual to invest on a 'unit-linked' basis, rather like a unit trust. Managed funds offered the investor much greater transparency than the traditional life fund approach, in which investment strategy and valuation is wholly a matter for the company.

It was at this point that the pendulum swung decisively away from protection as the industry reinvented itself as a savings medium, cleverly wrapping these new investment-based products in the familiar and trusted language of protection. Investors were still 'policyholders', monies invested remained 'premiums' and the protection element emphasized, even though in many cases it had become an insignificant part of the total package. In short, the term 'life insurance' is now a misnomer. It does not describe what the industry does. The life insurers continue to sell or devise products that are intrinsically complex and difficult for the consumer to understand, using phrases like 'with-profits' and 'endowment' whose meaning is not readily apparent. Words like 'bond' are freely applied to insurance products, doubtless designed to imply an association with something that is guaranteed. Little attempt has been made to create simpler products with names that actually say what they do. Compared with the life insurance business, the pensions industry is a model of transparency!

> Words like 'bond' are freely applied to insurance products, doubtless designed to imply an association with something that is guaranteed.

All this begs the obvious question: given the industry's penchant for obfuscation, why has it been so successful in capturing new business and gaining more funds to manage? And successful it has been, with strong growth in the second half of the 1990s. Figure 4.2 shows the trend.

The reasons for the continued health of the life insurance industry in Britain can be grouped under three headings:

■ *Effective mass marketing*. The life insurance industry is a highly efficient selling machine. There exists within it a well-established tradition of proactive mass marketing, dating back to the 'Man from the Pru' who collected premiums door to door. Distribution through

THE CITY

Figure 4.2 Long-term annual insurance premium income in the UK, 1993–2000

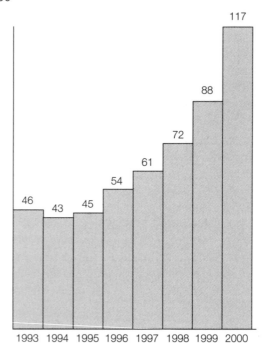

Source: Insurance Trends, Association of British Insurers, January 2002

multiple channels is seen as crucial: a widely accepted industry adage asserts that ' life insurance is sold, not bought'. High up-front commissions for salesmen and independent financial advisers (IFAs) provide a powerful incentive, clearly sufficient to offset the intrinsic opacity of many of the products. In some countries, such as France and Spain, the distribution system is largely in the hands of the banks, in a combination dubbed 'bancassurance'. Equally, in the UK, there is increasing evidence of 'cross-dressing' – banks moving into insurance, and insurers moving into banking.

■ *The right connotations*. In spite of having moved a long way from its roots, life insurance has succeeded in retaining a residual aura of solidity, security, prudence and tax efficiency. Investment products enjoy a 'halo effect' from the protection associations of insurance. Equally, there is a general perception that the tax advantages of a life policy are greater than they are (a leftover perhaps from the days when premiums attracted tax relief, a concession that was abolished in 1984). In fact, tax incentives remain a significant influence on life insurance growth in most European countries but play a lesser role in the UK and the US nowadays.

■ *Innovation and diversification*. To its credit, the insurance industry has been adept at spotting opportunities and rapidly creating products to fill them (sometimes with unintended consequences, as with the personal pensions misselling scandal in the 1980s). A good example is the success that insurance companies are having with group personal pensions (GPPs), a fast-growing segment of the pensions industry. Originally aimed at smaller employers wanting to contract out the administration and investment management of a DC scheme, GPPs are now making inroads into larger companies looking to set up a DC plan alongside an existing DB scheme. Diversification has taken the form of a move into unit trusts, investment trusts and tax-efficient savings vehicles, either by internal development or acquisition.

The investment activities of life insurers have moved a long way from their origins in the 'back room' of a company more interested in selling policies and undertaking actuarial assessments than worrying about investment performance. The main life fund – in which all policyholders were invested – was shielded from outside scrutiny, a far cry from the situation today when the performance of unit-linked funds, publishing daily valuations, can easily be compared. Life funds are still important as they contain the premiums of traditional, non-unitized with-profits policies but managed funds have grown substantially.

During the 1980s insurance companies began to view investment management as an activity in its own right. Many came to the conclusion that, in order to compete effectively for segregated funds (and for fund managers), the investment department needed to be more independent. In particular, it was essential to convince the investment consultants that these units were no longer tainted by the staid, ultra-cautious image of the life companies. Companies such as Prudential and Legal & General created separate investment companies – with their own career path and remuneration policies – and went after external pension fund mandates, head-on against the professional fund managers. In the 1990s they were followed by the larger mutuals, including Standard Life and Scottish Widows. Sometimes unit trusts and investment trusts were grafted on to give a further boost to funds under management. The result is that the investment activities of the larger insurers are now reliant on assets from several sources – including outside mandates – rather than the single (internal) source in the traditional life insurance model.

Insurance companies could have adopted an alternative strategy and chosen to reduce their fund management operations, farming out responsibility for this aspect of their business to others. Currently, as performance pressures build on investment teams, this is an approach that is beginning to receive greater attention. Life insurers' core competence, after all, lies at the 'front end' of the business, not in investment management. In the US insurance companies commonly make use of external asset management firms to boost the quality and width of their product appeal. Several years ago, Skandia Life, the large international Swedish insurance company, chose not to manage money itself but allow its British-based clients to select from no fewer than 200 funds managed by others. In 1998, National Mutual Life Assurance, one of the smaller UK life companies, decided to assign all its equities management to Goldman Sachs, Schroders, J.P. Morgan Chase and State Street, arguing that higher charges to clients would be offset by better performance. Understandably, the trend towards outsourcing investment management is particularly pronounced among smaller and medium-sized life insurers. Even among the larger companies the concept is receiving consideration, if only as a supplement to the range of internal funds on offer.

> The investment activities of the larger insurers are now reliant on assets from several sources – including outside mandates – rather than the single (internal) source in the traditional life insurance model.

What investment options are offered by insurance-managed DC personal and occupational pension schemes? In marked contrast to an IRA or 401(k), there is little possibility of direct investment in individual equities selected by the participant. (One option does exist permitting direct equity investment: a self-invested personal pension plan, or SIPP, which is becoming increasingly popular at the top end of the market.) A typical pension fund provides the contributor with a choice of 10 unit-linked fund options, Skandia being the obvious exception. But these plans do not offer the flexibility of a 401(k), either in terms of information flow or the ability to move money between funds.

How do life insurance companies behave in investment terms? Like pension funds, cash inflows and outflows are reasonably predictable. In principle, insurance companies hold a higher proportion of their assets in fixed interest than pension funds, due to their need to 'match' specific, known policy pay-outs in their life funds with gilts. Property was historically favoured by life companies and, even now, the allocation tends to run at a higher level than for pension funds. Insurance companies follow a rather more cautious investment strategy than pension funds and are able to take a longer-term perspective, in the absence of pressure from – unaware and presumably unconcerned – policyholders for performance. But all this only applies to the original business of life insurers – to their life funds. The increasing importance of unit-linked funds with a higher equity content and a transparent performance record has altered the balance of funds under management. Averaging over all types of fund, the asset allocation policy of insurance companies does not now differ that much from pension funds. The one big difference, as we have noted, is that, due largely to the influx of money into equity-oriented, unit-linked contracts, UK insurance companies have been buyers of equities as UK pension funds sell them.

The appeal of the collective

Mutual funds originated in the US at the end of the 19th century and were introduced to the UK in 1931 by M&G (then known as Municipal & General). Unit trusts (or mutual funds) are 'open ended', which means that the number of shares or units in the fund is not fixed but varies according to investor demand. Also, the price of the fund always faithfully reflects the value of the underlying assets – equities, bonds and so on. Unit trusts are strictly regulated, in fact more stringently than either pension funds or insurance companies.

The alternative form of collective investment organization is the 'closed-end' fund. Investment trusts, invented in the 1860s, are closed-end funds. An investment trust is a normal quoted company whose business is investment rather than, say, factories making pet food. Closed-end funds have a fixed number of shares, which means that changes in supply and demand cannot be accommodated by creating or reducing the number of shares. Instead, the company's share price in the stock market takes the strain. There is consequently no intrinsic relationship between the price of the fund and the value (calculated as the price per share) of the assets within it. If there are generally more sellers than buyers in an investment trust – which has been the case for some years now – the share price of the trust will stand at a discount to the value of the assets. If, say, the discount is 15 per cent the new investor is being offered 100p worth of assets for 85p, which seems a good idea but a little odd! This discount (or premium) swings around and is not amenable to analysis. Given the difficulties inherent in selling the closed-end concept to retail investors, it is not entirely surprising that they have been eclipsed by the simpler and more transparent open-ended funds.

In Britain, unit trusts have enjoyed excellent growth on the back of the cult of the equity, driven in the second half of the 1990s by sales of tax-advantaged personal equity plans (PEPs) and now individual savings accounts (ISAs). Sales have, inevitably, been hit by the downturn in markets, having peaked in the third quarter of 2000. The number of funds has pro-liferated (to nearly 2,000) as has the degree of specialization, with sector groupings for ease of comparison. Equity funds dominate, accounting for 80 per cent of unit trust portfolios. The currently popular corporate bond funds only became eligible for PEP status in 1995. In fact, bond and money market funds were virtually non-existent until 1990, when a change in the tax regime made it worthwhile for managers to promote them.

> In Britain, unit trusts have enjoyed excellent growth on the back of the cult of the equity, driven in the second half of the 1990s by sales of tax-advantaged personal equity plans (PEPs) and now individual savings accounts (ISAs).

How big is the unit trust business? Total funds in early 2002 stood at £230 billion, up from £63 billion in 1992 (although some of this growth is, of course, market related). These figures, however, need to be treated with caution. The structure of the UK unit trust industry has been distorted by its incestuous relationship with the life companies, driven by the shifting tax advantages of one or other kind of investment fund. Just as unit trust groups use life 'wrappers' for funds when it suits, so life companies have, since 1980, used unit trusts as a tax-efficient container for life fund equities. The overlap between the two is considerable and hard to disentangle.

Difficult as it is for us to imagine, the US mutual fund industry was actu-ally an endangered species in the late 1970s. Since then, however, it has been a remarkable growth story and the close to $7 trillion of assets held in 2001(up from just over $1 trillion in 1990) exceeds the sum held on deposit in US banks. The number of mutual funds on offer is now a staggering 8,000. Initially, success came mainly from selling fixed income and money market funds. Subsequently, the 1990s bull market and the increasing influ-ence of 401(k) plans – which have a bias towards equities – raised the pro-portion of stock funds. Then, in 2000, for the first time in recent memory, assets taken out of mutual funds exceeded those flowing in. Hardest hit were stock funds, as disillusioned investors reacted to the decline in equity values. Confronted with lower demand, and burdened with overcapacity, the American mutual fund industry is struggling to adjust.

The leading mutual fund house is Fidelity, followed by Vanguard Group. Observing the growth, everyone has wanted to get into the act. During the 1990s, the retail securities firms swiftly captured a healthy slice of the busi-ness by leveraging their powerful selling networks. The industry has also attracted commercial banks, as for example in 1994 when Mellon Financial bought Dreyfus, then the sixth largest mutual fund company.

European legislation has created a new structure for mutual funds seek-ing to operate on a pan-European basis. Many European mutual funds are registered and based in Luxembourg, which has deliberately set out to attract this business. Called an OEIC (for open-ended investment company, pronounced 'oik') it rests not on trust law but on a specially framed company law. An important difference is that the units have one price for both buyers and sellers – as do American mutual funds – unlike the higher (buying) and lower (selling) price system used by unit trusts. The concept is undoubtedly gaining ground: at the end of 2001 32 per cent of the open-ended funds on offer from UK-based providers used the OEIC structure. OEICs are a halfway house between unit trusts and investment trusts. The key features of each are summarized in Table 4.2.

Table 4.2 Comparison of UK-based collective investment fund structures

Feature	Unit trusts	OEICs	Investment trusts
Legal structure	Trust	Company	Company
Nature of fund	Fund expands and contracts on demand	Fund expands and contracts on demand	Fixed number of shares in issue
Investor's holdings	Units	Shares	Shares
Independent supervision	By trustee	By depository; optional independent directors	Stock exchange requires independent directors
Investment restrictions	Clearly defined rules on what investments the manager may make	Clearly defined rules on what investments the manager may make	Almost unlimited investments allowed subject to approval by the board
Stock exchange listing	Not listed in practice	Not listed in practice	Listed
Price system	Dual price: different buy and sell prices	Single price	Dual price: different buy and sell prices
Frequency of valuation	Normally daily	Normally daily	Normally once a month
Price	Reflects value of investments in fund (net asset value) + charges calculated in spread	Reflects value of investments in fund (net asset value) with charges shown separately	Will vary according to market sentiment and charges are shown separately

Source: Abstracted from table in *Effective Investment*, Association of Unit Trusts and Investment Funds (AUTIF), (now the Investment Management Association), September 1999

The problems of the investment trust industry are rooted in its history. Until the 1950s investment trusts were the preferred form of collective investment for the private investor. In fact, having been put into cold storage by the authorities for the duration of World War II, unit trusts were not allowed to advertise for new money until their rebirth in 1957. Right from their early days, many investment trusts were extremely adventurous, investing in the high-risk, emerging markets of the time (especially the US, the hairiest of them all!). In the 1960s, spotting an opportunity to extend their shareholder base to the rapidly expanding pension funds and insurance companies, investment trusts began to promote themselves as a way of allowing them to invest in geographical areas and complex sectors in which they had no expertise. For the insurance companies and the pension funds managed in-house by corporate personnel – lacking the resources of the professional fund managers – this pitch had a distinct appeal. They bought heavily into the industry and soon ended up with a 75 per cent ownership.

> For the insurance companies and the pension funds managed in-house by corporate personnel – lacking the resources of the professional fund managers – this pitch had a distinct appeal.

Then, during the 1980s, this process went into reverse. Insurance companies built up their own expertise and many plan sponsors moved to external management. The original rationale for investment disappeared and they have been sellers of investment trust shares ever since. In the meantime, the investment trust had lost its appeal to the retail investor, whose heart had been captured by the unashamedly self-promoting, youthful and dashing unit trust movement. Attempts have been made to revive the retail investor. These have been only modestly successful, in part because the nature and status of investment trusts as companies makes it difficult for them to compete on even terms. Institutions are still substantial owners of investment trusts and continue to reduce their holdings. In contrast to unit trusts, investment trusts can be bid for like any other quoted company. Equally, they can choose to wind themselves up. This means the industry is under constant pressure to reduce its size (which is, in any event, only one-third of the unit trust industry).

As investors, how do unit trusts and investment trusts behave? The short answer is, 'Very differently!' The innate structure of a unit trust/mutual fund means that it is bound to be more short term than a pension or insurance fund. Unitholders view them as a source of liquidity. Cash inflows and outflows ('redemptions' in the trade) are unpredictable (although 401(k) plans have improved the position for US mutual funds). Like insurance companies, unit trusts have generally been buyers of UK equities. Unit trusts invariably hold minimal cash (why would unitholders pay for something they could just as well do for themselves?) so a rush of redemptions means that shares in the underlying portfolio must be sold. The stocks that are sold will tend to be the liquid stocks, not necessarily those the fund manager would prefer to sell, and the quality of the overall portfolio can suffer.

Prices are published in the quality newspapers daily so unitholders can easily follow the fortunes of their fund. Unit trust fund managers are under constant pressure from their marketing colleagues who need to show a good performance to sell additional units. The manager also has to contend with the well-known retail investment syndrome. Investors pile in when share prices are going up and sell when they go down – when they should be doing the reverse! The result of all this is that unit trust managers trade more than pension fund and insurance fund managers, which means that they have a disproportionately greater influence on the equity market than their ownership share (around 6 per cent) would imply.

Investment trusts, by contrast, are intrinsically stable animals. They experience none of the cash inflow and outflow pressures. As such, the structure is ideal for investment in longer-term, illiquid assets, either small (and exotic) countries where it is difficult to buy and sell, or in sectors such as venture capital. Investment trusts have had to specialize to survive, which means that their UK equity portfolios are concentrated on a narrow range of stocks, frequently the smaller and less liquid. They have little need to trade. In terms of their influence on stock market activity, investment trusts are of minor consequence.

> Investment trusts have had to specialize to survive, which means that their UK equity portfolios are concentrated on a narrow range of stocks, frequently the smaller and less liquid.

Overseas investors learn to love London

As the institutions acquire more and more assets, it is inevitable that they extend the degree of control they exert over companies. The Conference Board, a prestigious New York-based research organization, has attempted to measure the current position in the four largest Western economies (see Table 4.3). Including all shareholders, concentration in France and Germany is comparable to that in the US and the UK. But in continental Europe corporate, founder and government shareholdings distort the picture. Taking financial institutions only, the degree of concentration of investor power appears to be highest in the UK, followed by the US, then Germany and then France. (The UK figure is low compared with the 75 per cent institutional ownership we estimated in Chapter 1, principally because the calculation excludes foreign institutional investors).

Table 4.3 Estimates of proportion of equity of top 25 corporations held by financial and non-financial institutional investors

	US	UK	France	Germany
Financial institutions	57.2%	57.7%	31.6%	24.9%
Non-financial institutions	5.6%	6.8%	30.2%	17.8%
Totals	**62.8%**	**64.5%**	**61.8%**	**42.7%**

Note: 'Non-financial institutions' refers to family stakes, corporate cross-holdings and government holdings.
Source: Institutional Investment Report, The Conference Board, April 2000

International investment became easier during the 1990s, and as it did so, it tended to become higher profile and more 'activist'. Many large continental European companies have a high foreign ownership percentage. In France, for example, foreign investors control more than 40 per cent of the capital of the 40 largest companies, reflecting the absence of a domestic funded pensions industry. By comparison, foreign ownership of the US equity market is a modest 11 per cent. The UK experienced a particularly marked increase in overseas interest between 1994 and 2000, which lifted the foreign component from 16 per cent to 32 per cent of equity market capitalization. US institutional investors are much in evidence: for example, at British Airways, where four leading American asset managers hold over 25 per cent of the equity.

The massive increase in US foreign equity investment during the 1990s was partly due to the rise in the number and availability of what are called American Depositary Receipts (ADRs), or sometimes American Depositary Shares. An ADR is simply a receipt issued by a US bank that represents a foreign share. First introduced as far back as 1927 (the first one was for the London store, Selfridges) an ADR is packaged to provide the investor with something that looks and acts just like a US domestic stock. Prices are in dollars, trading is in dollars, dividends are in dollars, and so on. The 'depositary receipt' approach can be applied to any company that wants its shares traded outside its home market in any centre it chooses – although in practice the American market is the magnet for most non-US companies. In fact, an ADR is essential for any company with serious designs on the US investor base as many American institutional investors must hold ADRs rather than the domestically registered and traded shares of foreign issuers.

The number of companies offering ADRs grew dramatically during the early 1990s, making it much easier for US institutions (and private investors) to invest internationally. ADRs now account for over 10 per cent of the daily trading volume of the New York Stock Exchange. From the perspective of the company issuing them, they are valuable as currency for raising capital from US investors and for making acquisitions of US quoted companies. Both BP and Vodafone used their ADRs to fund the acquisitions of Amoco and AirTouch respectively during 1998 and 1999.

As we noted in Chapter 1, the emergence of a more interventionist approach to foreign equity investment is essentially an American phenomenon. It is mostly associated with a small number of large funds that are prepared to press management for better performance, privately and, if necessary, publicly. Certain large US institutional investors, with substantial stakes in companies they favour in 'UK plc', are particularly identified with the 'activist' cause. They are Franklin-Templeton, Capital Group and Fidelity. Led by the California Public Employees Retirement System (invariably abbreviated to 'CalPERS', or, by its critics to 'Scalpers') US state and local government pension funds are also committed standard bearers of the interventionist philosophy. American public pension funds are a growing force in stock markets as, through the nineties, they moved out of bonds and devoted an increasing proportion of their assets to equities, both domestic and internationally.

> American public pension funds are a growing force in stock markets as, through the nineties, they moved out of bonds

Investment management
The art and practice of relativity

- Who are the investors?

- Concentrate, concentrate, concentrate

- Why benchmarks are the fund manager's burden

- Getting business – the consultant as gatekeeper

- Introducing the wonderful economics of fund management

- The perils of index mesmerization

And that's all the news from Lake Wobegon, where all the women are strong, all the men are good-looking, and all the children are above-average.

(Garrison Keiller, the American humourist, signing off
from his weekly radio show)

The power of asset managers continues to strengthen ... Two years ago we reported that the assets managed by the five largest firms was greater than the size of the UK and French economies combined. Today, this is represented by just three organizations – a concentration that is rather striking.

(Julia Hobart, editor, European Pension Fund Managers Guide,
William M. Mercer Limited, employee benefits consultancy,
press release, 15 May 2001)

Who are the investors?

The names of many of the largest institutional investors will be familiar from the analysis we have done so far. This section puts those names, and others, into context, treating fund management as an industry like any other. Institutional asset management can be looked at from several different angles. In the last chapter we concentrated on the sources of funding. The focus of this chapter is on the organizations responsible for the management of these funds. In addition, the 'mix' between source and management differs from country to country.

Vertical integration is the norm – organizations generally manage the assets that they themselves have gathered. Pension funds are the one big exception though, as we noted in the last chapter, vertical integration is no longer the automatic model for insurance companies. The majority of pension funds subcontract the management of their assets to professional money managers. In the UK, the trend away from internal management is very well established, spurred partly by the difficulty of recruiting and retaining expensive fund management talent. Today 'self-managed' pension funds (as they are called in the trade) account for less than 10 per cent of total DB pension fund assets. This category does, however, contain some large and influential investors, such as Hermes, the fund responsible for the pensions of British Telecom and Post Office employees, with £45 billion of assets. In continental Europe, by contrast, internal management is the rule, although external management is gaining ground.

The US asset management 'mix' is rather different. Vertical integration is still the model for insurance companies and mutual funds but with many more exceptions. Largely due to the success of the 401(k), mutual funds are relatively a much more significant source of funds than in the UK. The pattern for pension funds is also different. Rather surprisingly in the land of free enterprise, public pension funds play a key role, accounting for 15 per cent of all US institutional assets. Looking at pension funds overall, internal management is more prevalent than in the UK although the sheer size of the American pensions industry means that there is still plenty of business for money managers to fight over.

It should be apparent by now that the investment management industry is a complex matrix. A decade ago asset management was essentially a local activity – it is now a global activity. Most sizeable fund management organizations look after several types of funds, often sourced from several countries and quite possibly managed from more than one centre. As a result, it makes less and less sense to consider the UK in isolation. Many continental European banks choose to control their group-wide fund management activities from London. The reasons have much to do with depth of experience, availability of talent and strength of supporting services. In several cases, the presence in fund management has been achieved by acquisition, either of a British fund management group per se or, as we noted in earlier chapters, via a move to secure an Anglo-Saxon investment banking platform.

Investment management – unlike investment banking or securities – has a simple measure of organizational scale: funds under management. (In CitySpeak this is often abbreviated to FUM; in StreetSpeak, assets under management, or AUM.) Institutional investors are ranked by the total funds for which they are responsible. Within the industry, the FUM number is frequently viewed as a symbol of corporate virility. Size brings with it certain benefits, if only in terms of financial strength and client perception. Of course, from the point of view of the client it is performance that matters. Sadly, as is so often the case, size and performance are not necessarily correlated!

> The problem with FUM is that, being based on the current market prices of securities and subject to fluctuating exchange rates, it is a continually moving target.

The problem with FUM is that, being based on the current market prices of securities and subject to fluctuating exchange rates, it is a continually moving target. Fortunately, portfolios are sufficiently similar for this not to matter too much in practice – the absolute numbers for each competitor may change but generally the relative positions remain the same. Much more important are client gains and losses and, especially in recent years, M&A activity. Rather than rely on client changes, which tend to be relatively slow and incremental, fund management groups have been busy buying each other (for reasons we cover later in this chapter) and the rankings have changed significantly over the last decade as a result (see Table 5.1 for the current UK position).

It is clear from the table that the leading UK-based fund managers are quite a mixed bunch. (Note that the FUM figure refers to the worldwide total, not just the UK). In terms of money management – those firms active in the marketplace for external mandates – five groups dominated the UK pension fund management business during the 1990s. The 'Big Five' were Merrill Lynch (formerly Mercury Asset Management), Schroders, Phillips & Drew (rebranded early in 2002 as UBS Global Asset Management), Gartmore and Morgan Grenfell (now called Deutsche Asset Management). However, this statement needs to be heavily qualified. Two of those on the list, Barclays Global Investors and Legal & General, have been extremely successful in capturing pension fund business with a different kind of fund management product – what is called passive management or indexation (also, more colloquially, 'tracker' funds). Traditional fund management is 'active' in that it tries to outperform some kind of yardstick,

Table 5.1 The 10 leading UK-based institutional investors

Investor	Total FUM ($bn)	Types of fund	Comment
Barclays	801	Pension, mutual funds	Barclays Global Investors is owned by Barclays Bank
Amvescap	408	Mutual, pension funds	UK-listed, American-run asset management group
Aviva	329	Insurance, pension, mutual funds	The new name for CGNU, quoted insurance company
Prudential/ M&G	235	Insurance, mutual funds	UK-listed insurance company
Schroders	198	Pension, mutual funds	UK-listed asset management company
Lloyds TSB	182	Mutual, insurance, pension funds	Fund management arm of UK-quoted commercial bank
Legal & General	165	Insurance, pension, mutual funds	UK-listed insurance company
Standard Life	123	Insurance, pension funds	Europe's largest mutual insurer
HSBC	123	Pension, mutual funds	Asset management arm of UK/Hong Kong commercial bank
F & C	111	Pension, mutual funds	Eureko, the pan-European financial group, uses F & C to manage all its assets from London

Source: P & I/Watson Wyatt World 500, Pensions & Investments, 3 September 2001; corporate websites

often an index of some sort. Passive management operates on the principle that, in a world of instant information, this is a difficult – and probably fruitless – exercise. A passive fund merely attempts to match the performance of the index. US pension and mutual funds turned to passive management in a big way in the mid-1980s and the idea was taken up by UK funds about a decade later. We look more closely at passive management/indexation and its implications in a later section.

Table 5.2 shows the leading asset managers in a European context. Given the complex matrix that characterizes the industry, it is not surprising that there are many overlaps. This produces some oddities given that roughly half of all institutional assets are located in the US. For example, Amvescap is a London-based company, with its primary listing in the UK that, for historical reasons, manages relatively little in the way of UK assets.

Looking specifically at the US-owned asset managers, there are some well-known names, such as Fidelity and Merrill Lynch (see Table 5.3). There are also several less familiar ones, like Vanguard, whose business is essen-

Table 5.2 The 10 leading Europe-based institutional investors

Investor	Total FUM ($bn)	Types of fund	Comment
UBS	1,533	Pension, mutual funds	Operates now under a single brand: UBS Global Asset Management
Allianz	928	Insurance, pension, mutual funds	Allianz Dresdner Asset Management formed after Allianz, Germany's largest insurer, acquired Dresdner Bank in 2001
Crédit Suisse	867	Pension, insurance, mutual funds	Assets boosted by purchase of DLJ Asset Management in 2000
Deutsche Bank	863	Pension, mutual funds	Deutsche's acquisition of Scudder from Zurich Financial Services in 2001 significantly increased FUM
AXA	840	Mutual, insurance, pension funds	Paris-based international insurance group with large US presence
Barclays	801	Pension, mutual funds	UK-controlled with two-thirds of assets for US clients and run from San Francisco
ING	468	Insurance, pension funds	Dutch-owned financial services group with substantial insurance interests in the US
Amvescap	408	Mutual, pension funds	Trades as Invesco outside the US, where the majority of assets are located
Aviva	329	Insurance, pension, mutual funds	Morley Fund Management, the UK-based asset management arm, is responsible for around half FUM
CDC Ixis	298	Insurance, pension funds	French asset manager, part government-owned, with nearly half its assets in North America

Source: P & I/Watson Wyatt World 500, Pensions & Investments, 3 September 2001; corporate websites

Table 5.3 The 10 leading US-based institutional investors

Investor	Total FUM ($bn)	Types of fund	Comment
Fidelity	1,037	Mutual, pension funds	Private, Boston-based mutual funds industry leader
State Street	750	Pension funds	Boston-based bank turned asset management house
J.P. Morgan Chase	638	Pension, mutual funds	Acquisitions of J.P. Morgan and Flemings greatly lifted asset management operation
Vanguard	587	Mutual funds	Mutually-owned, Number 2 in mutual funds; pioneer of indexation
Capital Group	561	Mutual, pension funds	Long-established Los Angeles asset manager, early into international markets
Merrill Lynch	557	Mutual, pension funds	Acquisition of Mercury in the UK in 1997 to form Merrill Lynch Investment Managers (MLIM) greatly increased institutional assets
Mellon Financial	530	Pension, mutual funds	Grown rapidly in asset management through acquisition
Morgan Stanley	457	Pension, mutual funds	Subsidiary of investment bank rebranded as Morgan Stanley Investment Management in 2000
Citigroup	431	Insurance, mutual, pension funds	The merger of Citibank with Travelers insurance
Prudential Financial	371	Insurance funds	Large insurance group, now listed after demutualization in 2001

Source: P & I/Watson Wyatt World 500, Pensions & Investments, 3 September 2001; corporate websites

tially focused on the vast US market, although nearly all the American asset managers are now pursuing international expansion.

Who are the largest institutional investors worldwide? This is always a matter of debate given definitional problems, particularly those surrounding the huge private banking (fund management for wealthy individuals) business conducted by the two big Swiss banks. However, most would agree that, including private banking assets, the senior bracket would include UBS, Fidelity, Allianz, Crédit Suisse, Deutsche Bank and AXA. All operate internationally but the one that best illustrates the global character of the fund management industry is the French insurance group, AXA, with its controlling interest in New York quoted Alliance Capital Managers, one of the largest and most successful asset managers on Wall Street, combined with substantial European funds under management in France and Britain.

Concentrate, concentrate, concentrate

The UK fund management business is highly concentrated. This high level of concentration is particularly marked in pension funds and insurance companies. In 1996 Schroder Securities (as it then was) calculated that the top 10 pension fund managers were responsible for 63 per cent of all pension fund money invested in the UK equity market. The figure for insurance funds was even higher – 10 organizations controlled 83 per cent of all the insurance money invested in UK shares. Overall, Schroders concluded that:

> Some 50 fund management groups control around half of the UK equity market, with the top 20–30 domestic funds controlling around one-third of the market. This is a very concentrated ownership in contrast to other major markets like the US or Japan.

Since then, there is no doubt that, mostly through acquisition – though client gains and losses have also been important – the big have continued to get bigger. Examples are the takeover of M&G by Prudential in 1999 and the merger in 2000 of CGU and Norwich Union to form CGNU, which in July 2002 renamed itself Aviva. Barclays, Legal & General and others offering indexed funds, notably the US bank, State Street, made major market share inroads in the second half of the 1990s. Meanwhile, firms like Merrill Lynch Investment Managers and Schroders, with a heavy reliance on traditional balanced management, have lost ground. Table 5.4 compares the equity market influence of the leading fund management groups in the UK and the US, showing that institutional control of the UK equity market is more pronounced than in the US. It also indicates that there has been further concentration since the Schroders survey in 1996.

Why is the UK fund management industry so concentrated? And why is it more consolidated than its equivalent across the Atlantic?

Why is the UK fund management industry so concentrated? And why is it more consolidated than its equivalent across the Atlantic? The recent

Table 5.4 UK and US equity market shares by fund management group

UK Investor	Ownership of domestic equity market	US Investor	Ownership of domestic equity market
Legal & General	2.5%	Fidelity	3.1%
Barclays	2.4%	Barclays	2.2%
M&G	2.1%	Deutsche Bank	1.7%
MLIM	2.0%	Alliance (AXA)	1.5%
Aviva	1.8%	State Street	1.4%
Top 5	**10.8%**	**Top 5**	**9.9%**
Standard Life	1.7%	Putnam	1.3%
Lloyds TSB	1.7%	Capital Group	1.2%
Deutsche Bank	1.6%	Citigroup	1.1%
Schroders	1.5%	Mellon Financial	1.0%
Henderson (AMP)	1.1%	Vanguard	0.9%
Top 10	**18.4%**	**Top 10**	**15.4%**
AXA	1.1%	Morgan Stanley	0.9%
Capital International	1.1%	Pimco etc. (Allianz)	0.8%
Fidelity	1.1%	Wellington	0.7%
Threadneedle (Zurich)	1.0%	TIAA-CREF	0.7%
State Street	0.8%	J.P. Morgan Chase	0.7%
Top 15	**23.5%**	**Top 15**	**19.2%**

Sources: Merrill Lynch, UK Manager Holdings by Index, April 2002; Institutional Investor Report, The Conference Board, January 2000 and supplementary information

increase in concentration owes a good deal to the onward march of the indexers. Boosted by the inflow of money into equity-linked and traditional life funds, several of the larger insurers have also gained market share. M&A activity has also been important. But it also has to do with the way the pension fund business has operated in the UK. The prevalence of balanced management meant that even the largest plan sponsors only employed a few managers. And, encouraged by the investment consultants, trustees have tended to go for the same few managers. At their peak in 1997, it is estimated that the Big Five pension fund managers controlled about two-thirds of externally managed pension fund assets.

One unfortunate consequence of this cartel (as some have described it) is that it has been exceedingly difficult for new firms to break into the pension fund management business. Only a few have succeeded and those that did sold out in due course. Two examples are Geoffrey Morley & Partners and Newton Fund Managers, both founded in the 1970s by strong-minded individuals who left existing fund management companies. Morley was acquired by Commercial Union (now part of Aviva) while Newton was sold to Mellon Financial in 1998. In general, the firms that were prominent in this business in the 1980s are still among the leaders. The competitive structure changed remarkably little over 20 years but is now facing a powerful challenge from US money managers, offering both specialist active and passive products.

The US asset management experience is completely different. In America, the traditional DB pension fund management industry has been characterized not by concentration but by fragmentation. Over the last 20 years, it has been surprisingly easy for individuals or groups to set up as independent money managers (known as investment 'boutiques' or sometimes investment counsellors) and win business from plan sponsors. Some of these have risen through the rankings to become significant competitors. Many have sold out to larger organizations but there remains a vibrant core of independent firms. New ones are entering all the time.

The reasons for this fragmentation and fluidity lie in the 1974 ERISA pensions legislation. Trustees, with consultant encouragement, interpreted ERISA as a clarion call for diversification. Diversification spreads risk by allocating assets to a wide variety of managers, each possessing different skills and investing in assets that are, hopefully, 'imperfectly correlated' (the share prices do not move together but react differently to the same series of events). As it rolled on, the diversification bandwagon created, in effect, the specialist approach to fund management favoured in the US.

US pension fund assets were originally managed by bank trust departments and insurance companies. In the early 1980s, motivated by ERISA and the desire to improve investment performance, many pension plans took their assets away from the banks and parcelled them out to numerous speciality money managers, each generally offering only one product. Fragmentation was the result. Over 750 firms manage and compete for institutional tax-exempt assets. Surveys suggest that the industry contains 1,350 independently-owned units with at least $100 million of assets under their control. Consequently, there may be in aggregate two or three thousand fund management firms in the US compared with, perhaps, 150 or so participants in the UK. The Myners Review concluded that concentration was becoming less of an issue in the UK as specialist management gained ground but made no reference to the fragmented nature of the industry on the other side of the Atlantic.

Some of these firms concentrate on equities, others on fixed income, but these classes are subdivided into sub-classes, such as international equities or emerging markets, and then further into what is referred to in the US as 'investment style'. 'Style' is a term that is used freely and extensively in American asset management circles. In recent years it is a term that has become familiar to US retail investors. Style is a function of the specialist management approach. To differentiate themselves, equity managers specialized in a particular investment style. 'Value' and 'growth' are styles as are numerous variations on the same theme, such as 'midcap value', 'large-cap growth', 'international smallcap', 'aggressive growth' or something called 'GARP' (growth at a reasonable price). Even indexation can be regarded as a style. US institutional investors define themselves primarily by their investment style.

As with so many other terms in StreetSpeak (or CitySpeak) the definition of 'investment style' is elastic. It can be – and has been – extended to cover sector rotation, market timing (where the investor tries to predict and ride general market trends), contrarian investing (going against conventional wisdom) as well as others. Sometimes style is used to denote a sector strategy, such as a fund focused on energy stocks, or a geographical area. A further style is 'momentum investing' – buying into stocks showing a marked upward trend in earnings, trading volume and/or share price, often in a sector that is moving up. Momentum investing has much in common with passive management/indexation.

> Style is a function of the specialist management approach. To differentiate themselves, equity managers specialized in a particular investment style.

The contrast between the relative rigidity of the UK fund management scene and the breadth, diversity and geographical dispersion of the American industry is best illustrated by brief profiles of three asset managers operating happily at a level below the top echelon.

- *Janus Capital*. Founded in 1969 and based in Denver, Janus runs retail and institutional funds worth $160 billion. It is owned by a listed financial company. A growth style manager, it did well in the technology boom but assets have since fallen sharply.

- *Brandes Investment Partners*. Based in San Diego since being set up in 1974, Brandes is a committed value investor. It has $55 billion under management, nearly all DB pension assets. Brandes has been an active seeker of value in the UK. For example, it successfully participated in the share-price recovery of Marks & Spencer, owning more than 9 per cent at one point.

■ *Kopp Investment Advisors*. Located in Edina, Minnesota, Kopp is a smallcap growth-style manager with $5 billion in institutional and mutual fund assets. It was founded in 1990 by Lee Kopp, a stock-broker at a regional brokerage firm.

Plan sponsors moved into passive management in the mid-1980s as it became clear that, for large funds especially, an ERISA-induced multi-manager structure could be both costly and unwieldy. Even today, General Motors, admittedly a very large fund with over $100 billion of assets, employs no fewer than 70 external managers. However, plan sponsors did not dismantle the specialist approach. Instead, many moved to a system that involved splitting the fund into a passive core surrounded by a carefully selected group of style-differentiated, specialist active managers. Commonly, the figure is between 10 and 20, each responsible for a small portion of the fund. The objective is to achieve the best of both worlds – index performance plus diversification and (hopefully) that bit of extra performance for the fund that active management provides. Higher fees for specialist management are offset by the low cost of indexation, which can be done either internally or externally (although the tendency is to place mandates with outside managers because they are prepared to do it so cheaply). This is known as the *core–satellite* approach. Indexation led naturally to core–satellite and core–satellite means style-based, specialist investment management.

Core–satellite is at the heart of the challenge that the US money managers are currently mounting, assisted by certain of the investment consultants, against the incumbent UK balanced managers. Some plan sponsors have gone for a half-way house of balanced surrounded by specialists. But many have moved towards indexing a substantial part of the fund, fuelled by the inability of the large balanced managers to beat the All-Share Index in recent years. Inevitably, once the principle of a passive core is accepted, it calls into question whether the trustees should retain balanced management for the remainder of the fund or go down the specialist route. All this is taking place, as we noted in the last chapter, against the background of an ongoing debate about how much responsibility trustees should take upon themselves (and, more specifically, the pensions professionals employed by the plan sponsor) for asset allocation and manager selection and oversight. Core–satellite – often starting with specialist overseas equity mandates – is currently gaining ground rapidly against balanced management.

Ironically, just as the award of more specialist mandates is beginning to expand opportunities for firms outside the Big Five UK pension fund managers – and so loosen up an excessively concentrated industry structure – the US fund management business is, to some extent, moving in the opposite direction. DB pension fund management has low entry barriers. There is little requirement for infrastructure or capital, given the ability to outsource administration. But this is not true of DC plans, which require a large up-front commitment in administration and systems. Passive investment, likewise, cannot be done by a boutique. However, while mutual fund groups dominate DC plan management, in the traditional mutual fund business the ability to 'rent' distribution has allowed small firms to enter and prosper.

As American 401(k) participants 'hand over' their money to mutual funds they are, in effect, responsible for creating greater asset management industry concentration. Also, in the DB area, there has been a swing away from the use of an excessive number of managers. (Larger sponsors employ dozens of managers. Contrast this with the UK where one to three balanced managers has been the norm, although some larger funds do employ more.) The difficulty and cost of monitoring has encouraged sponsors to award mandates to fewer managers, often to firms offering more than one investment style. Against this background, and taking into account the pressures exerted on the industry by the downturn in markets, it is hardly surprising that asset management is an active M&A market: there were over 100 transactions involving US managers in both 2000 and 2001. All in all, the US money management industry is undoubtedly consolidating but it has a long way to go before concentration becomes an issue, as it has been in the UK.

> While mutual fund groups dominate DC plan management, in the traditional mutual fund business the ability to 'rent' distribution has allowed small firms to enter and prosper.

Why benchmarks are the fund manager's burden

Anyone who hands money to someone else to manage needs to have some way of judging whether the manager has done a good or a bad job. The simple approach is to set an absolute target: say, 10 per cent total return annually. This is how hedge funds are assessed. Such an approach is fine for a fund whose very rationale is flexibility and speed of response. It does not work for an institutional fund that, due to size, liquidity issues, cost of dealing and other factors, resembles the proverbial supertanker, capable only of minor changes in the course it has set. The liquidity limitations we explained earlier mean that an institution cannot, for example, move quickly into cash if the fund manager anticipates a significant downturn in the market – and then nip back into securities as he scents the upturn. Institutional funds have no alternative but to ride the market's ups and downs, so the only way of assessing a fund's performance is how well it rides in comparison with an index of market movement or relative to all the other riders in the same carriage (those running similar portfolios).

The key point is: *institutional investors inhabit a relative world*. Fund managers' performance is measured against some kind of market index or against their peer group. 'Relativity' is a critical concept as it has a profound influence on their behaviour. It works fine in a bull market, when a manager who produces a return of 17 per cent in a year has clearly done better for his clients than one who only matches an index return of 15 per cent. In a bear market, however, the concept of outperformance is one that an outsider finds instinctively difficult to handle. If the market falls 10 per cent and our fund manager is down only 8 per cent he is a (relative) hero to his clients. But he has still lost 8 per cent of the money in the fund!

The generic term for the yardstick by which a fund is judged is its 'benchmark'. As we saw in Chapter 2, benchmark is used in the fixed income field to mean a reference point for pricing other securities. In a portfolio management context it is how performance is measured. When two fund managers meet for the first time and talk professionally, two questions tend to be asked early in the conversation. The first is: 'What is your universe?' 'Universe' refers to the limits that the manager has to abide by in terms of the type of securities he can buy and the geographical area he can invest in. For example, a fund manager may have a mandate that specifies largecap equities in Europe, Australasia and the Far East.

The second question is invariably: 'What is your benchmark?' The answer in the UK is frequently the FTSE Actuaries All-Share Index, which covers around 700 companies and accounts for 99 per cent of the capitalization of the London stock market. As far as the institutions are concerned, the 'All-Share' is the market. In the US the equivalent, widely used benchmark index is the Standard & Poor's (S&P) 500 Index. Professional investors rarely use the more popular indices, such as the FTSE 100 or the Dow Jones Industrial Average, as they were designed for a different purpose.

The alternative benchmark approach is the use of peer group comparisons, long favoured by British pension funds (although its usage is in decline). The criterion in this instance is an average, the average performance of a large number of pension funds, often representing a high proportion of the industry. The objective is to 'beat the averages' although the standard used is actually the median fund in the sample. Clearly, any kind of peer group performance measurement service needs a neutral third party to run it. In the UK, there are two such organizations: CAPS, established in 1984 by three firms of consulting actuaries, which was sold in January 2002 to Russell/Mellon, a joint venture already active in the performance information field; and the WM Company, part of Deutsche Bank. Both produce median numbers for each calendar quarter soon after the end of the quarter so that managers can rank their own performance. They also provide regular asset class statistics so that a manager can see how his asset allocation varies from that of the median fund.

In practice, the overall performance of fund management houses tends to be judged by their pooled fund, as this represents the visible tip of the pension fund iceberg. League tables are published soon after the end of the quarter. Fund managers are normally reluctant to disclose the performance of segregated funds but have no choice with regard to pooled funds, as these represent their public vehicle for capturing smaller clients. Unit trusts are in a slightly different position: they are normally measured against an index but peer group comparisons are extremely important in terms of getting new business.

It stands to reason that, in a relative world, a fund that creates a portfolio exactly in line with the benchmark against which it is being measured will perform exactly in line with the benchmark. This involves replication of asset allocation, sector allocation and, if possible, stock allocation. In reality, it is difficult to go beyond the level of sector allocation (although, in practice, this does not matter too much as many sectors are dominated, as we saw earlier, by a few stocks).

A fund manager takes his benchmark as the starting point. If his allocation to international bonds or, within equities, his sector allocation to, say, the oil and gas sector, is above or below the percentage benchmark allocation then the manager is said to be 'overweight' or 'underweight'. If it is the same, he has a 'neutral' or 'full' weighting. This nomenclature is applied equally to individual stocks. In a situation where Shell accounts for 3 per cent of the All-Share Index and a manager decides to put only 1.5 per cent of his fund in it he is effectively betting it will underperform. A 50 per cent underweighting is 'big bet'. If he is wrong, and it shoots up, the performance of the fund will suffer against the index – and against his competitors with neutral or overweight positions. The converse – overweighting a poorly performing stock – is, of course, equally true. Fund

> It stands to reason that, in a relative world, a fund that creates a portfolio exactly in line with the benchmark against which it is being measured will perform exactly in line with the benchmark.

managers talk less about how much money they have in a sector or an individual share, or what proportion of the fund the holding represents, than whether they are fully weighted, underweight or overweight. The following quote from an anonymous fund manager provides a vivid illustration of fund management reaction to the news, in early 1999, that Vodafone intended to merge with AirTouch of the US, greatly increasing its weighting in the All-Share and the telecommunications services sector.

> I'm surrounded by people who are all buying Vodafone in the wake of the AirTouch announcement. We all think it is expensive but we've got to buy it to maintain our weighting in the sector. The more we buy it the more the price rises, so we have to buy more. Worst of all is that in order to release funds to buy Vodafone we're having to sell really good small company shares that are flat on their backs and, of course, as we sell, we drive the prices down further.

('Tomorrow's giants', February 1999, a sequel to the Treasury's *Small Quoted Companies* report published in November 1998)

The problem with any benchmark is that it is apt to distort the behaviour of whatever it is attempting to measure. The asset allocation decision is, in reality, increasingly being driven by the relevant index or the peer group median. Trustees of balanced funds often set targets of, say, 1 per cent over the benchmark, that are very difficult to beat consistently. Others set an explicit objective not to underperform the median fund (which is obviously impossible for all managers, unless they are fortunate enough to live in Lake Wobegon where everyone is above-average!). Specialist fund managers are set more demanding targets: typically, 1.5 per cent or 2.0 per cent over the relevant index. In today's highly competitive environment, fund managers understandably react by playing safe. There is a widely held view in the fund management business that the downside risk is greater than the upside potential (what economists would call an 'asymmetry of outcomes'). The trick is not to hit winners but to avoid hitting losers. Pension fund managers believe they are better off in business terms if they fail to meet the target but do not fall below the benchmark rather than taking a higher risk to try and beat the target and increasing the probability of falling below the benchmark. A really bad year might lose them the mandate. Staying above – even just above – is everything.

As a consequence, fund managers are constantly looking over their shoulders at what everyone else is doing. This applies with particular force in a peer group performance environment, where the actions of one big manager can change the median benchmark. So when Phillips & Drew, with £50 billion under management, went heavily into cash it altered the benchmark. A manager who moved towards the benchmark might find himself underperforming against the market if it goes up and he is high in cash. An unnamed fund manager summed up this uncomfortable position as rather like claiming to be:

> OK if you're five feet under if your nearest competitor is six feet underground.

> (*Financial Times*, 13 May 1997)

All this leads to portfolios that do not differ greatly from the benchmark. Fund managers now talk of 'benchmark risk', referring to the risk they incur by deviating from a benchmark. This is a strange sort of risk compared with risk as defined earlier. It is the risk that a manager may fail to achieve the 'reward' of being demonstrably average! Managers who pursue this approach are called 'closet indexers' or 'index huggers'. (The difference between tree huggers and index huggers is that tree huggers are there to protect the tree while index huggers are there to protect themselves.) No one knows the proportion of pension funds run on a closet index basis but all the evidence suggests it is growing steadily. Quite often, closet indexing takes the form of maintaining neutral sector weightings while over- or underweighting individual stocks in the sector. So, for example, in food producers and processors, a decision might be made to counterbalance an underweight position in Unilever by overweighting Cadbury Schweppes and AB Foods.

> Quite often, closet indexing takes the form of maintaining neutral sector weightings while over- or underweighting individual stocks in the sector.

Increasingly, pressure is being exerted on pension funds by trustees and consultants not to take 'big bets' on the 10 largest capitalization UK stocks, accounting for over 40 per cent of the market. An analysis done by Schroder Securities demonstrated that, during 1998, UK pension funds moved decisively to reduce their risk by scaling back under- and overweight positions in the market. The analysis also suggested that life funds and self-managed pension funds practise closet indexing to a greater extent than externally managed funds. Active external managers who travel too far in this direction may find themselves facing the accusation that they are effectively running an indexed fund – in which case why use them when a passive manager will do it properly and more cheaply?

The median UK pension fund underperformed against the stock market when share-prices were going up and has only marginally outperformed the index as it declined. Why? A key element is increased volatility. Value stocks outperformed growth stocks in 2000 and 2001 after three years when the reverse was true. As we observed in Chapter 3, fund managers tend towards allegiance to one of these two philosophies. Even those who are not so committed rarely have the flexibility – or the prescience – to make the switch at the right time. On a shorter term basis, more vigorous and rapid sector rotation has made it difficult for pension funds to keep up with the trends, particularly as they themselves have been getting out of equities.

Getting business – the consultant as gatekeeper

Fund managers win or lose mandates largely on the basis of relative performance. Other factors sometimes intrude – poor administration or unsatisfactory client liaison, for example – but essentially it is performance that counts. In a formal sense the number that matters is the five-year track record – the average annualized return over the period against the benchmark. In practice, the one year and quarterly numbers are closely and continually scrutinized by investment consultants and trustees. Quarterly performance is, of course, a component of the vital five-year record. Within fund management houses, there is always talk about whether the current/previous quarter is/was 'a good quarter' or 'a bad quarter'. The differences between the total return numbers are often very small: as little as 0.1 per cent may separate, say, Schroders from Gartmore.

Everyone agrees that past performance is a poor guide to future performance. Fund managers will, inevitably, have good patches and bad patches. But, in the absence of a better method of assessment, past performance is primarily what determines whether a manager loses or gains business. In general, trustees are reluctant to change managers too frequently. Consultants often recommend a change once underperformance has been established but it is not uncommon for several years to elapse before the manager is sacked and a new appointment made. To be fair to trustees, change is both disruptive and expensive. Nor are trustees immune from the retail investor syndrome in which unit trusts are bought when share prices have peaked and sold when the market has bottomed. For 'unit trusts' substitute 'managers'.

In a balanced management environment, especially, gaining or losing market share is a slow business. However, it would be wrong to infer from this that the industry is not highly competitive. Any fund manager who fails to outperform – which effectively means most managers at any given time and every manager at some point – feels under threat and strives to squeeze out that extra ounce of performance to secure his position.

Investment consultants play a key role in all aspects of the pension fund business, including manager selection and performance measurement. Performance measurement is a complex area, with much scope for 'adjustment' by individual fund management houses seeking to present their numbers in the best possible light. The phrase that fund managers aspire to use as frequently as possible is 'upper quartile', such that it sometimes seems to apply to rather more than 25 per cent of the peer group sample!

How, precisely, are fund managers appointed by trustees? As in so many other areas of modern business, it is done via a 'beauty parade'. A sponsor, usually on the back of consultant advice, will decide it wants to review its managers. At this point the consultant becomes the conductor of the orchestra. The normal procedure is for the consultant to draw up a list of candidates. This will include the incumbent manager, unless they have done something that puts them truly beyond the pale. The next stage involves the completion of a detailed questionnaire prepared by the consultant. After assessment, the consultant draws up a shortlist of two to six managers who have the opportunity to present their case to the trustees in person. These meetings usually take place over a few days, with the investment consultant present, and the decision is made soon afterwards.

> Performance measurement is a complex area, with much scope for 'adjustment' by individual fund management houses seeking to present their numbers in the best possible light.

Consultants control around 90 per cent of pension fund manager appointments in the UK. It is they who decide who gets on to the shortlist. Although there are perhaps 20 firms active in UK investment consulting, manager selection for segregated pension funds is dominated by a small group, mirroring in some respects the situation that once prevailed in UK pension fund management. Watson Wyatt (a UK–US alliance) is probably the most influential in the larger schemes, followed by William M. Mercer, part of Marsh & MacLennan, the US insurance broker. Hewitt Bacon & Woodrow, part of Hewitt Associates, a large US employee benefits concern, is next. Hymans Robertson, a UK partnership, is in fourth place. According to Myners, these four account for at least 70 per cent of the market in investment consulting.

The investment consulting scene in the US is similar to that in Britain but, with more than 200 firms offering their services, the industry is less consolidated. William M. Mercer is the market leader but with a substantially lower share than it enjoys in the UK. Unlike the UK, most US investment consulting firms do not have an actuarial origin. For example, Frank Russell, an American consulting firm (now owned by a mutual insurer) that is active in the UK, started life in the 1930s as a financial advisory, insurance and mutual fund distribution company: it moved into investment consulting in the 1970s. This may be one reason why, generally, American investment consultants are not quite as powerful as their British counterparts. Fidelity discovered this to its cost when it first tried to promote itself to UK sponsors in the early 1990s. It committed the unpardonable faux pas of approaching sponsors directly without going via the consultants (an acceptable practice in the US). Consultant resistance forced it to climb down: it took several years for normal relations to be restored.

The Myners Review expressed concern at the consequences of concentration in UK investment consulting for the quality of advice given to trustees, arguing that it was 'relatively uniform' and 'insufficiently specialized'. On the other hand, the review did accept the industry's contention that it earns barely adequate margins. Prompted by Myners, investment consulting is currently going through a period of self-examination. One possible way forward, pioneered by Frank Russell, is the creation of a multi-manager service, in which the multi-manager is responsible for selecting, monitoring and, if necessary, deselecting from a roster of managers it has identified on behalf of trustees. This business is attractive because fees are related to funds under management: investment consulting operates on a time charge basis. Targeting smaller pension schemes, multi-management is growing rapidly from a low base. Consulting firms have, however, been reluctant to travel too rapidly down this path, conscious that it may raise conflicts with their existing client base. It may not be labelled or such but, in reality, several are moving gradually in the direction of multi-management.

Consultants act as gatekeepers to the all-important shortlist. Fund managers spend much more time marketing to the consultants than to pensions professionals in the sponsor or to trustees because that is where the power lies. Their position is analogous to that of a sluice gate in an irrigation system. Opening the gate allows your field to get watered and provides the opportunity to grow crops, if all the other conditions are right. Because the focus is on track record – which is quantifiable – rather than on softer issues, there is always a broad consensus of opinion among the leading consultants as to who is worthy of a shortlist place and who does not qualify. Of course, there is movement in and out but changes occur quite slowly. What this means is that, at any given time, all the major consultants are generally putting forward the same names to all their clients going through a manager selection process. Everyone in the business knows who is 'in' and who is 'out', if only because consultants are very willing to talk to the trade press, usually anonymously. Fund managers are banned from the charmed circle for a time until they earn or reclaim their place through good behaviour. A quotation from a press report about Gartmore, which suffered from poor performance for a time but improved substantially in 1999, is revealing:

> Consultants are beginning to let clients meet Gartmore again ... 'Hold' recommendations are appearing, although 'Buy' ones will be some way off. Several consultants remain hostile to the firm and Gartmore would do well not to get too excited about its immediate prospects.

> (*Financial News*, 12 April 1999)

What do trustees, relying heavily on consultant advice, look for in making a new appointment? Track record is obviously extremely important but less so at the shortlist stage as those with an inferior performance will already have been weeded out. Personal 'chemistry' – or the lack of it – between the trustees and the fund manager can often be a determining factor. In terms of how the fund management firm would actually run the portfolio, the consultants are keen on pinning down the way in which an organization goes about handling the mandate. Key words here are 'investment process' and 'philosophy'.

'Investment process' refers to the precise mechanism whereby investment decisions are made. For a balanced manager, whose universe is very wide, it is usually based on 'top-down' approach, starting with a world macro-economic view that leads to asset allocation taking into account country preferences, sector preferences and currency exposure. The process is driven by continually updated asset class and market return forecasts. Stock selection decisions are then made in the context of this framework. Other managers are more 'bottom-up'. They focus on stocks they favour, regardless of where they are located, and then 'test' them in a broader context. Every manager will claim that his investment process is disciplined – a word that is sprinkled like fairy dust across fund management websites and marketing material. Figure 5.1 shows the investment process employed by Merrill Lynch Investment Management. (Note the free-flowing, two-way, wholly democratic lines of communication. One could be forgiven for wondering whether it works quite so smoothly in practice!)

> **Every manager will claim that his investment process is disciplined – a word that is sprinkled like fairy dust across fund management websites and marketing material.**

'Philosophy' is broader and more difficult to define. It is essentially subjective, covering issues such as investment style, organizational structure, administration and investment process. Consultants and trustees place

Figure 5.1 The Merrill Lynch Investment Management investment process

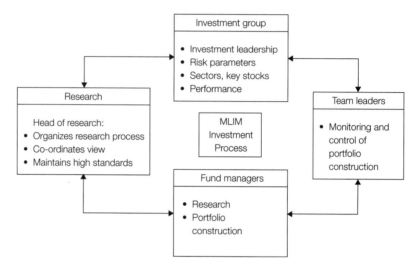

Source: Financial Times, 20 April 1999

great emphasis on consistency – does the organization pursue a line and stick to it? In a similar vein, continuity of personnel, especially fund management personnel, is something that is viewed as extremely important.

Consultants like to 'buy into' a house line that applies equally to all funds run by the organization. A management group running, say, 60 pension funds for 60 clients should, with a common philosophy and investment process, produce broadly similar returns for all those funds. For example, a range of +4.2 per cent to +6.5 per cent might be acceptable but a variation in performance of, say, 5 per cent would be regarded as a distinct negative. In the industry this spread between funds is known as the 'dispersion'. Trustees, closely advised by consultants, like managers who can demonstrate low dispersion. This inevitably leads to an increased emphasis on central decision-making.

The contrast between Schroders, which has a reputation for being centralized, and Merrill Lynch Investment Managers, whose fund managers have traditionally enjoyed considerable freedom, is instructive. Either through good luck or good judgement, dispersion did not emerge as an issue for MLIM until 1998, when consultants and trustees looked at the numbers for 1997. There were wide variations in fund performance and MLIM was forced to tighten up its investment process, issuing edicts on sector weightings which left much less scope for deviant behaviour by individual managers. Dispersion narrowed in 1998 but not before two leading consultants removed the firm from their shortlists. Most significantly, one of their largest clients, the Unilever pension fund, which had suffered a massive 10.5 per cent underperformance against its benchmark in 1997, sacked MLIM and instituted legal proceedings for £100 million in damages alleging negligence. The dispute captured the attention of the press, if only because it was billed as a battle between two strong-minded women: Wendy Mayall of Unilever and Carol Galley of MLIM.

For six weeks at the end of 2001, until a settlement was reached for a reported £70m, evidence given in the High Court revealed the innermost workings of MLIM (in its previous incarnation of Mercury Asset Management) between 1995 and 1997. What emerged was both fascinating and damaging. (Indeed, it is difficult to imagine Merrill Lynch's thought processes in allowing the dispute to get as far as a public hearing, rather than settle before it got to court.) Clearly, Mercury was run on very loose lines, even by the relatively lax standards of the day in the British (balanced) pension fund management business. Formal risk controls were few and inadequate. The fund manager handling the Unilever portfolio was allowed to take lots of 'big bets' – all of which, in 1997, went the wrong way. There was no attempt to control dispersion. A leading consultant commented subsequently:

> Mercury was a franchise. There wasn't anything called the Mercury house line.

> (*Financial Times*, 20 April 1999)

Many of the press reports during and after the case tended to give the impression that the way it was then is the way it is now. Nothing could be further from the truth. What emerged in court was a snapshot of an era that has now passed. The UK fund management industry has changed dramatically in the last few years. There is a much more professional approach to risk management. A large part of this shift is attributable to competitive pressure from US asset management firms, where rigorous, quantitative risk controls have long been an integral part of the service. Today, any UK firm unable to demonstrate its commitment to these techniques would not be regarded by the investment consultants or their clients as a serious contender.

In some respects the investment consultants have been a force for change, encouraging conservative trustees to take on more responsibility and move in new directions. All the major consulting firms have argued for a while that trustees should spread their risk by using a greater range of investment managers, including passive managers. Watson Wyatt, in particular, has been an active promoter of the core–satellite approach and an American-type structure of an effective supervisory investment committee and/or a chief investment officer. But, in other ways, they have been on the side of inertia. Non-mainstream, alternative assets have received scant attention. Any change or uncertainty at an investment manager tends to be viewed as a negative. Consultants have, until recently, been reluctant to persuade trustees to put even small amounts of money with new firms, even those staffed by successful fund managers who have broken away from elsewhere. US investment consultants have been much more prepared to back start-ups run by a manager with a known track record (admittedly easier to do in an environment in which specialization is the norm).

> All the major consulting firms have argued for a while that trustees should spread their risk by using a greater range of investment managers, including passive managers.

As specialist management catches on, and consultants adopt a more flexible attitude to shortlists, the position of the Big Five is steadily being eroded by, among others, a new breed of up-and-coming firms. Examples are: SG Asset Management, 70 per cent owned by the French bank Société Générale and headed by Nicola Horlick of Morgan Grenfell fame; Henderson Investors, part of the largest Australian insurer, AMP; and Baillie Gifford, an Edinburgh-based independent partnership. Successful managers are leaving established organizations for smaller firms, attracted principally by the prospect of owning a significant slice of the equity. Newer and smaller contenders are gaining mandates but the real winners continue to be the indexers and the Americans, led by Capital International and Fidelity.

What has been the effect of all this on fund managers? The combination of conservative trustees wedded to balanced management – at least until recently – and high-profile consultants anxious to demonstrate their worth has created, in actuality, an environment with powerful incentives in favour of risk aversion and conformity. Outperformance is rewarded but only if it is consistent quarter by quarter, not too variable and with minimal dispersion – a difficult feat! Small wonder pension fund managers dare not put a foot wrong for fear of being cast into the outer darkness.

Introducing the wonderful economics of fund management

There must be few businesses where the seller can do what everyone agrees is a poor job for his customers and continue to earn, for some considerable time afterwards, higher revenues and profits. Fund management is one of these lucky businesses. The reason for this is the way in which fund management fees are structured. It also reflects client inertia in both wholesale and retail asset management. Plan sponsors or individual investors do not readily desert an underperforming manager, especially if the value of the fund is up on where they started.

Pension funds, managed funds and investment funds mostly operate on an ad valorem basis. Fees are levied as a percentage of funds under management, not on a fixed fee or fixed fee plus bonus basis, so when share prices go up fees go up. Around 70 per cent of UK pension funds use an ad valorem payment structure. According to the Fund Managers Association (now the Investment Management Association) the average annual fee rate for managing a £200 million equity portfolio is about 30 basis points (0.3 per cent) of funds under management. The fee for a large fund will be considerably lower. Sponsors usually pay quarterly based on the FUM figure at the end of the quarter. US money management fees are much higher: a range of 0.5 per cent to 0.75 per cent is common. In large part, this differential reflects the orientation towards specialist managers who are set more demanding targets. Cross-border comparisons of fee levels are notoriously difficult but, even allowing for this, it does seem that the American money management industry has successfully established a 'high fee culture' that clients generally do not dispute.

The effect of the ad valorem fee structure is, of course, that, in a bull market, fees continue to rise even if the fund underperforms. Fund managers call this the 'endowment effect'. Revenue increases until client defections are so great that they are sufficient to offset the beneficial impact of rising share prices. The easiest way of appreciating the unusual nature of this arrangement is to imagine a situation in which the owner of a house goes away for a year and hires a housesitter to look after the pets and water the plants. The housesitter is asked to keep the house in good condition, and make improvements where necessary to maintain – and hopefully improve – the value of the property relative to the rest of the neighbourhood. The housesitter is paid £600 a quarter. If the value of the house appreciates over the year from £400,000 to £500,000 because house prices in general have gone up it would not occur to the house owner to pay the sitter 25 per cent more merely for being there while this was happening! He might give the sitter a cash bonus if he thought he had done a particularly good job of looking after the house. If we substitute 'pension fund' for 'owner' and 'fund manager' for 'sitter' the arrangement would have been 0.6 per cent of the value of the house per annum rather than a fixed fee of £2,400. The sitter would have earned an additional £600 for doing no more than he was asked to do.

Given the endowment effect and its stable and predictable cash flow characteristics, it is easy to see why financial institutions find fund management attractive. Unsurprisingly, private client fund management, notably the service offered by the Swiss banks, is right at the top of the profitability scale. On average, fund management groups produce pre-interest margins on sales around 30 per cent, though, faced with lower markets and rising costs, they are currently under pressure. When fund management companies change hands the price is usually expressed as a percentage of FUM. Retail managers are more profitable and sell for a higher percentage of FUM than institutional managers.

> If the value of the house appreciates over the year from £400,000 to £500,000 because house prices in general have gone up it would not occur to the house owner to pay the sitter 25 per cent more merely for being there while this was happening!

All this begs the obvious question: Why have clients tolerated a system of payment that is – for most of the time – so patently advantageous to the manager? Even in the US fixed or performance-based fees are not that common. There is no simple answer. One reason is that performance-related fees are attractive but complicated to implement. Another may be that UK sponsors felt that, in a balanced management environment, they could negotiate a low percentage fee. Now, however, it does seem that performance-linked mandates are gaining greater acceptance. Pension funds appear more willing to tolerate the (potentially) higher cost, especially where they are able to offset it against an increased allocation to lower-fee passive and fixed income management. For fund managers, they offer a welcome opportunity to restore margins.

Institutional fund management is under fee pressure. It is also under pressure on the cost front as the pendulum swings away from DB and life fund management to DC and managed funds business, in which the individual has a direct relationship with the fund management organization. The upside from the fund manager's point of view is that performance moves lower down the priority scale: individual investors are less able and less inclined to scrutinize performance with a fine-tooth comb. The downside is that much more emphasis needs to be placed on branding, distribution and information systems, all of which require capital. In such an environment, size is an advantage. Many recent acquisitions and mergers in fund management have been driven by the need for scale, in distribution especially. Lloyds TSB bought Scottish Widows to take advantage of its excellent reputation in the all-important IFA market. Merrill Lynch bought Mercury to secure a top position in institutional asset management and obtain a brand it could push through its US retail network.

Unfortunately, the economics of fund management are not quite so simple, leading to an important point. In terms of actually running funds, size does not necessarily bring benefits and, worse still, can often be a disadvantage. Fund management is not like other businesses because the end product, investment returns, is not positively correlated with scale. Large equity funds are unwieldy to manage and restricted in what they can do by liquidity problems. Studies show an established and identifiable inverse relationship between size of fund – and indeed size of organization – and performance. One key factor is that bigger management companies derive less benefit from good investment ideas because of the difficulty of spreading them across a number of funds. For obvious reasons, this lack of correlation between size and performance is something that the major branded sellers of asset management services make no effort to inject into the public consciousness.

There is a well-known tendency in the industry for successful fund management companies to take on new business in excess of the amount the existing team can realistically handle. The story of what happened to Fidelity in the mid-1990s illustrates the point:

> Size had become a handicap. Many Fidelity funds had grown so large they could no longer manoeuvre through the market as they had in the past ... incredible performance led investors to pour money into Fidelity at unprecedented rates. Faced with billions of dollars in new cash, many mutual fund managers in 1994 began side-stepping Fidelity's traditional approach of investing in a diversified array of hundreds of fast-growing small and mid-size companies in favour of making big bets on whole sectors of the economy, such as technology stocks or government bonds.

Many Fidelity funds had grown so large they could no longer manoeuvre through the market as they had in the past ... incredible performance led investors to pour money into Fidelity at unprecedented rates.

(Excerpted from the 14 September 1998 issue of *Business Week* by special permission. © 2000 by McGraw-Hill, Inc.)

New management restored the position by closing Fidelity's four biggest funds to new investors. More significantly, recognizing that going back to the old way of stockpicking was simply not an option for a company with (then) $480 billion in equity assets and 326 fund managers and analysts, the investment focus shifted to largecap growth stocks, such as Coca-Cola and Microsoft. The results have been positive but some commentators argue that many of the larger Fidelity funds bear more than a passing resemblance to the S&P 500 Index. The simple and uncomfortable truth for active managers is: *size is good for capturing funds but not for managing them.*

Despite the rise in importance of distribution and technology, by far the largest single cost for asset management firms is 'people cost', particularly the cost of employing fund managers and analysts. A survey by the Investment Management Association (IMA) in 2000 suggested a UK-based fund management employment figure of 22,200, of whom just over 3,700 were classified as 'investment managers'. Fund managers (and analysts) need to hold a certificate, having passed a professional exam organized by the United Kingdom Society of Investment Professionals (UKSIP). Salary and bonus levels are high, especially in the US where successful mutual fund managers can become media personalities, exemplified by Peter Lynch, the high-profile manager of Fidelity's Magellan fund, in his heyday. Other mutual fund groups, such as Capital and Putnam (the asset management subsidiary of Marsh & McLennan, the owner of W.M. Mercer), make a conscious effort to prevent their star managers from becoming embroiled in the media circus.

A critical development in investment management in the 1990s has, as we noted in Chapter 2, been the rise in importance of the buy-side analyst. Fund managers are increasingly wary of the sell-side analysts employed by the investment banks and prefer to rely on internally generated research. Buy-side researchers seek to develop direct relationships with companies in which their firm is invested or might wish to invest, ideally via regular contact on a one-to-one basis. The extent to which they are able to gain access depends on the reputation of the firm, the size of their shareholding – or potential shareholding – and the expertise and experience of their analysts in the relevant sector. As we shall see in Chapter 7, companies treat buy-side analysts very differently from sell-side analysts.

Unfortunately, the IMA survey does not split the 'investment managers' figure between fund managers and buy-side analysts. Some firms, notably Prudential and Schroders, have maintained a commitment to buy-side research since the 1970s but the great majority of UK fund managers are relatively recent converts. UK fund management groups are some way behind the US in terms of their allocation of resources to buy-side research, although the trend is running strongly in that direction. A database of money managers maintained by the authoritative US industry journal Pensions & Investments indicates that, out of 19,000 personnel directly involved in managing portfolios in 2000, no fewer than 42 per cent were classified as analysts. Some leading US houses employ twice as many analysts as portfolio managers.

The commitment to intensive, rigorous, bottom-up, buy-side research has deep roots at many of the longer established American asset management firms, such as Capital Group, Fidelity or T. Rowe Price, where the tradition of independent in-house research goes back 20 years or more. In these organizations buy-side research is seen as a career in itself rather than, as elsewhere, merely a stepping stone to fund management. In the 1990s others followed their example. Demonstration of a competent buy-side research capability is now regarded as a sine qua non for any US firm that is serious about winning institutional, or indeed retail, business. In the UK, a commitment to buy-side research is rapidly coming to be regarded as 'best practice'.

A further significant trend in asset management during the 1990s has been the focus on securities trading costs. In an environment in which 0.1 per cent extra performance can make all the difference in the league tables, the ability to execute a trade as cheaply as possible becomes a priority. Institutions have responded by moving from a structure in which each fund manager was responsible for buying and selling the shares in his fund or funds to one in which execution of trades is done through a central dealing desk. By the end of the 1990s every UK fund management organization of significance had converted to central dealing. In doing so, they have maintained a constant pressure on commission rates. This process has been given a further impetus by the Myners Review, which encouraged trustees to look closely at the transaction costs incurred by their managers. The shift to central dealing and the enhanced status of the buy-side analyst have narrowed the traditional role of the fund manager, although, as we see in Chapter 6, in other respects it has expanded.

> This process has been given a further impetus by the Myners Review, which encouraged trustees to look closely at the transaction costs incurred by their managers.

The perils of index mesmerization

Indices (or, in StreetSpeak, 'indexes') can be constructed in different ways and used for a variety of purposes. Weighting by market capitalization has become a generally accepted standard, which means that larger stocks have a disproportionate influence. We noted in Chapter 3 just how skewed indices have become. To put this into perspective, a 5 per cent rise in BP, the largest stock on the London market, has the same impact on the FTSE 100 Index as a doubling of the share price of Safeway (standing around number 80 at April 2002).

Some indices – the familiar ones quoted daily – are mainly market trend indicators, some are designed specifically to act as portfolio benchmarks, while others are there to provide a platform for derivatives (futures and options) trading. The more venerable ones often originated (in the US especially) as loss-leading newspaper promotional devices. Only in Britain did the actuaries get into the business early on, a position they retain via an association with FTSE International, a joint venture between the *Financial Times* and the London Stock Exchange. Today, cheap and easy-to-use computing power allows an index to be created to cover pretty well any specific requirement, however exotic or obscure. Twenty years ago indices were an unglamorous backwater, comprising a few well-known country-based series designed to track the performance of national stock markets. Not so now. Index construction and operation has become so vital to the functioning of the investment management industry that it has even acquired a kind of down-to-earth sex appeal!

Indices are now big business, with a handful of providers battling to become the standard in what is regarded as virgin index territory: for example, Europe following the introduction of the euro. The major opposing armies, dedicated to capturing the hearts and minds of institutional investors, are Morgan Stanley Capital International, Dow Jones, Standard & Poor's and FTSE International. All except FTSE International are commercial organizations with broad interests that need to take care that their index business is, and is seen to be, independent. Indices have proliferated to the point where there are now literally thousands of them, covering individual countries (down to the smallest emerging market), global markets, regions, asset classes, sectors domestically and on an international basis, company size categories and investment styles plus customized benchmarks for performance measurement (increasingly favoured by pension fund trustees). For the professional investor, for whom beating benchmarks is the name of the game, index watching can easily turn into an obsession.

The simplest way of understanding indices is to think of them in terms of three basic categories (with a lot of overlaps):

■ Headline indices, containing a relatively small number of 'blue chips' with a high 'brand recognition factor' among retail investors.

■ Mid-level indices, with anything from 30 to 300 liquid, actively traded stocks, often designed to serve as the basis of stock index futures trading.

■ Benchmark indices for portfolio management purposes, with a wider coverage.

The original British 'headline' index was the FT Ordinary (30 share) Index, dating back to 1935. It is still calculated but, following the introduction of the FTSE 100 ('Footsie') Index in 1984, no one takes any notice of it. Surprisingly, its American equivalent, *the* long-running Dow Jones Industrial Average (DJIA), retains its status as the popular Wall Street indicator, even though it is an anachronism. It is astonishingly primitive by today's standards with some strange features. The oddest of these is that the 30 stocks in it are equally weighted by price, which means that a given percentage rise (or fall) in a high-priced stock has a greater influence on the index than the same percentage change in a lower priced stock! Nor is it any longer just an industrial index (it contains American Express, J.P. Morgan Chase and Citigroup). Changes in 'the Dow' are rare and lag significantly behind changes in the US economy. Only in November 1999 did it deign to include Microsoft and Intel, even though they had ranked as Numbers 1 and 3 in US stock market capitalization for several years.

It is not generally appreciated that fund management demand for derivatives is driven primarily by liquidity considerations, rather than the desire to indulge in 'speculative' activity. The creation of the 'Footsie' owes much to institutional demand for a derivatives instrument with good coverage of the UK equity market. Through the FTSE Index futures contract (as it is called) a fund manager who is, for example, bullish on UK equities over the next month can buy, say, £100 million worth of stock instead of buying a representative selection of companies, which would almost certainly be more difficult and more time consuming. The futures contract often has better liquidity than the underlying stocks. The same applies to any other stock market. An investor who is bullish of Germany would buy the DAX futures contact based on the DAX 30-share German Stock Index.

> A benchmark index needs to have certain characteristics that are not present in many other indices. For example, it must have the ability to calculate total return.

For the institutional fund manager the indices that matter are the benchmark indices: the FTSE Actuaries All-Share Index in the UK and the Standard & Poor's 500 Index in the US. The All-Share has been calculated since 1962 and the S&P since 1957. A benchmark index needs to have certain characteristics that are not present in many other indices. For example, it must have the ability to calculate total return. There is no 'real time' requirement as there is for an index underlying a derivative contract – daily calculation is sufficient. While the status of the All-Share as the UK benchmark index is not often challenged, the S&P 500 has been losing ground to style index benchmarks.

Indexation is a phenomenon that has risen to prominence on the back of an increasing dependence on, and fascination with, indices. No one knows exactly how much of the stock market is currently owned by tracker funds, both institutional and retail. Best guesses are 10–15 per cent in the UK and closer to 20 per cent in the US. Index funds continue to gain adherents, although the curve has flattened out. In the US it is a largely mature market. Even in the UK there is evidence of a decline in the rate of conversion. A key element in index fund expansion is the core–satellite trend, with its associated shift to passive management. Another reason for continued growth in the UK is that DC scheme members are inclined to select index funds.

There is, of course, a risk that index funds could come to account for such a large proportion of the stock market that there would be no one to lead – and nothing for them to follow! However, we are currently some way away from that point. On top of these figures we need to add the closet indexers. At a guess, this might raise the proportion of the UK equity market subject to these influences to 30 per cent or more. But there is no way of assessing the value of institutional funds that practise something approximating to indexation while professing their undying love for active management.

Unlike active management, indexation is a purely quantitative process, relying heavily on computers and software. Indeed, index funds are a subset of a broader category of (in StreetSpeak) 'quant' funds, employing a 'black box', scientific approach to investment. Indexers are the faithful foot soldiers of the investment management industry. Where others lead, they blindly follow. Better still, an index army is prepared to march on a stomach that is nearly empty. Being reliant on technology rather than people, index funds are cheap to run. Additionally, they benefit from low turnover/transaction costs. Fees run anywhere from one-third to one-tenth of the levels charged for active management. Passive management is profitable even at this level because there are huge economies of scale and entry barriers are significant. Having said that, passive management is not a licence to print money. Margins are significantly lower than those earned by active investors. The tough economics of passive management were highlighted by Gartmore when it sold its passive business to State Street in July 2001, citing as reasons insufficient scale and meagre returns.

Those who run index funds do not pretend it is an exciting business to be in. Patti Dunn, former Chairman of Barclays Global Investors (headquartered in San Francisco following Barclays acquisition of the Wells Fargo passive management operation in 1995) is disarmingly frank about the sort of people it attracts.

We are like the designated driver at a big party. We are not the fun people.

(Interview in the *Financial Times*, 21 May 1999)

It is tempting to assume that tracking an index is straightforward. It is, in fact, extremely difficult. There is a constant scramble to buy or sell stock to 'rebalance' the fund, in response to changes in index constituents and the issue and cancellation of shares by companies. Those managers following the All-Share – that is, in fact, the majority of indexers – normally opt to buy a representative sample that hopefully parallels the performance of the index. Consequently, passive management suffers from a virulent and persistent disease called 'tracking error'. Mainly for liquidity reasons, it is surprisingly difficult to create a fund that performs exactly in line with the index it is tracking. Plan sponsors demand low levels of variance and it is not unknown for a passive manager to be fired for allowing tracking error to become too large.

Corporate behaviour, as well as investment behaviour, is increasingly driven by index considerations. The investment bankers advising a company that is large enough to be a significant index constituent on an IPO or a transfer of its primary listing will put index inclusion right at the top of the discussion agenda. (Theoretically, a company's primary listing determines which index it is in.) For the five big South African companies that transferred their primary stock market listing from Johannesburg to London in the late 1990s inclusion in the Footsie (and, more importantly, in the All-Share) was an absolutely critical element in their planning. Membership guarantees a demand from both explicit and closet indexers. It is doubtful they would have gone

> Corporate behaviour, as well as investment behaviour, is increasingly driven by index considerations.

ahead if they had been refused entry. When, in 1992, HSBC bought Midland Bank it somehow achieved the neat trick of retaining two primary listings, so that it benefits from inclusion in both the main UK indices and Hong Kong's Hang Seng Index. Getting into the right index – or, even better, more than one – is a critical issue for any company wanting to build a strong investor following.

Changes in index membership are closely monitored by institutional investors and significantly influence investment decision-making. Entry or removal from a key index undoubtedly affects short-term share price performance. With the rise of indexation the job of the equity strategist has changed its emphasis. As well as spending time looking at macroeconomic variables and 'big picture' items like equity supply and demand they also focus on the probable demand for individual stocks based on changes in their index weightings. This kind of analysis works particularly well when a large-scale share-for-share ('paper') takeover occurs. Vodafone's successful bids for AirTouch and Mannesmann both resulted in an approximate doubling of the company's market capitalization as the former shareholders received newly issued Vodafone shares. Suddenly, if it did nothing, a fully weighted UK institution (assuming it held no AirTouch or Mannesmann) found itself only 50 per cent weighted. A detailed analysis of the leading UK institutions, looking closely at their closet indexing tendencies, allowed strategists to make predictions of the amount of money that would go into Vodafone as institutions moved to rebuild weightings to previous levels.

> Increasingly, major shares move up or down for a time for index reasons, unconnected with the merits or demerits of that company as an investment.

So pervasive is indexation – both overt and covert – that fund management behaviour in the big stocks that are critical to portfolio performance can be predicted with a high degree of accuracy. Increasingly, major shares move up or down for a time for index reasons, unconnected with the merits or demerits of that company as an investment. The index imperative has comparable implications for corporate strategy, as companies feel the pressure to buy or merge in an effort to stay above the FTSE 100 (or FTSE 250) 'radar screen'.

Institutional attitudes
Why fund managers behave as they do

■ It has all got much more nerdy

■ What turns fund managers on – and off

■ Promises, promises

■ The art of managing shareholder expectations

■ The emergence of the New Industrial Compact

■ Why the Inexorable Logic of fund management means that small is no longer beautiful

■ Can we solve the small company dilemma?

You might think that institutions, with their large staffs of highly-paid and experienced professionals, would be a force for reason and stability in financial markets. They are not ... A story told 40 years ago illustrates why investment professionals behave as they do: An oil prospector, moving to his heavenly reward, was met by St. Peter with bad news. 'You're qualified for residence,' said St. Peter 'but, as you can see, the compound reserved for oilmen is packed. There's no way to squeeze you in.' After thinking for a moment, the prospector asked if he might say just four words to the present occupants. That seemed harmless to St. Peter, so the prospector cupped his hands and yelled, 'Oil discovered in hell.' Immediately the gate to the compound opened and all the oilmen marched out to head for the nether regions. Impressed, St. Peter invited the prospector to move himself in and make himself comfortable. The prospector paused. 'No,' he said, 'I think I'll go along with the rest of the boys. There might be some truth in that rumour after all.'

(Warren Buffett, the legendary American investor, in his annual Letter to the Shareholders of Berkshire Hathaway Inc., 1985)

It has all got much more nerdy

The title of this section is a quote from a fund manager looking back at the last 20 years. Over this period, the practice of equity fund management has been greatly changed by the 'quant revolution'. Compared with what he did in the 1980s, a fund manager now has huge amounts of data on which to base a decision. Everything, from portfolios to companies, is capable of being mathematically modelled. Clients do not just seek above-average returns, they expect the manager to monitor risk – stock, sector and country – on a continuous basis. Investment management is increasingly about control, about process and systems. The bold and heroic stockpicker, passionate about the companies in which he placed his trust, has been largely replaced by a more considered, more analytical type of individual. Gone are the days when Tom O'Connell of GRE Insurance, one of the best known City fund managers of the 1970s and 1980s, could put a substantial chunk of his fund into up-and-coming companies like Racal or Siebe, many times their benchmark weighting. But active stock selection had its downside. It was easy for a fund manager to 'fall in love with his stock'. His emotional involvement with the company and its management made selling difficult when the time came.

> A fund manager now has huge amounts of data on which to base a decision. Everything, from portfolios to companies, is capable of being mathematically modelled.

Today's fund manager tries to stand back from the fray. He is less likely to be turned on by what companies do or the people who run them. The spreadsheet model constructed to replicate a company's finances plays a large part in his thinking. Fund managers are far less inclined to take anything that is said to them, either by corporate executives or securities analysts/sales personnel, at face value. Corporate contact is more formalized but this is largely because companies, under pressure to equalize and control the flow of information, endeavour to structure the whole process of investor relations. The portfolio decision-making element in the fund manager's role has been greatly eroded by the rise of the buy-side analyst, central dealing, a surge in administrative and regulatory obligations and the need to maintain a high marketing profile.

Fund management is a continuum, from indexation at one end to 'traditional' active management at the other end. Today's 'traditional' managers are significant users of quantitative tools, as are the new breed of hedge fund managers whose growing influence on the London market became the subject of public debate in 2001. (Indeed, so important have hedge funds become that, in CitySpeak, conventional active equity funds are now referred to as 'long only' to distinguish them from those for whom 'going short' is a tool of the trade). None of this means that stockpicking is dead. It is distinctly alive but has to operate in a much more controlled context. Fund managers still talk graphically about 'torpedoes' (stocks that plunge unexpectedly, creating a large hole in the portfolio) and 'angels' (the reverse). At the other end of the spectrum, pure quantitative techniques have evolved into index beating strategies, that go by the name of 'active quant'. Most fund managers consider their profession to be an indefinable blend of art and science. In an interview Bill Mott, a highly-regarded equity manager at Credit Suisse Asset Management with a long-term record of outperformance (who holds, incidentally, a Ph.D in quantum physics) put it like this:

> There are no rules; I like to kiss and cuddle the numbers. I try to be pragmatic and hope that, from a framework of knowledge and hard work, I can make some sensible decisions. But I can't tell you how I do it.

(*Financial Times*, 9 February 2002)

Fund managers are faced with intensifying performance pressures in a rapidly changing world awash with information. The understandable reaction to the task of handling all the information inputs that might affect any one of, say, 100 companies is to reduce each company to a few essentials. In the mind of the fund manager, each company name has, at any particular point in time, attached to it a set of 'bullet points', probably between two and five. Decisions to buy or sell are made on the basis of how new information affects one or more of these characteristics. These bullet points form the kernel of the investment 'story' (in StreetSpeak, the 'investment case' or 'investment thesis') that persuades the fund manager to buy the stock in the first place.

For example, the UK mining sector contains three large companies: Rio Tinto, BHP Billiton and Anglo American. The last two are relatively recent arrivals. Anglo American moved its primary listing from Johannesburg to London in 1999. Billiton did the same and subsequently merged with BHP of Australia using what is called a 'dual-listed structure' (it has primary listings in both London and Sydney, as does Rio Tinto). All mining companies are cyclical (profits are closely related to commodity prices as mining costs are fixed) and currencies (especially the Australian dollar and the South African rand) have a strong influence so these are bullet points that apply to all three.

Rio Tinto is the familiar, well-regarded 'quality stock' in the sector. If a fund manager decided to put money into the mining sector 'Rios' would be

the obvious first port of call. A further bullet point is the company's exposure to the price of copper. Fund managers buy and sell Rio Tinto on the
back of movements in the copper price because it is information that is continuous and easily accessible. In fact, copper is less important than iron ore
or coal to Rio Tinto but there is no world market price for either of these.
For BHP Billiton the bullet points are the well-diversified product portfolio it
now has, including significant earnings from oil and gas, and a management that is seen as more adventurous than cautious but reliable Rio Tinto.
Anglo American remains heavily exposed to South Africa (70 per cent of
profits), is more oriented to precious metals and has an aversion to debt
(gearing is much lower than its fellow miners). Nor, given the history of
family control via a complex corporate structure, are investors convinced it
has shed its inbred boardroom culture. Management is often a key bullet
point for fund managers. Companies are strongly identified with the personalities of the people who run them, especially the chief executive. Fund
managers respond to signals that tell them whether a certain bullet point
has become more positive or more negative for the
company.

> Companies are strongly identified with the personalities of the people who run them, especially the chief executive.

The practice of fund management rests, as in any
other profession, on certain assumptions. One of
these is that the only thing that matters is getting the
direction of the share price right. This is perfectly
understandable as the only criterion for judging a
manager's performance is the performance of his
fund. Whether the manager made the right (buy or
sell) decision for the right reasons is irrelevant. To use
a well-worn City phrase, it is perfectly acceptable to 'get it right for the
wrong reasons'. A common instance is when a manager buys an ailing
stock because he believes it is on the road to recovery and, gratefully but
unexpectedly, finds himself on the receiving end of a bid that pushes the
price up, say, 30 per cent. Or when a fund manager makes a poor investment but ends up with a profit simply because the company has been
caught up in a market or sector upturn. The manager receives full credit for
'getting it right'. How or why is of little consequence.

Compare our fund manager with an executive in, say, publishing who
estimates the first issue sales of a new monthly magazine at 100,000
copies. If the actual figure turns out to be 150,000 because the main
article happens to relate to something in the news that week or a competitor magazine fails to appear, the executive is regarded as lucky rather
than clever. This is because he is not measured – or paid – on the basis of
150,000 but on the basis of having reached his 100,000 target. The extra
50,000 is a bonus that may not last. The problem with 'getting it right for

the wrong reasons' is that the focus is entirely on the result rather than what lies behind the result, obscuring longer-term trends (as we see in the context of smaller companies, covered later in this chapter).

What turns fund managers on – and off

The institutional investor's Valhalla is a world in which every stock in the portfolio outperforms by, say, 10 per cent every quarter ad infinitum. This is obviously impossible. We are once again in Lake Wobegon where every-one is above-average. A few stocks in a portfolio might enjoy consistent outperformance – but only for a time. Every share price fluctuates, if for no other reason than the temptation to take profits. Additionally, fund man-agers are reluctant to let an outperforming stock become too large a per-centage of the fund. It goes against the principle of risk reduction through diversification. To keep the holding within reasonable bounds they often sell small amounts as it goes up ('top slicing' in the jargon).

In the imperfect world in which they are obliged to operate how do fund managers make their stock selection decisions? What do they look for in a company? Conversely, what are the things that put them off? The factors involved can be divided into 'hard' and 'soft'. Hard items are those that are more factual, often financial. Soft items are those that are less easy to define, more a matter of (individual or general) perception, often people related, ultimately with an instinctive/emotional content. Fund managers – like all managers – prefer to believe they make decisions primarily on the basis of hard factor evaluation ('We employ a disciplined investment process'). In reality, as elsewhere, soft factors play an extremely important role. The City has a long tradition of making business judgements on the basis of people judgements, as per David Kynaston's description of London before Big Bang.

> Unless there was an overpowering reason to do otherwise, which was seldom, chaps stuck to dealing with chaps whom they knew, liked and, above all, trusted.

('Insider dealings and the governor's eyebrows', *Financial Times*, 31 July 1999)

This ethos retains its influence today in the evaluation of investments. At board level, the City interface with a company will normally be the chief executive in a double act with his finance director. While the CEO talks 'big picture' the finance director deals with questions of detail and spends more of his time attending to the needs of the sell-side analysts. The character, reputation and trustworthiness of these individuals is of paramount importance to institutions in making their investment decisions. As we saw in the last section, 'management' normally figures as a key bullet point in the mind of the fund manager. Companies, inevitably, tend to be viewed in terms of the personalities who run them. To a considerable degree, in the mind of a fund manager, BP is Lord Browne, Rentokil Initial is Sir Clive Thompson, British Airways was – until he was fired in March 2000 – Robert Ayling. However, not all firms are led by, and identified with, such strong personalities. The City's preoccupation with personalities is both good and bad (as we see in the next section).

Looking first at the hard factors what are the things that institutions focus on?

■ *The right numerical stuff*. Good financial numbers and ratios, both historic and forecast, are crucial. Sales and earnings per share growth rates (preferably accompanied by the magic words 'double-digit') come high on the list, as do cash flow and margin trends. Profitability ratios assessing whether a firm is earning in excess of its cost of capital have gained in importance in recent years. Anything that threatens to dilute future earnings/cost of capital and especially EPS trends is regarded as a negative. 'Dilution' commonly occurs when a company makes an acquisition, typically when the number of shares issued to pay for the target more than offsets the expected contribution to earnings. If a company was forecast to report an EPS of 25p for next year and, as a result of a deal, the forecast EPS is now 24p, it is said to be suffering dilution. Fund managers like earnings-enhancing (in StreetSpeak, 'accretive' or 'anti-dilutive') acquisitions. Dilution is a dirty word in the institutional lexicon. Fortunately, its unwelcome impact can be offset by 'synergies'. Putting two and two together should always add up to more than four – otherwise there would be no point in doing it! Nowadays companies engaged in an M&A deal helpfully provide investors with a public estimate of the 'synergistic benefits'. Cost-saving synergies are easier to quantify than any prospective enhancement to revenues.

> 'Dilution' commonly occurs when a company makes an acquisition, typically when the number of shares issued to pay for the target more than offsets the expected contribution to earnings.

■ *Forget yesterday*. Fund managers are always looking forward. Many – in their professional lives – would subscribe to Henry Ford's view that 'History is bunk!' A company's track record is only one of many inputs into the City's estimation of the future. This is particularly so when a company goes through a troubled patch. Few outside the City realize that investors would much rather see a complete clearing of the decks – however expensive or painful – than the perpetuation of a running sore. New management usually finds it easier to adopt a deck-clearing approach than incumbent management. Once the deed is done a share price often responds positively. When, in 1996, Rolls-Royce wrote off £280 million to get out of the power business the share price rose.

■ *Keep it simple*. Anglo-Saxon investors thoroughly dislike the messy and byzantine corporate structures found in most other stock markets, typified by intricate cross-holdings, 'strategic' stakes and minority positions in quoted companies. Such structures are common in continental European markets and places like South Africa and Canada, principally because family-based enterprises still play an important role in these economies. But, under pressure from American and British investors for simplicity, transparency and more comparable and reliable accounting information, things are changing fast. Continental firms are moving towards neater structures. And those that already have such structures are responding to investor demands for increased transparency by improving their reporting of business segment results. For example, in 1998, ABB, the large Swedish–Swiss engineering company, changed its structure from three to eight divisions, principally to allow investors to see more clearly how individual parts of the business perform. A further reorganization in 2001 maintained this level of transparency.

■ *Purity usually pays off*. Generally, fund managers prefer 'pure plays' – companies that have a single business focus. Indeed, 'focus' is a word much favoured by today's investors. Intel is almost entirely focused on making semiconductors. 'Exposure' is also a term that is used freely and extensively. When a fund manager buys into a company he is buying exposure to the industry that company is in and the geographical area in which it operates. Pearson, for example, offers exposure to the burgeoning demand for online education, together with a major presence in the vast US market. Fund managers consciously invest in companies that give them the exposure they seek. In the 1960s investors were convinced that conglomerates represented the pinnacle of capitalist achievement, based on their counterbalanced exposure to different industries. (Amazingly, some survive: the most successful is General Electric of the US, with interests from jet engines through television broadcasting to financial services, which all goes to prove that superior EPS growth will overcome the deepest investor prejudice!) But today's fund managers do not want corporate management to select their exposures for them. They want to be able to pick and choose between a range of quoted companies that have stripped themselves down to their core business and are, as a consequence, focused. They want simple and understandable investment propositions. Hence the pressure – when markets are receptive – for the divestment of non-core operations, demergers, spin-offs, tracking stock, carve-outs and all the other confusing terminology of investment banking. Fund managers expect chief executives to manage their business portfolio much as they themselves manage an equity portfolio.

■ *Stories in boxes are best*. As part of the process of reducing the information inflow to essentials, investors like to categorize companies in terms of their stories. This approach is particularly helpful to the fund manager evaluating an IPO, as there is no existing story. There are various categories. 'Growth' is an easy and obvious one. 'New management' is another obvious story, probably allied to 'recovery', 'turnaround' or 'financial restructuring'.

Investors also like 'consolidation' stories, where one or two companies take it upon themselves to buy up their weaker brethren in an industry. Investment in a consolidator should prove attractive as the industry's economics improve. Investment in a company that may be consolidated has a more immediate reward if and when the company is bid for. Some investors respond to 'themes', covering types of companies or sectors, like energy conservation or global consolidation in financial services.

> Some investors respond to 'themes', covering types of companies or sectors, like energy conservation or global consolidation in financial services.

■ *Stay biddable*. Institutions like to receive bids, even if they decide to reject them. The corollary is that they are resolutely opposed to anything that prevents a company from being acquired, such as a large family or corporate stake. Nowadays, in the absence of such a barrier, no company, whatever its size, is safe. Ever since BTR's successful 1983 takeover of Thomas Tilling, an old-style conglomerate convinced it was too large and well connected to be bid for, it has been clear that any company is vulnerable. Even if it is never bid for, a company's P/E is often higher than it would otherwise be if there is no obvious blocking mechanism. The existence of a large minority stake held by a potential bidder is good news for the share price. To persuade them to sell, a bidder needs to pay the existing shareholders a 'control premium' over and above the prevailing market price. In the UK, this premium has generally ranged between 20 per cent and 40 per cent. Sell-side analysts who have encouraged institutions to buy a stock that has subsequently fallen are not slow to highlight 'bid possibilities' in an effort to get the share price moving in the right direction. A useful technique is a research report containing a break-up or sum-of-parts valuation, revealing 'hidden value' at the current, lower price.

■ *Size, diversity (and, of course, liquidity) are good.* As we explained earlier, institutions prefer large to small. Diversity of products and customers is also a positive provided the company does not stray beyond the bounds of purity (however that is defined). This can give rise to some interesting linguistic gymnastics, illustrated by Rexam, the UK listed international packaging company, when it described itself (in its 1997 annual report) as 'a diversified and yet focused group'!

■ *Associate with quality.* Any company benefits from an association with recognizable 'blue chip' names, preferably as customers or, better still, equity stakeholders. The aura that attaches to them rubs off on the stock concerned. Investors feel more comfortable buying a speciality chemical company selling pharmaceutical ingredients to GlaxoSmithKline or Pfizer rather than one whose business is with second or third rank drug producers. Quoted property companies proudly list their blue chip tenants. It is a case of glitz by association!

■ *Some types of business have more appeal.* In a mature economy like the UK, institutional investors exhibit preferences for certain types of business. Together with growth, quality of earnings is accorded a high priority. Fund managers like businesses with recurring revenues from maintenance and service, or the sale of spares or consumables. Anything with a 'commodity' tag is a big turn-off while, conversely, anything with a 'speciality' (in the US, 'specialty') label is immediately welcomed as providing a degree of protection from cyclical and competitive forces. The inevitable consequence is that the term has been devalued. Pretty well every company courting investors portrays itself as offering speciality products in niche markets!

■ *Corporate modesty wins applause.* The business structure favoured by institutions is the decentralized organization run by a small, lean head office. Vodafone Group is run from an unpretentious building in the Thames Valley town of Newbury. Large and wasteful headquarters are out. Older fund managers remember too many instances of corporate folie de grandeur (Vickers and P&O are but two among many) followed by a deterioration in business and share price underperformance.

The soft factors that institutions take into account when making a decision to invest in a particular company are, by their nature, more difficult to define:

- *'Quality of management' is a key ingredient.* Fund managers talk about a particular firm as having 'high-quality management'. Quality of management – much more than quality of earnings – is an elusive concept. To an extent, it is a function of the numbers that the company produces. A firm that consistently reports higher growth rates and/or better operating ratios than its competitors can, quite reasonably, be assumed to have high-quality management. But quality of management is much more than the bare numbers. It covers the whole relationship between the senior management, especially the CEO and FD, and the City. That relationship is based on a further important term in CitySpeak – the concept of delivery. When evaluating a company fund managers will focus on the track record and personality of the chief executive, asking themselves the question, 'Does he deliver?' In effect, the institutions regard themselves as having a contractual relationship with the CEO. We explain how this relationship works in the next section.

- *Be seen to be doing things.* Unlike stockbrokers or investment bankers – who depend for a living on activity-based fees, trades and commissions – fund managers get paid even if they make no purchases or sales. Indeed, transactions cost money so there is an incentive to avoid activity. Consequently, it would be reasonable to suppose that many fund managers agree with Warren Buffett's proposition that he makes 'more money when snoring than when active'. Picking solid, reliable companies and holding on to them, as he does, would seem to be a sensible and logical strategy. However, in practice, fund managers frequently favour companies that engage in what the City euphemistically calls 'corporate activity'.

> In practice, fund managers frequently favour companies that engage in what the City euphemistically calls 'corporate activity'.

Other than in sectors with high organic growth the City views M&A as a key element in corporate strategy. But, in part, this is irrational behaviour. Institutions persist in supporting takeovers despite the evidence that at least half create no discernible shareholder value.

M&A deals and other strategic moves are disruptive. They risk changing the basis on which the investment was made in the first place, prompting purchases or sales. The fact is that big, bold moves are exciting – and fund managers are as prone to adrenalin surges as anyone else! Activity is frequently viewed as evidence of firm leadership. Nor should we underestimate the influence of the securities houses, keen to generate trades. Brokers thrive on change, preferably a discontinuity sufficient to cause a fund manager to re-evaluate his position on a stock. That is what creates business. Analysts, traders and equity salespeople therefore 'talk' M&A to fund managers and to the press because deals are good for them. In the clamour to attract institutional attention worthy but inactive companies can easily be overlooked. A company that does not engage in significant corporate activity or similarly bold moves risks being labelled by the City as 'boring' – even if it is a consistent grower. The truth is that institutions like EPS growth *and* the excitement that deal making generates. As Lex put it (on 9 July 1997): 'As a tonic for underperforming shares, a bit of corporate activity is hard to beat.'

■ *Strategy, what crimes are committed in thy name!* Strategy is probably the most overused – and abused – word in the business lexicon. Companies only make 'strategic' acquisitions. All decisions are 'strategic' decisions. Often it has come to mean nothing more than 'important', as in 'I'm in strategic planning.' Who would willingly admit to being in tactical planning? 'Strategy' is used in CitySpeak as freely and as loosely as elsewhere. Investors are, of course, vitally interested in a company's strategy as are – from another perspective – investment bankers. When fund managers ask a CEO to explain a company's strategy they are really asking how he plans to keep earnings moving ahead over the longer term. M&A activity may well be a part of the answer but not necessarily, depending on the industry. For example, at Next, the hugely successful clothing retailer that is a constituent of the FTSE 100, the strategy is to keep growing EPS by relocating to larger stores and extending existing stores. At Rio Tinto the strategy is to develop large-scale, low-cost, open-cast mines (supplemented by acquisition from time to time). In most sectors, though, strategy is more or less synonymous with M&A activity. If a company announces it is conducting a 'strategic review' the City immediately assumes this is the prelude to disposals, a merger, joint venture or sale of the company. When Lex describes Whitbread as 'the most strategically active of the big brewers' it is clearly referring to its deal-making record. In investment banking, strategy has only one meaning – 'What do you want to buy and what might you sell?'

■ *Promises are always worth more than reality*. Investors have an instinctive affinity for stocks offering a pot of gold at the end of the rainbow, as these have the potential to transform a humdrum portfolio. That is why investor enthusiasm is invariably greater if there are no earnings on which to base a valuation, as was the case with most internet or biotechnology stocks during the 'New Economy' boom. Silicon Valley entrepreneurs no longer offered investors a business plan, only a 'business model' – which helped to deflect those annoying questions about revenues and profits! A company that actually reported profits ran the terrible risk of being assessed by conventional yardsticks. An astronomic P/E can often bring a share price down to earth with a bump. A company whose share price is buoyed up by hype and no numbers is well advised to keep it that way. In the stock market it is better to travel hopefully than to arrive!

Promises, promises

Fund managers regard regular contact on a one-to-one basis with senior management in companies in which they are invested (or may wish to be invested) as being of overwhelming importance. Other sources of information, including the inputs received from sell-side analysts, play a relatively minor role (more details in Chapter 7). The relationship is quite formalized. Normally, a major fund management firm will be visited by several hundred companies each year. In addition, corporate events, such as takeovers or management changes, may prompt ad hoc meetings. Large companies see perhaps 40 institutions on a one-to-one basis during the course of a year. Typically, the chief executive (or possibly executive chairman) probably accompanied by his finance director and/or his investor relations executive – all sizeable companies have IR departments – will sit across a table from a group of fund managers and buy-side analysts. Meetings usually last about an hour. These meetings are predominately about longer-term strategy rather than short-term earnings performance.

Fund managers not only want to understand the strategy being pursued, they also need to make a judgement on management's ability to achieve that strategy. In City parlance, can the management team – or often just the CEO – 'deliver' for shareholders? The answer to this question is heavily dependent on an assessment of management's personal qualities – capability, reliability, motivation, integrity and, above all else, reputation and track record. (To an extent, this assessment will extend to the chairman and the other non-executives on the board, on the basis that they too have shareholders' interests in mind.) In essence, 'delivery' means doing what you said you were going to do. Institutions see managers as being accountable to them via an implicit contract. Companies make 'promises' relating to the future rate of profit and/or sales growth and, perhaps, also the trend in margins or acquisition activity. (Sometimes a company chooses – not always wisely – to make these 'promises' public, such as Rentokil Initial's well-known 20 per cent annual growth commitment, now discarded.) Questions at each meeting will refer to 'promises' made at previous meetings.

> The answer to this question is heavily dependent on an assessment of management's personal qualities – capability, reliability, motivation, integrity and, above all else, reputation and track record.

After a few years it becomes apparent who delivers and who does not. A new management coming into a difficult situation will, as a rule, be given a 'grace period' of at least 18 months, after which hard evidence of improvement is expected. Normally, the maximum time horizon is three years. There is also an appreciation that certain industries are inherently more predictable than others, for which some adjustment is made. Previous experience of management's ability to deliver is a key ingredient in the institutional assessment of a company. To a considerable degree, the phrase 'quality of management' encapsulates the City's view of who delivers and who does not.

A chief executive who delivers is given full credit and becomes an institutional (and public) hero as the share price responds. (Sometimes – usually in the context of a smaller, acquisitive company – the CEO is said to have attracted a 'City following' or 'fan club'.) He is then in a position to move on to another company in need of his services if he so wishes. A typical instance was the appointment, in September 1999, of Crispin Davis as Chief Executive of Reed Elsevier, the Anglo-Dutch professional publishing company whose shares had underperformed for a considerable time. Davis had demonstrably 'delivered' at his previous company, Aegis Group, an international media-buying company, which was in severe difficulties when he arrived, taking the market capitalization from £180 million to £1.5 billion in five years.

Two further examples illustrate institutional hero status in practice. In 1994 Stuart Wallis was appointed CEO of Fisons, an ailing pharmaceutical company. Within 14 months he had more than doubled the share price by selling it to Rhône-Poulenc, a French competitor. Since then, he has been associated with several midcap companies. Generally, 'shareholder-friendly' (in CitySpeak) corporate executives tend to stay within the same broad sector. But some are more mobile. Sir Peter Davis, an archetypal institutional hero, is a case in point. Starting at Sainsbury's in the 1970s he moved from food retailing to publishing (Reed International), then financial services (Prudential) and finally, in March 2000, back to Sainsbury's.

For the ambitious chief executive, being in the good books of the institutions is a tradable commodity. A parallel market exists for finance directors. A board of directors seeking a new CEO or FD needs to be cognizant of who would be acceptable to the institutions and who would not. Reputation and track record provide comfort to fund managers but do not, as they know only too well, guarantee future performance. There are plenty of examples of 'serial deliverers' whose reputations became tarnished as they moved on. During the 1980s, Andrew Teare was a hero at Rugby, the building materials company, did a less impressive job at the industrial minerals company, English China Clays, in the early 1990s and was pushed out ignominiously at Rank, the leisure group, after less than three years, in October 1998. A management team that fails to deliver loses credibility in the eyes of the City. 'Credibility' is a further important concept in CitySpeak. Loss of credibility is a serious matter, evidenced by a languishing share price. However, unlike virginity, it can be restored. Sir Geoff Mulcahy, CEO of Kingfisher, survived numerous calls for his head in the dark days of 1995. By 1998, after several sets of sparkling results, he had been thoroughly rehabilitated. Following further criticism, he finally departed in 2002.

The City's identification of companies with personalities is both good and bad. There is absolutely no doubt that powerful, inspirational individuals can have a profound impact on organizations in a relatively short time. The belief that this is so is consistent with City experience and tradition. But the cult of personality can easily be taken too far. The City invariably underestimates the influence of senior managers in a company, particularly line managers at or just below board level. They may be exposed to analysts and fund managers from time to time but barely figure in the investment equation. If these people are of low calibre or disaffected it will impact the results. With its single-minded focus on the CEO and FD, the City rarely picks up on what is really happening inside a company. For example, the fact that Liam Strong, brought in to revitalize the ailing retailer Sears in the early 1990s, had difficulty in retaining senior management never came to light at the time.

> The City invariably underestimates the influence of senior managers in a company, particularly line managers at or just below board level.

An essential attribute of the modern chief executive is the ability to present the company's case coherently and effectively to the City and the media.

The modern finance director, with a detailed knowledge of the business and the strategy being pursued, occupies a crucial supporting role. There is no necessary relationship between presentational skills and managerial/financial skills, although it is reasonable to assume that presentational skills are needed internally as well as externally. It is tempting to assume that a good presenter is a good manager but he may not be. The Americans frequently solve this problem by appointing a CEO ('Mr Outside') and a chief operating officer (COO or 'Mr Inside'). So important is the presentational element nowadays that jobs can be won or lost on that basis. In October 1997 Glaxo Wellcome (according to an article in Director magazine in August 1999) reversed a decision made 10 months earlier to groom Sean Lance, its managing director, for the job of chief executive following negative feedback from investors on his presentation skills.

A final aspect of the cult of personality is the pressure it puts on the CEO to be corporately active. As we saw in the last section, somewhat perversely, investors like activity. Equally, an incoming chief executive understandably feels the need to make his mark on an organization: a 'transforming' deal in City parlance. (There is often a similar impulse as he nears the exit.) Our new CEO is surrounded by cheerleaders – investment bankers and securities analysts – waving banners with MORE CORPORATE ACTIVITY PLEASE written on them. As we saw in Chapter 3, investment bankers present companies with a continual stream of unsolicited M&A ideas, suggesting who they might buy (and how). Remember also that M&A fees are overwhelmingly success weighted. Fees are broadly related to size of deal so there is a powerful incentive to secure big deals – and see them through.

Investment bankers are singularly adept at massaging the egos that can play a large part in the initiation of an M&A deal. They understand that corporate strategy is often influenced by a chief executive's personal agenda, suitably dressed up as something grander. And anyway, for CEOs doing deals is more fun. Peter Drucker, the legendary thinker on management matters, summed it up beautifully in an interview with *Time* magazine:

> I will tell you a secret: Dealmaking beats working. Dealmaking is exciting and fun, and working is grubby. Running anything is primarily an enormous amount of grubby detail work ... dealmaking is romantic, sexy. That's why you have deals that make no sense.

(Quoted in Warren Buffett's Letter to Shareholders, 1995)

There is no doubt that chief executives do sometimes make bids primarily because they think the City wants them to do a deal. It may not be the right deal, or it may be the right deal at the wrong price!

The art of managing shareholder expectations

Institutions primarily view delivery in an operational sense – management getting the strategy and the numbers right. But what fund managers really want is the consequence of delivery, in the form of an improved share price performance. In recent years this desire has become absorbed into the concept of 'shareholder value'. Shareholder value was originally defined mechanistically, referring to the ability of a corporation to generate returns greater than its cost of capital. In academic circles it is still viewed in these terms. Then, in the early 1990s, it became bound up with the much broader concept that institutional shareholders should play a more active role in monitoring and disciplining companies in which they are invested.

Originating in the US, this clarion call for shareholder activism soon acquired the convenient, catch-all tag of 'corporate governance'. As with shareholder value, the initial focus of corporate governance was on mechanistic and structural issues: shareholder voting, the respective roles of CEO and chairman, composition of board committees, the nature of the contract with top management and so on.

Then, quite logically, as investors turned their attention from issues of structure to financial performance, corporate governance 'adopted' shareholder value. In America, pressure was put on companies to create more efficient capital structures via share buy-backs and higher leverage, a practice that soon spread internationally with the victory of the 'US model'. Then, for many institutions, the sense of the question, 'Are you committed to enhancing shareholder value?' gravitated quite naturally from its narrow technical meaning to something akin to, 'Do you have our interest in the share price performance of your (our!) company truly at heart?' When institutional investors ask management about attitudes to shareholder value they often mean more than creating the right capital structure, more than maximizing the asset value of the enterprise, more than the maximization of profitability – they are asking for a commitment on a 'best efforts' basis to maximizing the share price (or, if not the share price, the cash returns to shareholders from restructuring or selling the business). Total return is, after all, how they are judged.

Reinterpretation of shareholder value to mean a commitment to total return has the useful benefit that the interests of owners and managers are wholly aligned. It is unlikely to be expressed exactly in these terms but the underlying message coming through to CEOs can often be: 'Your job is to do everything in your power to maximize the value of your stock on our behalf.' None of this is intended to suggest that institutions are inflexible. They recognize that firms can be buffeted by forces outside their control. But, ultimately, management is expected to perform just as they are expected to perform.

> The underlying message coming through to CEOs can often be: 'Your job is to do everything in your power to maximize the value of your stock on our behalf.'

Every CEO and FD is obliged to worship publicly at the altar of shareholder value. But how are chief executives supposed to maximize the value of something over which they have no direct influence? Shareholder value in these terms is not merely a matter of squeezing as much juice as possible out of the corporate lemon, it is as much about doing things – and being seen to do them – in a way that most appeals to investors. Fund managers not only want firms to be proficient in delivering the news to them, they also want companies to be equally skilled at getting the investor relations message over to other institutions. It is their buying that will push the price up. This is achieved through the management of expectations, in regard to EPS growth and all other aspects of the business. The astute, shareholder value-driven company not only produces good news, it also tries to ensure the best possible investor, analyst and media reaction to that news. This needs to be – and usually is – a highly organized process.

At the core of this approach is the management of earnings expectations. As we noted in Chapter 2, the notion that analysts make independent estimates is a myth. To a considerable degree, sell-side analysts are not much more than a conduit for the company's own assessment of how it will do. For a company a good maxim is: 'Always endeavour to overshoot your estimates.' This is obviously easier for a company in a reasonably predictable growth business than one operating in a volatile trading environment. The job of the investor relations department is to manage this process in keeping with the 'no surprises' principle.

From the perspective of the institutions and the company a number just ahead of forecasts and a modest but positive share price response is the most desirable outcome. When results are declared, beating forecasts is not the only element governing the share price reaction. Analysts and investors also look closely at the dividend announcement – a raised dividend is viewed as a tangible expression of corporate confidence – and the statement on current and future trading. If the news is bad the trick is to deliver it if at all possible in a way that minimizes its impact, so that the share price drifts down rather than becoming the focal point of media attention. For a company, the management of expectations is a fine line. Promise too much and you risk a loss of credibility. Promise too little and you risk being accused of lacking both capability and ambition.

Buy-backs, demergers, special dividends, divestments, 'strategic' acquisitions and initiatives, major contracts and other corporate events can also, if handled properly, have a beneficial impact on share price performance. Press announcements, presentations to the City and media, friendly sell-side analyst reports, informal journalist briefings, well-placed feature articles, and marketing campaigns to attract new institutional investors are all tools of the trade. Once again, timing is everything. Finance directors and corporate IR executives, advised by their retained financial PR consultants, deliberately release information on a 'drip feed' basis so as to optimize its impact.

Sell-side analysts talk about a company's 'newsflow' (another example of the American fondness for joined-up words, like restroom). In principle, plenty of newsflow is good, absence of newsflow is bad. Some companies have a reputation for handling newsflow and the management of expectations with consummate skill. BP is one such company. Others commit the crime of wrongfooting the City too often and acquire a reputation for perennially disappointing the market or, worse still, ineptitude. Racal Electronics offers a salutary lesson as does, more recently, Marconi. Once a stock market darling, Racal spent the 1990s struggling unsuccessfully to get back into the institutions' good books. Few tears were shed when, in early 2000, it lost its independence to a bid from the French electronics group, Thales. Marconi's decision to say nothing at its AGM in July 2001, even though it knew the first quarter of its financial year had been heavily loss-making, was, in the eyes of the City, a hanging offence. From a fund management perspective failure to warn is a greater crime than the warning itself.

The emergence of the New Industrial Compact

During the 1970s and 1980s the relationship between the institutions and British industry was largely an indirect one. Face-to-face contact was organized by stockbrokers, via lunches or meetings at which a group of institutions listened to, and participated in, the civilized questioning of corporate executives. Then, when bid fever gripped the City in the mid-1980s, industrialists felt let down by those same institutions, accusing them of 'short-termism' in their eagerness to accept takeover bids and their unwillingness to back companies prepared to invest in the future at the expense of today's profits. 'Short-termism' became the subject of a vigorous public debate, which raged for several years in the late 1980s and early 1990s.

In 1990, when recession hit, institutions found themselves forced to adopt a more interventionist stance towards their investments. Previously, the automatic reaction to an underperforming company was to sell the shares in the market or, better still, to a bidder. But increasingly, lack of liquidity precluded the first option while, in a recession, predators were thin on the ground. By 1992 the institutions had engineered the departure of a substantial number of management teams they regarded as below par, often using the need to raise equity as leverage. In keeping with the British tradition of quiet diplomacy much of this was conducted behind closed doors. Certain institutions were – and still are – more prepared than others to take the initiative in 'corporate governance'. The reasons are essentially pragmatic. Self-managed pension funds are in the vanguard, followed by insurance companies. It is, after all, 'their' money – they are not simply professional managers. At the other end of the spectrum, the asset management subsidiaries of investment or commercial banks may feel inhibited by the possible effect of their actions on commercial relationships elsewhere in the bank.

> 'Short-termism' became the subject of a vigorous public debate, which raged for several years in the late 1980s and early 1990s.

The experience of this period – and the public discussion of 'short-termism' – persuaded shareholders and companies that much was to be gained from a regular and open dialogue, without the intervention of a securities firm (with a different agenda). Management began to reveal its longer-term plans and targets to its shareholders. It did not take long for these to be translated into self-generated performance benchmarks ('promises') against which they could be measured, just as the institutions are themselves judged.

What of 'short-termism' now? Since the early 1990s the issue has virtually disappeared from public view. Rarely does a business leader make any comment on the timescales of institutional shareholders. Does this mean that 'short-termism' never existed? Or that the institutions have adjusted to industrial horizons? The truth is that it did and still does exist, although in a modified form. Its influence has been tempered by increased liquidity constraints and a considerably more constructive and understanding relationship between industry and its institutional investors.

Ironically, fund managers would, in an ideal world, like to take more short-term bets but are inhibited by limited liquidity. To an extent then, the bigger fund managers have become longer term by default. It would be wrong, however, to take this argument too far. External pension fund managers, unit trust and unit-linked managers are under constant and intense pressure to maximize current performance. The current quarter is what matters, perhaps the next quarter, certainly not next year's equivalent quarter. Confronted with the prospect of an uplift in the value of his portfolio from a bid, or a decline in performance as a company reports a short-term blip in an upward trend, the gut reaction of a professional fund manager will be to go for whatever enhances or protects his current performance figures. He may, in the event, be swayed by other considerations but the initial reaction will be the bird in the hand. 'Short-termism' lives on but perhaps not in quite the same form as it did before.

Industrialists no longer make speeches about 'short-termism' because the rules of the game have changed. The 1990s saw the emergence of a New Industrial Compact between senior management and institutional investors. Today's CEOs and FDs accept the process of regular dialogue, the mantra of shareholder value, target setting and performance appraisal as a fact of life. A valuable paper in Accounting and Business Research by Dr Richard G. Barker (1999) at Cambridge University's Judge Institute of Management concluded that, when questioned, most finance directors perceive fund managers as having time horizons similar to themselves. Inevitably, the evidence points to the conclusion that managers have adjusted to institutional timescales rather than vice versa. What is clear, however, is that where once there was a mismatch, there is now an identity of interest.

One consequence of the New Industrial Compact is that the period of tenure for CEOs and FDs has become shorter. A study by Cranfield School of Management in June 1999 concluded that the average tenure of FTSE 100 chief executives was just over four years, compared with just under six years for the FTSE 250. Since then, there is absolutely no doubt that – in an environment of disappointing results and falling share prices – the average 'time in job' has registered a further decline. Commenting on what affects the length of a CEO's tenure the report said:

> Most of the CEOs from quoted companies cite the performance of the share price as the key factor affecting their tenure. CEOs from the top 100 quoted companies comment they are under mounting pressure from both the City and the media.

Running a quoted company of any significant size has become a high-risk activity. Failure to match the earnings and share price 'promises' made to institutions within, probably, three years will lead to pressure being applied (probably via the non-executive directors, who are frequently executive directors of other quoted companies) for summary ejection. Alternatively, a languishing share price may lead to a bid which, even if agreed, will probably result in the surrender of the top job. If hostile, the outcome will almost certainly be dismissal.

Why then are managers prepared to accept a job that may not last long, in which an undue amount of time must be devoted to responding to the constant demands of shareholders, sell-side analysts and the media? The answer is twofold: ambition and money. Chief executives thrive on challenges, are personally resilient and enjoy the public exercise of power. They no longer expect job security. Nowadays tenures can be short even when an executive has done what is acknowledged to be a good job. They also accept that, from time to time, they may be forced to run the gauntlet of the press (something that those whose earnings are unpublished, like entertainers or investment bankers, are spared!). The need to stay in semi-permanent presentation mode might not appeal but it is a necessary and unavoidable part of the job. Small wonder then that a rising number of executives are electing to leave the public arena for quieter pastures, notably private equity.

> A languishing share price may lead to a bid which, even if agreed, will probably result in the surrender of the top job. If hostile, the outcome will almost certainly be dismissal.

The second element is the chance to earn a lot of money. In the financial arrangement implicit in the New Industrial Compact the rewards for success are extremely high, mostly in the form of incentive bonuses and, more especially, options. During the second half of the 1990s, in both the UK and the US, stock options came to account for up to half of the total remuneration of the board directors of larger quoted companies. Stock options link the opportunity to generate a very substantial capital sum directly to the performance of the share price. Long-term incentive plans are also normally linked to the share price. Institutions need to keep a close eye on these arrangements: there is concern at the insufficiently robust linkage, in some cases, between performance and reward. Unchecked, executives have a tendency to pay themselves more than they are worth (although, at root, fund managers recognize that high executive compensation is a small price to pay for a large addition to shareholder value). The modern CEO consequently has every interest in maximizing the share price for his owners because that is the mechanism through which he receives his real reward. And he gets the opportunity – if he is so inclined – to do it all over again!

Nor, in the New Industrial Compact, is failure a financial disaster, whatever its impact in career terms. The institutions recognize that the CEO job justifies a safety net. If the consequence of failure were the executive equivalent of penury fewer businessmen would be willing to take on the task. A high running salary and a significant payoff in the event of dismissal mean that the CEO can afford to take a chance. The point is well illustrated by the 'resignation' of Andrew Teare from Rank Group in October 1998. Having forfeited a salary in excess of £400,000 per annum, he received £874,000 (including the cost of his pension enhancement) as 'compensation for loss of office'. More recently, several instances of boardroom generosity to those who had patently presided over failure have provoked fund managers into taking a tougher line. Institutional intervention persuaded Marconi to negotiate a £300,000 pay-off to Lord Simpson, its former chief executive, in place of the £1 million to which he was contractually entitled.

If the shares fail to perform and the CEO receives or engineers a bid or a break-up of the business he benefits from stock options (and may still qualify as an institutional hero). The risk : reward ratio is not so much 'high risk, high reward' as (in financial terms at least) 'medium risk, high reward'. One experienced City fund manager considered the equation for a job in the upper echelons of 'UK plc' during the bull market of the late nineties to be roughly £3 million on success and £400,000 in the event of failure. Richard Donkin summed it up well:

> When times are good an underleveraged balance sheet is viewed as a negative, evidencing a lack of commitment to shareholder value; when conditions deteriorate that same balance sheet is suddenly hailed as a sign of strength.

This is the nub of the new contract for senior executives. The job has its risks but rewards are high and the P45 can look like a winning lottery ticket.

('Risks and rewards', *Financial Times*, 9 December 1998)

A separate but critical component in the New Industrial Compact is the degree of communication it demands. Managers are expected to confide in their institutional holders, to warn them of impending moves, or sound out their attitude towards a proposed corporate development. Any institution that is spoken to on this basis is, in CitySpeak, 'made an insider', which means it is unable to buy or sell the shares until the information becomes public (or is no longer relevant). Fund managers dislike being made insiders because it restricts their freedom of action but it is more than offset by their desire to be kept informed on a continuous basis.

Institutional investors are, as a breed, extremely demanding. Understandably so when one appreciates the pressures on them. Some corporate executives will privately admit that fund managers and analysts are hard – if not impossible – to please. If margins are low they ask why they are not higher; if margins are high they worry whether they can be sustained. When times are good an underleveraged balance sheet is viewed as a negative, evidencing a lack of commitment to shareholder value; when conditions deteriorate that same balance sheet is suddenly hailed as a sign of strength. Diversification is applauded so long as it is successful – if not, it soon becomes axiomatic that the company should have stuck to its core business! In the New Industrial Compact executives who harbour such views sensibly keep them to themselves. The upside is financial security, and quite possibly substantial wealth, while the downside would be an inability to get another job in a quoted company, anywhere!

Why the Inexorable Logic of fund management means that small is no longer beautiful

The proposition that 'small is beautiful' dates from 1973, echoing the title of E.F. Schumacher's book. It has since been adopted as a battle cry by the proponents of the 'US model' and is now regarded as axiomatic across Europe. Politicians of all persuasions love small companies. This is not just because they embody the capitalist virtues of entrepreneurship and innovation. The experience of the US economy over the last decade has convincingly demonstrated their powerful growth and employment-creating capabilities. From the perspective of a balanced or UK equities fund manager, small companies can inject excitement into a portfolio, offering the potential for high reward (admittedly accompanied by higher risk). Simple arithmetic suggests that small companies should be able to grow earnings at a faster rate than large ones. Instinctively, it seems reasonable to assume that the opportunity for profit is higher, as the stock market is less efficient at ironing out pricing anomalies at that level. Yet, despite a revival in 1999 and 2000, since the early 1990s smallcaps have significantly underperformed largecaps. In Britain, and to a lesser extent in America, there has been a massive decline in institutional interest in smaller companies. Why?

The reason is that, responding quite rationally to the environment in which they find themselves, fund managers inevitably end up making decisions that favour investment in large companies and run counter to investment in smaller companies. This is the 'Inexorable Logic' of fund management. It should be apparent from the last five chapters that institutions not only prefer large companies – liquidity constraints and market capitalization-based benchmarks mean that they have no alternative but to prefer large companies. Academic confirmation comes from two Harvard professors in a 1998 paper for the Boston-based National Bureau of Economic Research. Looking at the US over the period 1980–1996 they concluded that institutions show a strong and consistent preference for large, liquid stocks. What follows is a step-by-step guide through the complexities of the Inexorable Logic:

1   In round terms, the average UK institutional fund manager is responsible for eight separate portfolios worth £55 million each (data from PricewaterhouseCoopers' 1999 Investment Management Survey). For ease of management, an investment manager will normally create a very similar portfolio structure for each of these funds.

2   A typical UK equity portfolio contains between 50 and 120 stocks. In practice, this figure is heavily clustered around the 80–90 mark. (Specialist equity portfolios are usually more concentrated, with 20–60 stocks.) Experience shows that 80–90 is an optimum number, representing a balance between sensible diversification (and therefore risk reduction) and administrative practicality. More than this is unwieldy to manage, difficult to monitor and leads to increased costs.

3   The consequence is that the fund manager thinks in terms of a minimum percentage of the fund (or group of funds under his management) he is prepared to put into a single investment. In a 90-stock portfolio this would be 1.1 per cent of the value of the fund. In fund management jargon, this is his 'unit' of investment. A £400 million fund with 90 stocks would have a £4.5 million unit. An investment in a largecap stock will absorb several units. Every fund manager has the money amount of his unit fixed firmly in his mind. It is the basic building block from which his portfolio is constructed.

4   The problem for small companies arises because units are large and are getting larger. Big single funds, like life funds, self-managed pension funds, pooled pension funds or some unit trusts, have large unit sizes. For example, M&G's Recovery Fund, which has been going since 1969, is worth £1.1 billion and contains 100 stocks, so its unit is £11 million. Similarly, a £10 billion life fund might (assuming a 50 per cent allocation to UK equities) consider its unit as being in the region of £50 million. Sometimes managers of very large funds, like a £20 billion American-sourced ERISA fund invested in non-US

equities, will consciously decide to invest in more than the optimum number of stocks to cut the unit size, accepting the diseconomies involved. The argument is that liquidity problems and insufficient diversification more than offset the difficulty of handling, say, a 300-stock portfolio.

5   Large unit sizes apply just as much to money managers. This is because, as we saw in Chapter 5, they are under pressure from clients and investment consultants to demonstrate a consistent investment policy that reduces benchmark risk and dispersion. Centralized decision-making allied to central dealing mean that fund managers operate more or less in unison. If the firm makes a decision to lift its weighting in, say, AstraZeneca, then every manager has to build up the AstraZeneca weighting in all his funds. In effect, the business is run as a single portfolio. The unit that the organization deals in is determined by the total FUM and not by the size of the individual funds. And, as fund managers merge, unit sizes get larger, rising to £100 million or more. Breaking things up by creating smaller investment groups or dedicated smaller company funds are options but the downsides are higher costs and increased benchmark risk.

> If the firm makes a decision to lift its weighting in, say, AstraZeneca, then every manager has to build up the AstraZeneca weighting in all his funds.

6   All the major investment institutions run small company funds. However, many of these are retail and so suffer from a lack of interest, if not a reduction in size, when small companies are under a cloud. Pooled internal small company funds, with allocations from pension fund portfolios, are also important. But such funds can easily become very large, very quickly, with the attendant unit problems. The 2000 Reuters UK Smaller Company Survey showed that the 11 largest fund management groups each controlled at least £1.4 billion in UK smallcap funds. Twelve fund management groups accounted for 60 per cent of all institutional funds invested in small companies. With small companies accounting for only a few per cent of the market, no balanced or UK equity fund manager, benchmarked against the All-Share, is going to allocate a significant proportion of his portfolio to an in-house smallcap fund, particularly given the extra layer of cost involved.

7   One way in which the institutions have tried to handle the small company problem is by moving the definitional goalposts. Most UK fund managers now consider a company with a 'market cap' of less

than £400 million to be 'small'. Few outside the City would regard a £400 million company as small! Similarly, the midcap level has moved up to £1.5 billion. (Equivalent levels in the US are considerably higher.) Even at this level liquidity considerations are a critical issue, which is why so much emphasis is placed on the FTSE 100 stocks and their continental European equivalents.

8   A unit of, say, £50 million is not a problem for a buyer of BP. Equally, it is not a major issue for a buyer of Rio Tinto with a £14 billion 'market cap', although getting it in (or taking it out) without moving the price too much might take a few days or a few weeks. But it becomes a real problem further down the scale. Buying £50 million worth of a £500 million company with limited liquidity (and perhaps a restricted free float) will take a long time and a lot of patience, unless the buyer is fortunate enough to coincide with a large institutional holder who is anxious to sell. If successful, the buyer ends up with 10 per cent of the equity. In a £250 million company he would end up with 20 per cent of the equity. Simple arithmetic means that big institutions cannot buy companies below a certain size as they would end up with too large a percentage of the equity. Selling a stake of this size can be just as difficult as getting in, unless the fund manager is prepared to sell in one go at a substantial discount to the market price. In CitySpeak, the holder is 'locked in'. Like Siamese twins, the institution and the company are condemned to be part of each other whether they like it or not.

9   In the past a less concentrated fund management environment allowed investment institutions to limit their holdings in all but the smallest companies to well below 5 per cent, preferably keeping below the disclosable level of 3 per cent. At this level, they were just one of perhaps 10 or 20 institutional holders and retained (theoretically) the option of getting out if they changed their view. In large companies this 'keeping below the parapet' approach is still feasible. But, in smaller companies, for the leading equity managers, it is no longer possible. They are forced to act as owners rather than passive shareholders to a greater extent than they would wish. Due to their size, Schroders, M&G, MLIM, UBS, Standard Life, Fidelity and several others appear all over the place as 5 –15 per cent holders on the shareholder registers of small and midcap Britain.

10 As we saw in the last chapter, an equity fund manager's performance depends largely on getting the 'mega caps' right. Broadly, small companies account for a lowly 4 per cent of the market. Managers cannot afford to spend much time on companies (in which they may

have a large stake as a percentage of their equity) that account for an insignificant percentage of their fund. Even if a small company outperforms massively, it will not have a measurable impact on the value of the overall portfolio. A fund manager could legitimately put, say, 10 per cent of the fund into small companies in the hope of gaining that extra bit of performance. However, one problem is that evaluating and monitoring small companies is labour intensive. But a bigger problem is that, even if the fund manager were committed to this path, he would have difficulty in actually getting enough money into these companies to make the effort worthwhile. Small sectors suffer the same fate as small companies. The fund manager who philosophically accepts his failure to buy into a small sector, such as chemicals, in time to catch an upswing would be extremely put out at missing a similar outperformance by a large sector like banks, pharmaceuticals, telecommunications or energy. In short, it is much safer, simpler, cheaper and less time-consuming to make a bet on a big stock (or big sector) than a small one.

> It is much safer, simpler, cheaper and less time-consuming to make a bet on a big stock (or big sector) than a small one.

11   Index funds formalize and exacerbate the neglect of smaller companies. By definition, an index mandate excludes companies below the level of the index – around 1,700 stocks in the case of the All-Share. One reason why small companies have been weak in recent years is that, as passive managers take over active portfolios, they immediately dump unwanted stocks with little regard for price. The steady transfer of mandates by plan sponsors from active to passive acts, in effect, as a permanent depressant on smaller stocks. The ongoing asset allocation shift by pension funds from equities to bonds has a comparable downward impact on share prices. Smaller listed companies are more heavily owned by pension funds and are therefore more exposed to selling by them. In the case of large and medium-sized companies, foreign institutions are frequently to be found on the sidelines as potential buyers. They are less likely to be attracted to small caps.

12   The small company problem is further compounded by the way the securities business works, dominated, as it is, by investment banks with high cost structures. Stockbrokers rely on transactions to generate revenue. Limited liquidity means few transactions. They cannot justify spending time on companies in which there is little trade. Consequently, many small and mid-sized companies have only a

few analysts following them. (Large companies typically attract 25 or more sell-side analysts.) Even then, some of the coverage is effectively nominal, generating 'research' that is superficial in the extreme. Some smaller independent agency brokers do a better job but they too find it necessary to trade in larger stocks to get the revenue they need. Fund managers nowadays rely very substantially on their own internal research in making judgements on smaller companies, maintaining direct contact without the involvement of a broker.

Through a perfectly rational sequence of decisions, UK equity fund managers can end up with either no small or even midcap stocks in their portfolios – on the basis that they are not worth the bother – or with larger stakes than they would wish in illiquid small and medium-sized companies. This is not because they dislike the idea of investing in small companies. Many would welcome the opportunity to 'spice up' their portfolios, to do something a little different. But that is not what the business is about in today's world. They are boxed in, prisoners of circumstance.

Can we solve the small company dilemma?

Many reasons have been put forward for the longer-term underperformance of small companies. Some have validity but none comes anywhere near the explanatory power of the internal dynamics of institutional fund management – the Inexorable Logic. Fund managers talk about pan-European investment and the pressures to buy large, liquid continental European and international companies at the expense of smaller domestic stocks. It is a convenient message. The underlying truth, however, is more complex and less palatable: *investment institutions are getting out of smaller stocks because they do not wish to be in smaller stocks*.

Other explanations centre round the need for better communication between small companies and the City and changes in the regulatory regime. There is some merit in these arguments but they are essentially side issues. A more persuasive argument is the operational one – that larger companies are less risky and are currently capable of generating sustained EPS growth at higher rates than smaller companies. This explanation for the outperformance of big companies found particular favour in the US during the 'New Economy' boom, based on globalization, pricing power and the superior ability of large companies to control costs in a low-inflation environment.

The most compelling explanation is closely related to the impact of the Inexorable Logic – large companies benefit from a 'liquidity premium'.

Faced with the choice of owning a smallcap or largecap stock with equivalent earnings prospects, the vast majority of institutional investors would opt for the one that offered high daily volume and ease of entry and exit. Or, to put it another way, the P/E of the small stock would stand at a discount to that of the large, as a form of compensation for the extra difficulty and bother. In the eyes of a fund manager, the presence of liquidity has an identifiable value, a value that is 'tacked on to' the intrinsic value of the company.

> In the eyes of a fund manager, the presence of liquidity has an identifiable value, a value that is 'tacked on to' the intrinsic value of the company.

After several years of lacklustre performance compared with the All Share Index, 1999 and 2000 were banner years for small companies. Or so they appeared to be. Certainly, the smallcap indices did well relative to the broader market. The important question is: why? It is crucial to look closely at the shifting composition of the smallcap indices to understand exactly what went on. During this period some smaller stocks, notably ordinary, run-of-the-mill, cyclical manufacturing and service companies – the sort of companies that traditionally dominated the lower end of UK stock market capitalization – barely responded to the general mood of unbridled optimism. Everything was focused on growth companies, with technology companies in the vanguard. IPOs, many of them technology-based, came thick and fast. Smallcaps (at the IPO price) rapidly bounded into the mid-cap category, pulling up the small company indices as they did so. The significant outperformance of the FTSE smallcap (and midcap) indices in 1999 and early 2000 was hailed by many as signalling a change in investor attitudes, a revival in institutional interest. But it proved to be no such thing. Three factors were behind the run-up.

- A sparkling performance by small – often new – growth stocks, largely but not entirely technology-based. At the peak of the dotcom boom, in April 2000, growth sectors accounted for 42 per cent of the FTSE Smallcap Index: in the early 1990s the equivalent figure was a lowly 18 per cent.

- Bids, mostly for ordinary small companies whose share prices had not participated in the general euphoria. Public-to-private deals (explained below) and acquisitions by overseas companies played a key role and have continued to be an important influence on share-price performance in the small and midcap arena.

- Sympathetic moves in many of the remaining ordinary small companies, fuelled by bid rumours or investor reappraisal in the light of bid activity.

Even though, by mid 2000, the key factor that had propelled the smaller stock indices to new heights had moved into reverse, the FTSE Smallcap still managed to outperform the All-Share for the year as a whole. But only by default – the Smallcap benefited from its low exposure to telecommunications, a sector that did much to drag down the performance of the FTSE 100 and the All-Share. In 2001 the small stock indices struggled to make progress, held back, in part, by an overweight population (relative to the broader indices) of 'walking wounded' former technology superstars. It readily became apparent that the City's enthusiasm for smaller stocks – or, at least, those possessing a growth 'tag' – had been no more than a brief and tumultuous love affair. Fund managers soon reverted to the polite but distant relationship that has characterized their attitude to smaller quoted companies for most of the last decade.

The lowly valued small company segment has been a happy hunting ground for overseas acquirers and, more especially, venture capital firms, pursuing so-called 'public to private' deals in which the quoted company is bought out for cash and releveraged. Venture capital/private equity firms raise money from institutional investors and from portfolio realizations ('exits' in the jargon), either IPOs or sales to other companies ('trade sale' in CitySpeak). Even though the climate for private equity has been more difficult since the start of 2001 – not least because of the dearth of IPOs – these investors still have considerable funds at their disposal.

For a corporate management mired in the stock market equivalent of no-man's land, an approach from a venture capital firm has definite attractions. Before the bid can go through, the institutional shareholders need to be convinced that the collusion between 'financial buyer' (CitySpeak for a fund-based purchaser as opposed to a corporate purchaser) and management does not mean they are being bought out 'on the cheap'. However, for institutions, the prospect of 'a solution' (to use a City euphemism for any kind of bid) has a distinct appeal. It is often seen as a useful opportunity to clean out from a portfolio companies that have contributed nothing to performance and which, frankly, represent little more than nuisance value.

> For institutions, the prospect of 'a solution' (to use a City euphemism for any kind of bid) has a distinct appeal.

Nor are institutional shareholders any longer mere onlookers in this process. They are active in letting it be known throughout the City that, at the right price, certain small and midcap stakes are available. Investment bankers are not slow to pick up these messages, speculatively taking the idea that such and such a stake is available to potential (corporate or financial) acquirers they know or have identified. Equally, institutions have been prepared to prod management teams in stranded companies in the direction of a buyer. To encourage discussions of a 'What if X approached you on your stake in Y?' nature some of the largest institutions have created a small 'corporate finance' function, whose job it is to field these enquiries. Others choose to funnel these conversations through one or two designated fund managers, usually those with responsibility for smaller companies. The corporate finance function operates behind a 'Chinese wall', acting as a buffer between the enquirers and the fund managers. Clearly, a fund manager who is made aware of any such possibility is privy to inside information and dare not trade in the stock until such time it is made public or – which is more likely – the possibility has gone away. Of course, if he is 'locked in' anyway by liquidity constraints this may not mean much in practice – but, as a matter of principle, fund managers dislike the restriction that being made an insider entails.

> The corporate finance function operates behind a 'Chinese wall', acting as a buffer between the enquirers and the fund managers.

Prudential, Hermes and a few others have long had a corporate finance function but at Fidelity, for example, it is a recent development. Soundings can be particularly valuable where one small quoted company wants to buy or merge with another small quoted company, using shares rather than cash. Is the institution prepared to accept and retain shares in the new entity? In general, amalgamation of this nature is encouraged and much has occurred. Better a 10 per cent stake in a £300 million company – with, hopefully, improved liquidity – than a 20 per cent stake in a £150 million company! The issue is less clear-cut if the institution holds both predator and prey. Whether the deal makes sense from the point of view of industrial logic is not per se an issue that is uppermost in the mind of the institution or institutions concerned.

What all this boils down to is that smaller UK quoted companies find themselves having to make their way in a tough and unforgiving environment. From a corporate perspective, share price valuations are lower than they should be and access to the equity market on acceptable terms, whether for initial or continuing funding, is severely restricted. And, if that is the case, what is the point in being quoted? The small company sector is an instance of what economists call 'market failure' – a mismatch between the increased concentration of fund management houses into larger units and the investment requirements of smaller listed companies. Sadly, the Myners Review chose not to address this issue, even though in its description of its remit, it specifically referred to:

factors encouraging institutional investors to follow industry-standard investment patterns which focus overwhelmingly on quoted equities and gilts and avoid investing in small and medium-sized enterprises and other smaller companies.

(Myners Review, March 2001, p. 4)

Instead, it devoted a substantial proportion of the report to private equity, undeniably an area neglected by the British investment industry but one in which there has been no 'market failure'. UK institutions may have been reluctant but US institutions have been more than willing to take up the slack. There has been no shortage of funds available for investment in unquoted companies. Ironically private equity firms are affected by the plight of smaller companies: an unreceptive stock market curtails their exit opportunities.

What is the solution? Our analysis of the Inexorable Logic demonstrates that the 'small company problem' is structural at root. Short of deconstructing the investment management industry back into its component parts (or the evolution of an industry with a multiplicity of diverse, thrusting competitors, more along American lines) there is no way of modifying its impact. The proposition that institutional neglect of smaller companies is a temporary phenomenon is tempting but, sadly, wrong. To conclude otherwise is to misunderstand the power of the Inexorable Logic.

The experience of the US, where there is more institutional interest in small companies than in the UK, offers some useful pointers. In 2001 – a year in which UK smallcaps underperformed – the Russell 2000 Index (a popular measure of small company performance) significantly outperformed the S&P 500. Smallcap value stocks did particularly well. Taking a 10-year view, though, the pattern is similar to that observed on the London market: large companies generally do better than their smaller brethren.

> One important element is the relatively higher proportion of private investors, many with the ability to invest their personal pension money in individual stocks, via IRA or 401(k) plans.

However, it does seem that the disparity is not as wide as it is in the UK. There are a number of reasons for this. One important element is the relatively higher proportion of private investors, many with the ability to invest their personal pension money in individual stocks, via IRA or 401(k) plans.

A second element is that institutional asset management is more diverse in the US, with many more decision points. The established position of specialist pension fund management means that there are several hundred funds offering smallcap mandates, drawing their funds from plan sponsors who are more stable in their style commitment than mutual funds, who must respond to the ebb and flow of retail investor fund preferences. (The Pensions & Investment magazine database indicates that there are approximately 250 smallcap managers – some admittedly parts of larger organizations – each with around $600 million of tax-exempt money under management.) Demand for smallcap (and midcap) managers remains strong, exemplified by the decision, in January 2002, of the $33 billion New York City Employees Retirement System to hire five active domestic smallcap equity managers to run a total of $300 million. Funding for this new asset class came from a reduced commitment to passive management. Responding to this demand, new, dedicated smallcap management firms continue to emerge.

Smaller stock investment in the US also benefits from the larger absolute universe of companies available there and the greater variety of benchmarks. American fund managers are less tied to the largecap-dominated benchmarks that hold sway in Europe. Apart from the Russell 2000, smallcap managers are often assessed against the Wilshire 5000 Index (which actually contains over 6,500 stocks). In the UK, as specialist management gains ground, dedicated smallcap mandates are being awarded. The current transition from balanced to specialist management offers the prospect of increased demand for smaller company shares from a breed of managers possessing both commitment and expertise. This is undoubtedly a positive development but it will take time for its impact to be felt.

Small companies have a mountain to climb. Countering the influence of the Inexorable Logic is a hard task, but it is not an impossible one. Change will occur on the institutional front but it would be unwise to rely on it. Any real solution must lie largely with individual investors as they do not suffer from the liquidity constraints that so beset and frustrate fund managers. US experience demonstrates that access to stocks through pension-based, tax-advantaged investments is not, of itself, a panacea, although the existence of such schemes must be beneficial. Tax incentives can be effective. In this context, the continued success of AIM (the London Stock Exchange's lightly-regulated Alternative Investment Market for young, growing companies) in persuading investors to support flotations is highly significant. During 2001 – a year noted for investors' unwillingness to participate in new issues – there were 91 IPOs on AIM. True, 78 companies debuted on the full list of the London Stock Exchange over the same period – but only nine of these were trading companies (all the rest were investment companies, such as Venture Capital Trusts). The reason for

> US experience demonstrates that access to stocks through pension-based, tax-advantaged investments is not, of itself, a panacea.

this disparity is simple: the generous tax reliefs available to investors in AIM stocks, either directly or through Venture Capital Trusts. If there is a solution to the 'small company problem' it lies with tax breaks for individuals, covering both capital gains and income, firmly directed at investment in smaller quoted companies.

Conveying the corporate message
How investment analysts lost the communications high ground and turned themselves into promoters

- Stockbroking in the new millennium

- How fund managers view research

- The analysis of analysis

- The eternal triangle of the analyst, the journalist and the corporation

A blind rabbit knows that most research is non fee-producing and that the pay-off only comes when research can be translated into fizzy investment banking mandates.

(Ian Kerr, *Financial News*, 5 July 1999)

Market capitalisation in the billions and stock market listings have replaced the $10m or so capitalisation of what were mainly partnerships just 20 years ago. The size of the firms (in the investment banking industry) has increased – CSFB alone has 14,400 employees now, as opposed to just 5,000 in 1996. And the expense base is huge. We spend, say, $16m a day just to turn the lights on and be able to work.

(Allan Wheat, former Chief Executive of Crédit Suisse First Boston, quoted in 'Views from the top', *Euromoney*, June 1999)

Stockbroking in the new millennium

Old-style City stockbroking was a wonderfully cozy existence. Equity analysts and equity salesmen enjoyed significant status as the 'natural' interface between companies and the investment institutions. Provided there was reasonable market volume it was pretty well impossible not to make good money. Then, in 1986, Big Bang came along, bringing price competition and a profound change in market structure. In actual fact, commissions on institutional broking trades soon settled down at a lower but acceptable level. What really hit broking revenues was a substantial shift to 'net' dealing, in which the institution goes direct to a market maker without paying commission at all. It continues to be important. This occurred because the new London system was modelled on the Nasdaq (National Association of Security Dealers Automated Quotation) trading system. Nasdaq, which had successfully competed with the New York Stock Exchange, especially in the area of high-tech stocks, is a net trading market, in contrast to the NYSE where broking commission is paid.

Following the 1987 crash it soon became apparent to the assortment of banks that had bought London stockbroking partnerships that losses were more or less inevitable in an environment of lower volume, reduced commission revenues and expanded capacity. Characteristically, the Americans responded by throwing money at the problem, nicely illustrated by the first paragraph of a high-profile recruitment advertisement for Citicorp (which contains what must rank as one of the most prescient Freudian slips of all time!):

> Following the 1987 crash it soon became apparent to the assortment of banks that had bought London stockbroking partnerships that losses were more or less inevitable.

One of the City's most exiting stockbroking firms, Citicorp Scrimgeour Vickers, has emerged phoenix-like from the flames of 1987 and ready to forge a dynamic new path into the 1990s.

(*Financial Times*, 30 March 1989)

In December 1989, less than a year after this incredibly upbeat message, Citicorp pulled out of London equities. Meanwhile, the European banks that had chosen to enter the scramble for London stockbroking firms, and the American investment banks that had set themselves up in London in the early 1980s, settled down for a long haul.

As Goldman Sachs, Morgan Stanley, Merrill Lynch and Salomon Brothers quietly built up their London equity operations they – crucially – did so with the benefit of a decade of domestic experience in coping with the rigours of a competitive equity market. In particular, they were familiar with market making and net trading from their activities on Nasdaq. The New York Stock Exchange had been through its version of Big Bang in 1975 (known as 'Mayday' because it happened on the first day of May). Mayday was a lot less radical than Big Bang. It involved the dismantling of the fixed commission scale but nothing else. Neither the market structure nor the regulatory environment changed. After Mayday institutional commission rates initially collapsed but subsequently stabilized. Then, starting in 1983, renewed institutional pressure forced rates down still further, a process that has continued ever since. By the mid-1980s it had become abundantly clear to the leading New York investment banks that a securities operation, employing highly paid analysts, salesmen and traders, stood little or no chance of making money out of institutions if it was solely reliant on the meagre commissions available from buying and selling shares. The following newspaper extract illustrates the degree of concern felt at the time:

> Since Mayday institutional trades have plummeted from 25 cents a share to 8 cents a share and institutional brokers say they cannot make money at that level. There is much confusion over what should be done – and some say they may even abandon the business entirely. Indeed, the only thing clear is that something is about to crack.

> (New York Times, 28 April 1985)

In fact, nothing did crack. Through a combination of aggressive marketing and fortunate timing the major US investment banks found new sources of revenue to justify the continued existence of their equity operations. For one thing, retail (where rates remained fixed) emerged as a significant, and relatively stable, generator of commission dollars. In the institutional arena, it soon became clear that the equities division could function effectively as a loss leader, by leveraging its ability to support the marketing and operational activities of other parts of the firm. The focus of their securities operations shifted towards securing investment banking business (both equity offerings, especially IPOs, and M&A mandates) and support for principal transactions, including proprietary trading and arbitrage activities. Analysts, with their sector knowledge and existing contacts with senior executives – in a context in which the executive was anxious to gain their approval – were ideally placed to introduce their investment banking colleagues to corporates and to contribute to the generation of investment banking ideas. By the time Morgan Stanley went public in 1986 only 8 per cent of its revenues came from equity commissions. This new approach clearly ran the risk that it would alienate institutional clients, who clearly needed careful handling, but, given how little they were prepared to pay, how could they expect to be accorded priority?

No longer encumbered by the illusion that broking and trading equities could be a profitable business in its own right the Americans pursued European corporate business with vigour, consciously using their equity expertise to spearhead their marketing drive. It was this that laid the foundation for the welter of high-profile M&A mandates from European companies that they captured in the late 1990s. In doing so they had to overcome a peculiar advantage that British securities firms had in terms of their relationship with quoted companies – the concept of the corporate (or 'house') broker. In London, where companies are required by the Stock Exchange to retain brokers, the corporate broking departments of securities firms act as an interface between companies and the stock market. They traditionally worked in tandem with the merchant bank advising the company. This separation is unknown on Wall Street where the investment banks perform both functions.

At Big Bang many doubted whether corporate broking would survive. It was assumed that corporates would opt for an American-style 'one-stop shop' approach. In fact, a surprising number of British companies resisted the idea of a single adviser, on the basis that 'two heads are better than one'. Cazenove, corporate broker to half of the 350 largest UK companies, survives. Merrill Lynch, on buying Smith New Court in 1995, was at first puzzled by the concept but decided subsequently it was worth preserving and developing. In fact, ironically, several of the US investment banks, which are often (rightly) accused of being too transaction oriented, now see corporate broking as a way of maintaining a longer-term relationship with a corporate client.

> Several of the US investment banks now see corporate broking as a way of maintaining a longer-term relationship with a corporate client.

It is standard practice among American and European international investment banks for the investment banking activity to cover 50 per cent of the cost base of the equities division – testifying to its key role in obtaining high-fee corporate business. Banks, such as J.P. Morgan, entering the equity research and trading business in the 1990s without the accumulated baggage of an existing operation, focused deliberately on those large, liquid and active sectors where they could use the equity research product to leverage their investment banking business. Organizationally, in recent years, many investment banks dropped the pretence that securities and investment banking operated independently. In March 2000, for example,

CSFB announced it was merging its equities and investment banking businesses into a single entity.

There is, inevitably and understandably, a widespread perception among the institutions that the secondary market operations of the investment banks are geared towards generating lucrative fees from primary market activity and M&A deals. Some European institutions are more sensitive to this issue than US and UK investors who, perhaps as a result of greater familiarity, take a more pragmatic view. They know that any stock recommendation is likely to be part of an investment banking agenda and treat it accordingly. If, for example, Goldman Sachs has a 'buy' recommendation out on a stock and its analysts and salesmen are selling it hard to investors, there is a cynical assumption that they are trying to get the price up ahead of an impending corporate deal. Equally, an analyst who has been 'brought over the (Chinese) wall' and made privy to an investment banking deal is not available to talk to his institutional clients, which generates suspicion and irritation.

Much of the value of the securities operations of the investment banks to the institutions lies not in their stock selection advice but in their ability to execute large and complex deals, especially where liquidity is an issue and they are prepared to act as principal to facilitate a trade. In addition, portfolio trading – the simultaneous trading on behalf of a single investor of a large number of individual stocks in, perhaps, many countries – is a fast expanding service. Portfolio trading is used when a plan sponsor moves managers or there is a major change in asset allocation. Involving hundreds or billions of pounds (and several hundred individual stocks) it can be very profitable for the bank that wins the mandate, whether acting as agent or principal.

Closely associated with this trend is the growing importance of derivatives in the execution of equity trades. Post Big Bang trading in liquid stocks is often done on a net basis and commission rates have declined. Volumes have been affected by the rise of passive management, as indexed funds trade less. Consequently, the return on capital from traditional market making (in CitySpeak, the 'cash' equities business) has fallen sharply, forcing firms to offer more complex and sophisticated products commanding better margins. At many firms cash and derivatives traders work together. The modern equity trader needs to understand derivatives, risk management and the significance of the research into the companies he trades.

Fortunately for the embattled 'cash' equities business, salvation has come from an unexpected quarter: hedge funds. As we noted in earlier chapters, the rise of hedge funds from obscurity in 1999 to their current status as a key driver of the London market has been both rapid and

remarkable. Looked at from the perspective of a securities division executive, hedge funds are manna from heaven – they deal often and they deal
big (at full commission rates). Consequently, their contribution to trading
flows and commission revenues is vastly greater than the (modest) quantum of funds under management would imply. Better still, the bulge
bracket investment banks quickly spotted an opportunity to provide hedge
funds with back-office services such as accounting, securities lending and,
latterly, what is called, rather politely, 'capital introduction' (effectively a
dating service for hedge funds wanting to meet potential investors). Newly-
formed hedge funds customarily appoint a bank as their 'prime broker',
whose job it is to supply all of these services. So, for example, when Gartmore set up its sixth hedge fund in March 2002, it selected Goldman Sachs
as its prime broker (Goldman was already prime broker to two of the existing five funds). For the securities divisions of the investment banks, facing
downward commission pressures on conventional institutional dealing, the
sudden emergence of hedge funds as a large and lucrative source of profits has been rather like giving an undernourished man two square meals a
day and a concentrated course of vitamin injections. Or, to put it another
way, in the words of the global head of equities at one of London's largest
investment banks:

> They are the dream client. They don't complain about commission
> rates and don't want much input from analysts. What they want is
> revved up sales people.

(Financial Times, 14 August 2001)

Estimates suggest that about 150 hedge funds
were formed in Europe in 2001, with around half of
the money raised going into long/short strategies.
Nearly all of these funds were launched by experienced managers from established organizations
seeking their independence. Few major fund management houses have succeeded in building a substantial hedge fund business alongside their existing
long-only operation: Gartmore is the outstanding
exception. Nor are hedge funds guaranteed money-
makers in difficult markets – as they are wont to
portray themselves – either for the investor or the
manager. As additional money flows in, and more managers chase the
same trading opportunities, average returns are falling. Many do not survive over the longer term. Small size and poor performance generate a fee
base that is insufficient to sustain the business.

> As additional money
> flows in, and more
> managers chase the
> same trading
> opportunities, average
> returns are falling.
> Many do not survive
> over the longer term.

Liquidity is crucially important to hedge funds, particularly in the context of short trading. Hedge funds are stockpickers but of a different kind from the conventional long-only fund. Some use fundamental analysis to decide what to buy and what to short. Others incline towards technical analysis or statistical analysis. All receive a high level of service from the brokers who cover them. The contact points are sales traders (sales personnel who sit alongside the market makers whose job it is to keep hedge fund and other trading-oriented clients informed on market movements and market thinking), specialist salespeople and also analysts. All provide advice and ideas on trading opportunities. At the major London securities firms, hedge funds figure prominently in their Top Ten list of commission generators.

Figure 7.1 summarizes the relationship between institutional Investors – be they the asset management arms of investment banks, independent fund management companies, hedge funds or whatever – and the securities operations of the investment banks (or, indeed, 'pure' broking firms servicing the institutional market).

How fund managers view research

Investment analysts no longer occupy the high ground between the City and industry. Sell-side analysts have been sidelined. They too have been disintermediated. It was once true that a company that had anything to tell the stock market and the press did so through its corporate broker plus a few others with whom it had a close relationship. The idea of using financial PR agencies to influence journalists came into its own only in the late 1980s. Direct contact with institutional shareholders is essentially a 1990s phenomenon.

Figure 7.1 The fund management-securities interface

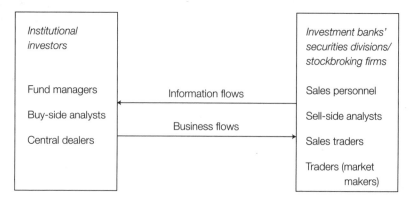

In an environment of equal access to information and easy electronic dissemination institutions have markedly less need for the services of a middleman. Once the jealously guarded preserve of sell-side analysts, company results meetings are routinely attended by buy-side analysts and fund managers. Most questions are asked by sell-side analysts, less to elicit information than to impress their institutional clients. Written presentation material is available to anyone who wants to look at it on corporate websites. 'Webcast' conference calls with management – still more common in the US – can be listened into by a broad audience: buy-side, sell-side, private investors (and, no doubt, competitors!). Ten or 15 years ago sell-side analysts and buy-side analysts did more or less the same thing. Today, as a consequence of disintermediation, their roles have significantly diverged. This is absolutely true of larger institutions but rather less so in the case of medium-sized and smaller fund managers, able to support a lower level of buy-side capability.

Old-style institutional stockbroking operated on the basis that what clients really wanted to hear was useful information that was not (yet) available to their competitors. After all, outperformance is all about buying into or getting out of a stock before the crowd. Previously it was possible for an analyst with a good relationship with his company – especially if he worked for the corporate broker – to obtain such information and disseminate it to his favoured clients. That is what they expected to get from their broker. An analyst who had such information was said to have the 'inside track'. Whether or not it could be described as insider information was a moot point. Not that it mattered much anyway in a more relaxed environment. But in today's controlled and regulated environment this is not an option: such information is a lot more difficult to obtain and, more to the point, using it is illegal. Analysts have lost what was once their central role.

Analysts use research notes to communicate information and advice to fund managers, backed up by telephone and personal contact. Equity sales personnel also speak to fund managers, conveying the analyst's thoughts and putting their own spin on the prospects for the share price. Nowadays much research is delivered online via the screen on the manager's desk. Excessive amounts of paper are still circulated although electronic delivery is gaining ground. In 1999, for example, Merrill Lynch decided to switch the distribution of all research reports under four pages long to electronic media. Buy-side customers want information faster but they also

> Previously it was possible for an analyst with a good relationship with his company – especially if he worked for the corporate broker – to obtain such information and disseminate it to his favoured clients.

want it in a form they can store and search easily – to manipulate and analyze as they wish.

Fund managers now spend less time reading research and listening to sell-side analysts. Much research adds little to what they know already and much is repetitive. Managers are more selective in what they read and who they talk to. Increasingly, they prefer direct contact with analysts, or sales-people specializing in the sector, rather than relying on an old-style generalist salesperson to communicate the analysts' views. In parallel, insti-tutional central dealers talk to sales traders. Fund managers and buy-side analysts remain circumspect, operating on the basis that most sell-side opinions have a subtext. Investors sense that analysts are primarily there to support current share prices – and find reasons why they should go higher! As John Plender, the Financial Times columnist, put it:

> The job of analysts, especially in a record-breaking bull market, is
> not to analyse but to provide post-hoc justification.

> (*Financial Times*, 1 May 1999)

In the US some busy asset managers will not talk directly to analysts but ask them to 'leave a stock-specific message of not more than 30 seconds'. At the end of their allotted time they are cut off! Fund managers, particu-larly those in the more substantial institutions, instead rely mainly on their own buy-side analysts.

Independent sell-side analysts prepared to say what they truly think are few and far between. Gone are the days when a brave analyst with a neg-ative view of Robert Maxwell's creation, the grandly named Maxwell Com-munications Corporation, would be prepared to publish a research note headed, '**C**an't **R**ecommend **A P**urchase!' Analysts with an independent cast of mind are not easy to find in the integrated investment banks, whose researchers frequently have too many other constituencies to satisfy. Some, such as those at UBS Warburg, do have a reputation for guarding their independence.

Generally, research objectivity is more in evidence in smaller stockbroking firms. One such is Collins Stewart, founded in 1991 and, since October 2000, a listed company on the London Stock Exchange. Headed by Terry Smith, who acquired a (well-deserved) reputation as a maverick in 1992 fol-lowing the publication of his critique of corporate accounting, 'Accounting for Growth', Collins Stewart pursues a resolutely independent line. Research is conducted on large UK and European companies free of any investment banking bias. Collins Stewart does, though, do investment banking work for small companies. (In reality, the decision not to let the lure of investment banking business affect research objectivity makes a virtue out of necessity

– a firm the size of Collins Stewart stands little chance of getting ECM or M&A work from largecap or even midcap companies.) The collapse of Marconi during 2001 can be seen as a vindication of the Collins Stewart philosophy. For two years before, as the share price scaled new heights and virtually every other analyst urged clients to buy the stock, Mustapha Omar, the Collins Stewart analyst, consistently and publicly recommended a 'sell'. In a tough securities market, the firm's willingness to go against the crowd is winning market share from the integrated investment banks.

The difficulty of finding an independent voice is particularly pronounced in the case of new issues. Investment banks keen to get into the offering syndicate – where fee levels are good – turn their analysts into promoters of the issue. A large syndicate will involve every significant investment bank – some observers cynically argue that syndicates are deliberately enlarged to stifle criticism! In 1999 when Freeserve, the internet service provider subsidiary of Dixons, went public amid dotcom fever with a 10-strong syndicate there was a single dissenting opinion (from WestLB Panmure). The desire on the part of issuers and their bankers to exercise total control over what is written became even more evident during the IPO of Orange in early 2001. Non-syndicate analysts complained vigorously that they were denied full financial information if they did not agree beforehand to submit their research for vetting before publication. It can be just as much of a problem in an M&A transaction. In the case of the three-way bid for NatWest seven of the top 10 banking teams were unable to express an opinion. Institutions like to hear contrary views and are concerned at the paucity of such views in the securities industry as it is now structured. Equally, analysts, if permitted, like to take a robust and independent line.

> A large syndicate will involve every significant investment bank – some observers cynically argue that syndicates are deliberately enlarged to stifle criticism!

When the stock market went up pretty well every day the lack of objectivity exhibited by the sell-side did not seem to matter. But the massive and sudden loss of value in heavily-promoted technology stocks in 2001 exposed the investing public on both sides of the Atlantic to what the institutional investor had known for some time – the essential worthlessness of analysts' recommendations. Fund managers knew that investment banking was driving many research opinions. The investing public did not. The upshot was a storm of criticism of sell-side analysts, a storm that has yet to abate.

Crucially, what is written and what is said are two different things. Even when equity research was unaffected by investment banking analysts were greatly influenced in what they wrote by the companies they were researching. Criticism of the company or a negative recommendation ran the risk of upsetting the relationship with the management, on whom the analyst relied for a high proportion of his information. There was inevitably a bias in favour of 'buy' recommendations, if only because rising share prices make everyone happy! Stockbrokers are, in any event, congenitally bullish. Analysis of a company that refused to co-operate was feasible in theory but, in practice, proved extremely difficult.

In today's market, with the analyst even more dependent on the company for information, forecasting earnings, or indeed maintaining an understanding of the dynamics of the business, without company co-operation would be impossible. The modern analyst is more conduit than commentator. He has little time to pursue anything that might be classified as independent research. A high proportion of the information he conveys to his clients comes straight from the company. When an analyst writes, 'We believe that Company X has an 18 per cent market share of a market projected to expand at 7 per cent per annum over the next five years', this can usually be translated as, 'The company told us this and I wrote it down.' More experienced analysts, admittedly, treat such information with a degree of scepticism, assessing it where possible against other data they may have gathered.

Fundamentally, unless a company is operating in an exceptionally simple and transparent industry – of which there are very few – the analyst has minimal chance of getting his forecast right without an enormous amount of help. Modern business is too complex with too many fast moving variables. Present-day analysts devote much time to adjusting and fine-tuning the financial models they themselves have created to forecast corporate performance. Investor relations executives actively assist them in maintaining and updating these models. In fact, some US corporations go so far as to appoint a member of the IR team to liaise with them specifically for this purpose.

In view of this, it is hardly a surprise that research notes are pretty bland documents. Written research has been emasculated by a stringent regulatory environment in which reports must be vetted internally by the in-house legal/compliance department (and, quite possibly, investment banking) before circulation. Privately, in speaking to fund managers, analysts may be willing to disclose their real view as opposed to the 'house view'. Sometimes the contrast is stark. For example, one analyst talking to a fund manager: 'We are putting out a "buy" recommendation on Company X – it is spelt S-E-L-L!' The desire to please everyone has made the written recommendation virtually worthless. As the Wall Street Journal put it in 1999:

Analysts don't simply assess stocks; they increasingly promote them . . . Analysts currently have a 'buy' or 'strong buy' on fully two-

thirds of the roughly 7,000 US stocks tracked by First Call, a Boston earnings and estimate tracking service. The percentage of 'sell' recommendations: just 1 per cent. The remainder are 'holds'.

('Heard on the Street', *Wall Street Journal*, 28 May 1999)

Since then, stung by intense public criticism, the proportion of 'sells' has increased. But not by much. In early 2002 Thomson Financial/First Call reported that 'sell' recommendations comprised 1.6 per cent of all ratings, up from 0.9 per cent in 2000.

No less an authority than Arthur Levitt, the former Chairman of the SEC, was even more direct, pointing to what he called 'a web of dysfunctional relationships' between sell-side analysts and the companies they research. Commenting on the importance of corporate relationships he said:

Any analyst who goes against the grain may find himself excluded from conference calls or worse, as I recently read, silenced by his own firm. Is it any wonder that today a 'sell' recommendation from an analyst is as common as a Barbra Streisand concert.

(Speech to the Economic Club of New York, 18 October 1999)

Actual written recommendations can be pretty arcane. What, to an outsider, is the difference between 'buy' and 'accumulate'? Does 'long-term buy' imply 'short-term sell'? (It probably does!) Long ago, analysts conjured up all kinds of ways of avoiding the dreaded sell word. A favourite City recommendation pre-Big Bang was 'weak hold'. Institutions understood the real meaning. Today the recommendation 'hold' or 'neutral' generally implies the same thing. In the Alice in Wonderland world of Wall Street it is an open secret that 'strong buy' means 'buy', 'buy' means 'hold' and 'hold' means 'sell'.

It is tempting to think that putting a disclaimer on the front of a research note highlighting the existence of an investment banking relationship between the bank and the company in question would solve the problem. Unfortunately not. As we saw in Chapter 3, investment banking relationships are highly mobile nowadays. Most large companies will award an investment banking mandate to any reputable bank that comes to them with a good idea and/or a creative way of doing it. Consequently, every substantial company is a potential corporate client. An analyst who upset a company that might turn into a significant source of investment banking fees would not survive for long.

> Any analyst who goes against the grain may find himself excluded from conference calls or worse, silenced by his own firm.

In the US, the outcry against analysts (which gathered momentum after the collapse of Enron) provoked Congress into setting up hearings into Wall Street research. In the summer of 2001, a subcommittee of the House of Representatives Committee on Financial Services took evidence from more than a dozen witnesses. The transcript makes fascinating reading. Clearly, the members of the committee were amazed – and sometimes aghast – at some of the practices disclosed, practices that were routine on Wall Street during the 1990s. Conflicts of interest were revealed, not only in relation to investment banking but also in regard to analysts' public stance on stocks and their private actions. Since these hearings, all the leading investment banks have announced policy changes aimed at reducing these conflicts.

Then, in February 2002, US stock market regulators laid out a series of rules designed to monitor and control the murky relationship between securities and investment banking. Wall Street, predictably, reacted by calling these measures excessive and, in any event, unworkable. But, by the spring of 2002, the pressure for radical reform – led by the attorney general for New York – had become unstoppable. The SEC responded by formulating new rules, based on those put forward by the stock market regulators. At the heart of these measures is a ban on the direct linking of analysts' pay to investment banking deals. In Britain, the Financial Services Authority (the new 'super-regulator' that came fully into being on 1 December 2001) announced a review of the rules governing conflicts at the investment banks under its jurisdiction.

Underlying all this is, of course, a more fundamental problem. The harsh economics of the securities business dictate that an analyst cannot ignore the requirements of investment banking if he wishes to retain his job and earn the money to which he has become accustomed. If an investment bank equity analyst had to rely on the commissions from share trading for his earnings he would be paid the same as a middle-ranking civil servant instead of a multiple of that number!

All in all, institutions have no illusions about sell-side analysts. They know that the objectivity of the average investment banking analyst is analogous to the objectivity of the film critic of *The Sun* reviewing the latest movie from 20th Century Fox – which also happens to be owned by Rupert Murdoch's News Corporation! Given the modest sums they are prepared to pay, fund managers can hardly expect to receive research reports that are full of originality and devoid of bias. However, despite all this, institutions – including some of the largest – do regard sell-side analysts as providing a useful service, as we see in the next section.

The analysis of analysis

The securities industry has experienced tremendous growth over the last 15 years. This is not because the customers wanted more output or were pre-pared to pay more for the product – as is normally the case – but because investment banks realized that the real money was to be made by selling services to the *suppliers* of the information. The researcher still has analyst status but functions in parallel as a 'door opener' for corporate business.

Huge excess capacity exists therefore in securities research because the size of the industry bears little relationship to customer demand. In both the UK and the US, institutional commission revenues available to securities firms continue to be squeezed. As we saw in Chapter 5, fund managers are under great pressure to minimize transaction costs.

What has been the growth in the number of sell-side analysts, how many analysts are there and how are they assessed? The annual Thomson Extel survey of fund managers' and finance directors' views of analysts is a good starting point. Extel has been collecting this information on a consistent basis since 1974. According to the survey, in 1999 the total number of sell-side analysts reached a staggering 6,000. In 1989 this same database had only 2,000 names on it. These figures, admittedly, reflect a generous defini-tion of 'analyst'. A more precise number is available from the 2002 Reuters/Institutional Investor European Equities Investment Survey. Based on data col-lected at the end of 2001, it identified just under 3,200 equity analysts covering European stocks, a modest 6 per cent drop from the year before.

Since mid 2000, falling share prices, lower volumes, tighter commissions – and, of course, the dearth of corporate business – have forced the investment banks into an examination of the func-tion and cost of sell-side research. Inevitably, jobs have been cut but not, it seems, to the extent of greatly affecting sector coverage. Overcapacity is still rife. Large companies are typically researched by 25 analysts. Even midcap companies can be followed by 10–15 analysts. Can it really be that every one – or even most – of these has something fresh and novel to contribute to the investment process, particularly in an envi-ronment in which corporate information is carefully controlled? The answer must surely be 'no'. Overcapacity will persist, however, if banks continue to believe that securities research is their entry ticket to corporate business.

The contribution made by research during the good times is still very much alive in the corporate memory of the investment banks. In the tech-nology sector, for example, analysts played a valuable role in identifying IPO

> Huge excess capacity exists therefore in securities research because the size of the industry bears little relationship to customer demand.

candidates for their investment banking colleagues. Some banks deliberately created spare capacity in big, active, international sectors such as telecoms, technology and insurance. Large teams, often organized on a pan-European or global basis, became increasingly common. When analysts were compromised by corporate work – and consequently unavailable to talk to fund managers – others were there to service clients. With the onset of more difficult conditions, many of these teams have been extensively trimmed.

Interestingly, further evidence of the comparative lack of interest shown by the buy-side in sell-side research comes from the fact that surprisingly few copies of the Thomson Extel survey are bought by institutions or companies – the audience it is supposedly aimed at! Most are bought by securities firms. Fund managers, especially the largest 20 or 30 institutions, rely mainly on their own internal surveys to determine the value they receive from sell-side inputs and the allocation of commission. The leading institutions conduct such surveys twice or four times a year. Sell-side analysts are told how they rank so that there is, in effect, a continuous feedback system. These views may – or may not – coincide with the rankings announced with great fanfare each year by Thomson Extel, Reuters/Institutional Investor and others.

This shift in the 'job spec' of the representative sell-side analyst from independent commentator to something closer to conduit and promoter does not suit everyone. Some move to smaller broking firms, or to investment banks that are less corporate led, where they enjoy greater freedom. In February 2000, for example, Merrill Lynch lost Richard Coleman, a star banking analyst, to the Dutch bank, ABN Amro, which has acquired a reputation for allowing its analysts free rein: a move, he said, prompted by the constant demands of the investment bankers.

Recent years have also seen a steady stream of experienced analysts moving out of securities into investment banking and fund management. Investment banking is a logical destination for an experienced sector analyst. As we observed in Chapter 3, corporate advisory departments are organized along sector lines. Industry specialization in investment banking is much like equity sector research, but with a different end point. The transition from sell-side to buy-side is an equally well-trodden path. In recent years, buy-side analysts have gained in influence at the expense of sell-side analysts (and fund managers). An extract from a piece written by an anonymous buy-side analyst reveals the reasons for moving.

> It's no joke being a sell-side analyst – I should know. I used to be
> one myself in my 20s, before I saw the light, did an MBA and
> moved to the buy-side. Your time is squeezed between many
> masters – the sales desk, the clients, the corporate finance
> department plus finding time to write and produce pieces of

*research on a range of public companies that frankly for the most
part are very uninspiring.*

Investment banks use analysts in a number of ways in order to market
their services. A substantial amount of research, particularly the larger,
more comprehensive company reports, is actually corporate rather than
investor-driven. The object is frequently more a matter of impressing the
company with the breadth and depth of the analyst's knowledge rather
than impressing investors. This is particularly true when an analyst (in
StreetSpeak) 'initiates coverage', which simply means that he is researching
the company for the first time at that firm. The decision to initiate coverage
is often governed, at least in part, by the perceived investment banking
potential. Companies are happy to co-operate with analysts in creating a
major research report, seeing it as a way of further promoting themselves
to institutional investors. However, as we observed earlier, investors may
actually be minimally influenced by such a document. Buy-side analysts may
find it tells them little they do not already know, or it is stuffed full of detail
they do not need to know!

Similarly, the various annual public UK analyst surveys are heavily used as
a marketing tool (and for assessing analyst remuneration!). When bidding
for underwriting or M&A business the underlying message of every investment bank is: 'If you want to sell this deal to investors and keep your share
price moving in the right direction you must have our analyst – who is top
ranked in this table or is number 3 in that table – on board.' It is usually
possible to find some survey that casts your analyst in a favourable light. In
other words, the active support of the securities arm
of the business is an integral part of the capital markets or M&A pitch. In an IPO, for example, the status
and distribution power of the securities division of an
investment bank does have some influence on the
institutions but it is easy to overestimate that influence. Using Goldman Sachs rather than, say, HSBC or
BNP Paribas will probably allow a company selling its
stock for the first time to gain better access to key
fund managers. But fund managers are wary, especially so post Enron and post the technology crash.
Particularly in the case of IPOs – a good fee generator so the selling machine is running at full throttle –
no investment bank has a spotless record. Every
sponsor, from Morgan Stanley to Cazenove, has had its share of issues that
have performed abysmally in the after-market. Yet, despite this, institutions

> **The decision to initiate coverage is often governed, at least in part, by the perceived investment banking potential. Companies are happy to co-operate with analysts in creating a major research report.**

display a tendency to buy IPOs they suspect to be overpriced. In the eternal contest between 'hope' and 'experience', 'hope' usually wins!

In their marketing to corporates, investment banks have successfully encouraged the notion that sell-side analysts are critical to the institutional buy or sell decision – when the truth is they are not! Many companies continue to believe that investors are – as they once were – led by advice from sell-side analysts. Nor do the institutions go out of their way to disabuse companies of this perception. One reason may lie in the fact that many are part of investment banks. A comment to a CEO by, say, a fund manager at Merrill Lynch Investment Managers suggesting that they pay scant attention to sell-side views undermines, by implication, the value of Merrill's own equity analysts. It would not be a career-enhancing move!

If institutions listen to sell-side analysts but are little influenced by their stock recommendations, in what ways do they find them useful? Fortunately, the annual analysts' survey conducted by the respected industry journal, *Institutional Investor*, asks asset managers this very question and tabulates the replies. The overall scores awarded by institutions operating in European markets, regardless of size, are shown in Table 7.1. (Equivalent US rankings are similar.)

For all the reasons we have covered so far in this chapter, stock selection merits only eighth place. (In the US survey it sits even lower, having been

Table 7.1 What investors really want (from sell-side analysts)

Overall rank	Attributes
1	Country/industry knowledge
2	Trustworthiness
3	Accessibility/responsiveness
4	Independence from corporate finance
5	Useful/timely calls
6	Written reports
7	Management access
8	Stock selection
9	Special services
10	Earnings estimates
11	Communication skills
12	Quality of sales force
13	Market making/execution
14	Primary market services

Source: All-Europe Research Team Survey 2002 (Institutional Investor website)

ranked number 2 as recently as 1998.) Earnings estimates come still further down the list. Companies are always prepared to offer consensus 'analysts' forecasts directly, frequently making the individual estimates available on their website. Note the high level of votes accorded to 'Independence from corporate finance', a recent addition to the list.

What fund managers do still value above all else is industry knowledge (allied in the case of Europe to country knowledge). Some sell-side analysts have been following their industry for a long time, acquiring an insight and a perspective that few buy-side analysts or fund managers have. They follow fewer stocks (usually between 10 and 20) and are in much more frequent contact with them, often developing over time a close relationship with the companies they cover. Surveys also reveal an increasing polarization of the industry. Investors focus their attention on a small number of well-regarded individuals mostly employed by the top securities houses, according few votes to the long tail of analysts who are primarily there because every organization that aspires to be called an investment bank must have its quota of researchers to parade in front of prospective corporate clients.

Sell-side analysts perform other useful functions. Their perspective, valuation approach and conclusions are valuable as an outside 'test' of an institution's internally-held view. Professional investors want analysts to challenge their assumptions – and the assumptions of the market. Those who simply go with the crowd have limited appeal. Analysts will do customized research for fund managers. Often, analysts will provide fund managers with their earnings model of a particular company, allowing them to 'flex' the inputs as they would wish and see the results. Broking firms organize sector-based conferences where buy-siders can listen to presentations from companies and analysts (described, rather intriguingly, in Table 7.1 as 'Special services'). Fund managers frequently find this to be an efficient way of keeping in touch with developments and trends. Analysts will also focus on thematic issues with implications for a range of sectors: for example, intellectual property rights.

> Investors focus their attention on a small number of well-regarded individuals mostly employed by the top securities houses.

Sell-side researchers are also a source of information on the attitudes of other institutions to a specific stock and can have a good sense of how a share is likely to perform. A fund manager or buy-side analyst needs to keep in touch with market thinking. It is well to remember that, in an institutional world, an investment outperforms only because other institutions decide to buy. Finally, there is no doubt that a 'push' on a particular stock by an analyst and his selling team can have a powerful effect on short-term share price performance. Liquidity constraints mean that even a small amount of institutional buying can have a significant impact on the share price. This could represent a buying – or even a selling – opportunity. The bottom line is: sell-side analysts do have a value to fund managers but it is a different and lesser value than they are generally believed to have.

The eternal triangle of the analyst, the journalist and the corporation

Companies talk to City analysts. Companies also speak to financial journalists. And journalists talk to analysts. This triangular framework characterizes the communications system used by management to convey its message to the investment institutions and the public at large. It is a ménage à trois that works because everyone gets something out of it. All three parties are content to maintain the fiction that sell-side analysts make independent forecasts of corporate profits (although, as we explain, recent developments have encouraged many companies to cast aside the veil of 'analysts' estimates').

In Chapter 6, we saw that the key skill required by today's companies in their dealings with institutions is the ability to manage expectations. The company-analyst relationship is an important element in this process, which starts with the investor relations department. IR first developed in America in the 1950s and transferred to the UK in the 1980s. All companies of any size have an IR department, with larger businesses employing half a dozen or more professionals. Their job is to 'present an accurate picture of corporate performance and prospects, thus allowing the investment community, through an informed market, to determine a realistic share price' (the definition used by the UK-based Investor Relations Society). Effective IR is, as we saw in the last chapter, the visible manifestation of a company's commitment to shareholder value. Investors expect management to take IR seriously. Surveys suggest that it occupies 10 per cent or more of a large company CEO's time, with perhaps double that for the finance director.

Investor relations is aimed at informing and influencing institutional investors, both directly and indirectly via sell-side analysts and the press. To supplement their in-house capability many companies use outside advisers: financial PR or IR consultancies. Financial PR agencies target financial journalists and sell-side analysts while IR consultancies concentrate on the buy-side – identifying fund managers who hold or might choose to buy the shares. Typically, a financial PR firm, in addition to developing relationships with journalists, will be employed to monitor City opinion by checking analysts' views before a company's results and then contacting them again after the results presentation. IR focuses on the needs and perceptions of institutional investors and tends to be more database driven. The ultimate objective is to place as many shares as possible in the hands of institutions that are believed to be longer-term holders.

In practice, there is no hard and fast line between these two activities. Most financial PR firms do some IR work, but they need to be careful not to be seen to be in conflict with the securities firms who are often responsible for recommending their services to corporate clients. Probably the most successful investor relations consultancy to emerge in London during the last decade, Makinson Cowell, consciously adopts an extraordinarily low profile. Its understanding of institutional psychology has resulted in a remarkable roster of blue chip clients and exceptional access to top management.

How do IR executives 'guide' analysts' forecasts so that fund managers can be kept informed of company thinking on its likely earnings performance? This is a tricky process, but recent developments have made it a little less so. In the past, management generally made use of heavy hints, either in the statement accompanying the figures or during subsequent presentations, to convey their view of future performance. Companies also do their best to make calculations easy for analysts. For example, if currencies are a major factor they will often provide a 'ready reckoner' along the lines of 'Every 10c rise in the US dollar is worth £5 million in additional annual profits to us.'

Events have moved on, however, since the end of 2000. In the US – and to some degree in the UK – the relationship between corporations, analysts and investors has undergone a sea-change. During the late 1990s, Arthur Levitt, the then Chairman of the SEC, became convinced that the way in which companies released information to the stock market (via 'nods and winks' to use his own words) was in urgent need of reform. His target was the time-honoured Wall Street practice of selective briefings – sell-side analysts and/or institutional investors, in groups or individually, receiving 'material' (price-sensitive) information ahead of the investing public. His solution (which, incidentally, he pushed through against opposition from some of his fellow commissioners) was a new rule called Regulation Fair Disclosure ('Reg. FD' or just 'FD' for short). FD came into force in October 2000 amid dire warnings from Wall Street that it would kill the 'natural' information flow between companies and investors.

> In the past, management generally made use of heavy hints, either in the statement accompanying the figures or during subsequent presentations, to convey their view of future performance.

What FD does is say to a listed company: if you have anything material to disclose you must do so to everyone, promptly and simultaneously. The small investor should no longer be disadvantaged. Changes in earnings expectations are clearly 'material'. In the past, American companies would feed their forecasts to analysts who, putting their own spin on it, would then filter the revised EPS number into the market. And so, a new – lower or higher – consensus estimate was born! Understandably, the sell-side were more than happy to go along with this charade – so gaining a reputation for clairvoyance they did not deserve. Now, a process that occurred behind closed doors has been driven into the open. FD did not insist that companies make public forecasts – such forecasts are a byproduct of the ban on selective disclosure. Private guidance has been replaced by public guidance.

US companies now customarily issue earnings guidance, quarterly or more frequently. From nowhere in 2000, the term 'earnings guidance' has risen to become a lynchpin of StreetSpeak. It can take various forms. A company's ability to provide guidance will, of course, vary – some industries are more predictable than others. Often it is quite precise, as when Microsoft said in April 2002 that it expected its EPS for the financial year ending 30 June 2003 to be in the range $1.89 to $1.92. Others continue to rely on the tried and tested formula of saying they are 'comfortable' with Street consensus estimates (asset managers know the effect is much the same). There are good reasons why some companies prefer to stick to the indirect approach. The use of 'analysts' estimates' acts as a shield between the company and potentially angry or disappointed investors. (The use of the analyst as a cut-out is based on a principle that will be familiar to any reader of Cold War espionage literature: 'plausible deniability'.) 'Targets' are also much in vogue. For example, Procter & Gamble's 'long-term earnings growth target of double digits'. Interestingly, everyone goes out of their way to avoid using the F-word: forecast. But that is what they are doing.

Regulation FD has been responsible for an active, sometimes emotionally charged, debate in US investor and corporate circles. Has the impact on the stock market been positive or negative? Surveys suggest that opinion is divided and that no definitive judgement can yet be made. Some say the quantity and quality of information provided by companies has declined. Others maintain it has improved. Companies are certainly more careful about what they say. Presentations are routinely scripted and rehearsed in an effort to avoid the FD minefield. Another thing FD has done is expose the myth of the analyst as forecaster, further emasculating the analyst's role. One positive is that, to counter this, analysts are being forced to do more original research, ferreting out useful information from within their industry, as analysts did before many of them

> From nowhere in 2000, the term 'earnings guidance' has risen to become a lynchpin of StreetSpeak. It can take various forms.

opted for the easy life relaying hot news from closed meetings to a waiting clientele.

In practice, FD seems unlikely to survive in the longer term. Harvey Pitt, the new Chairman of the SEC (appointed by the Bush administration) is on record as a critic of the rule, although he is not in disagreement with the underlying philosophy. Instead, his focus is on the need for companies to update investors on a real-time basis, a larger issue than FD. For the moment the SEC seems content to leave FD as it is. And Wall Street has – reluctantly – learned to live with it.

In Britain, FD has undoubtedly had an influence. In fact, the UK rules on the dissemination of price-sensitive information (which have been in existence since 1994 as part of the Stock Exchange's Listing Rules) are broadly equivalent to FD. However, in true British fashion they have been enforced flexibly (which, as far as one can see, means hardly at all). Under the new regime that came into operation on 1 December 2001, the Financial Services Authority can impose an unlimited fine on anyone found guilty of the new civil offence of financial market abuse, which has implications for selective disclosure. Many larger British companies – often with sizeable US share-holdings – have chosen to modify their reporting behaviour to something akin to FD. Companies accept that institutional investors now expect more precise public guidance on future financial performance – and are giving it to them. One effect of the new regime has been to enhance the importance of IR within companies. When – and what – to announce becomes a matter of fine judgement. Knowing what is price-sensitive involves a good appreciation of current market sentiment and perception, which is why the internal IR role has become much more central. In mid 2002, uncertainty remained about how the new regime will work in practice.

We saw in the previous chapter how institutions, through their desire to be kept informed at all times, want this process to be as seamless as possible. Regular newsflow is vital, in active support of the 'no surprises' culture. BP is an acknowledged master of the art:

There are rarely any nasty surprises from his [Sir John Browne's] company. Instead investors are expertly drip-fed a series of pleasant surprises, while bad news – such as write-downs on questionable investments – are usually tucked away amid a welter of positive developments.

(Robert Corzine, 'Oil's takeover king', *Financial Times*, 3 April 1999)

Responding to investor demands for frequent updates, many large and medium-sized companies now issue (in addition to twice-yearly, or quarterly, results) 'trading statements' or 'trading updates' to fill in those parts of the calendar when there would otherwise have been no news. BP, for example, is a generous provider of information: four end quarter trading updates followed, a few weeks later, by full quarterly results. The real purpose of these trading updates is, of course, to manage expectations. Such announcements are usually put out not much before the end of the trading period to which they relate – by which point most companies have a pretty shrewd idea of the profit number they are likely to report in two or three months' time. In the more difficult trading conditions that have prevailed since 2000, many of these updates have been recharacterized – by the press at least – as 'profit warnings'. As we observed earlier, the name of the game is managing estimates to a number that can be modestly exceeded. By the time the actual profit is reported – and the share price hopefully responds as earnings come in above expectation – the fact that forecasts had been massaged downwards two months previously is largely forgotten.

> Reality is, in fact, rather more complex as sell-side analysts and investors continuously attempt to second-guess the numbers indicated to them by IR personnel.

Reality is, in fact, rather more complex as sell-side analysts and investors continuously attempt to second-guess the numbers indicated to them by IR personnel. As ever, Wall Street illustrates the management of expectations in its most extreme form. What Arthur Levitt called 'a culture of gamesmanship' (in a speech to the Economic Club of New York in October 1999) is rife. That all this occurs is no secret, even outside Wall Street, as an extract from an editorial in *Business Week*, which is widely read in the corporate world, illustrates:

> These days, Wall Street is gaming the quarterly-profits cycle. Beating estimated earnings, not real profits, is the driving force in the market. Corporate IR specialists work through analysts to manage expectations of upcoming earnings. Lower those expectations and then beat them by 10 per cent or so, and bingo! Your stock goes up. Do it quarter after quarter and you get a reputation for delivering to shareholders – even if your stock price is not keeping up with Standard & Poor's 500-stock index or your industry group.

> (Excerpted from the 23 November 1998 issue of *Business Week* by special permission. © 2000 by McGraw-Hill, Inc.)

This dynamic interaction between corporation and analyst resembles a bizarre mating ritual that each year becomes a little more frenzied! Companies issue 'pre-announcement announcements' just weeks or even days before results are due to get analysts to reduce estimates to a number that can be beaten. One consequence is Wall Street's obsession with the trend revealed by pre-announcements – whether up, down or simply reaffirming existing earnings guidance. The risk in this strategy is that, after a while, analysts and investors make compensating adjustments. Unofficial EPS numbers (so-called 'whisper numbers') begin to circulate round Wall Street and on dedicated websites just before the announcement date. Shares in companies that beat their official estimate but fail to hit their whisper number can be hit hard. Very much a focal point during the internet boom, 'whisper' websites are today less influential than they were.

The nature of the company-journalist relationship has changed in the last 10 years. What used to be called a 'leak' – something that was generally inadvertent and embarrassing – has been woven into the fabric of modern corporate communications. Informal briefings to journalists are designed to maintain frequent and positive newsflow. The information so provided may relate to profits but, more especially, impending or possible corporate moves. These stories emanate from 'sources' or 'sources close to the company' or 'advisers to the company' (often a euphemism for financial PR) or just appear in the media without any provenance. In theory, under the new 'market abuse' regime, such disclosure ahead of a proper public announcement should cease. It has not – although, to be fair, the volume has dried up.

The most obvious impact has been on the quality Sunday newspapers. Holding back stories for the weekend press – when readers have more time to absorb them – is a practice deeply embedded in the psyche of the British financial PR business. Many of the pieces that appear are not price-sensitive but some are. For example, on 17 February 2002, *The Sunday Times* revealed that Innogy, the UK's second largest retail energy business, was in bid talks with the German utility company, RWE, having failed to agree a price a few months earlier. It was clear from the story that Innogy would regard a price in the region of £3 billion as acceptable. Innogy issued a press release that same day, confirming it had 'received approaches'. That this information was price-sensitive cannot be denied: the Innogy share price rose 20 per cent when the stock market opened the next day. Who stood to gain from this disclosure? It is difficult to resist the conclusion that the out-of-the-blue appearance of this well-informed piece, clearly written from an Innogy angle, was a deliberate strategy designed to put pressure on RWE to conclude a deal, speedily and at the 'right' price. Five

> The most obvious impact has been on the quality Sunday newspapers. Holding back stories for the weekend press – when readers have more time to absorb them – is a practice deeply embedded in the psyche of the British financial PR business.

weeks later RWE agreed to pay £3.1 billion for Innogy. Similarly, EMI illustrates how news continues to be 'trailed' to mitigate its impact. The contents of the company's strategic review – including a halving of the dividend – appeared in press articles for several days before the announcement was made. Unsurprisingly, on the day (20 March 2002) the share price barely moved.

As in politics, much is not actually announced nowadays. The financial pages are full of phrases like 'will announce' or 'is expected to announce' or, more intriguingly, 'is set to unveil' or 'is considering'. Viewed in an institutional context this process of drip-feeding to defuse makes perfect sense. An obviously well-informed newspaper story is more likely to capture the attention of a busy fund manager when he is fresh – and gives him time to think about his reaction. A change in strategy or a prospective bid is more easily digested over the Sunday breakfast table. Human beings naturally prefer time to adjust to something new. From the corporate perspective, it provides an opportunity to test City reaction. Informal briefings have raised the authority of financial journalists because they are seen to be a key channel through which companies convey the corporate message. The following quote from an article on the financial PR business explains how this works:

> A sensitive story . . . may be fed to a selected journalist exclusively with the implicit understanding this will secure sympathetic treatment.
>
> (Richard Tomkins, 'Money, money, money – it's a PR's world', Financial Times, 17 September 1999)

Journalists talk to both companies and analysts. The journalist-analyst relationship is beneficial to both parties, but particularly for the journalist. Investment commentators, such as Lex and Questor in the Daily Telegraph, rely heavily on sell-side researchers for both analysis and views. It is a valuable relationship because it enables them to appear to be extraordinarily well informed on the basis of a few telephone calls. This is a further reason why companies continue to find analysts useful. When news is announced, the normal format is a presentation to analysts (and investors) followed by a press presentation. The first presentation is designed for those with a good level of knowledge about the company and its industry. The second is more superficial. After the press presentation, a journalist can call an analyst for explanation and interpretation, reducing the communications burden on the company.

News and market commentary journalists make extensive use of analysts' views, including direct quotes, mostly on an unattributable basis. In these days of consensus, the phrase 'analysts say' finds much favour. Easily the most prolific source of pithy comment is the ever-quotable 'one analyst'. For a company that feels unhappy about the comments made there is no comeback on 'one analyst'. Interestingly, there is a rough inverse relationship between the power of an investment bank or agency stockbroking firm and the frequency of analyst press mentions. The analysts at Goldman Sachs or Morgan Stanley do not generally seek press publicity. At the other end of the spectrum, analysts at some smaller, agency stockbroking firms are clearly happy to attach their names to anything that is printed.

One obvious reason is that those houses with a minor market presence need the publicity. Additionally, those at the top of the tree are highly sensitive to the risk of upsetting actual or potential investment banking clients. But it also has to do with a firm's antecedents. Unlike Goldman Sachs or Morgan Stanley, where the securities business grew up essentially as the handmaiden of investment banking, UBS Warburg secured its substantial UK presence in securities through acquisition (at Big Bang). There is, as a consequence, a greater tradition of analytical independence.

For the analyst, the journalistic relationship offers a further opportunity to influence investor opinion, anonymously if he so wishes, so completing this mutually convenient triangular connection. Investment institutions may lie outside the triangle but have no illusions about what happens. Maintaining a veil over how it works in reality has advantages for all concerned. In StreetSpeak it would be called a 'win-win-win' situation!

> Analysts at some smaller, agency stockbroking firms are clearly happy to attach their names to anything that is printed.

Final thoughts

Like it is

This book has endeavoured to shed light on the equity component of the City, with the emphasis on providing key insights into institutional investor psychology and the forces that govern the functioning of modern stock markets. The essential backcloth to all this is the victory of the 'US model'. More and more, both in the business world and generally, things are done the American way. Given the context, it is not surprising that US firms enjoy competitive dominance in securities, investment banking and, increasingly, investment management.

A good many themes have emerged from our analysis. Of these, four are central to an understanding of the behaviour of equity markets in an institutional environment:

1 The appreciation that investor perception is invariably more powerful than reality. In stock markets what *might* be true is more important than what is true. Perception is, of course, an important element in any marketplace but has an especially profound influence on one that is institutionally driven. Investors, aided and abetted by companies and securities analysts, create a constantly evolving framework of expectations against which reality is continuously judged. The Great Expectation Machine is the formalization of this process.

> Investors, aided and abetted by companies and securities analysts, create a constantly evolving framework of expectations against which reality is continuously judged.

2 Growth is the god to whom institutional investors pay homage. The prospect of annual increases in EPS stretching as far as the horizon (and beyond) has an allure that institutional investors find hard to resist. Growth creates size, and size, fuelled by overt and closet indexing, generates its own momentum. For companies, however, the pursuit of growth can become a treadmill, as they strive to meet earnings expectations. To please investors desirous of owning sleek, reliable growth machines CEOs are under constant pressure to jettison the low-growth businesses in their portfolio. The market is a hard taskmaster. Institutional dynamics and fund management psychology mean that managers can easily be tempted to invest in a 'blue sky' company that is little more than a bunch of promises rather than plodding reality. Whatever their reservations, they dare not miss out on a stock that seemingly offers the potential to provide their portfolio with that significant edge in the performance stakes. Performance pressures and weighting considerations accentuate this trend.

3 It is essential not to underestimate the importance of liquidity in equity markets. It is a huge and critical consideration for institutional

investors. For smallcap and midcap companies lacking that vital growth tag it lies at the root of the problem they encounter in attracting the attention of the City. For fund managers the absence of liquidity is a permanent bugbear – a severe restraint on their ability to invest wherever and whenever they so wish. Yet liquidity receives no attention in their promotional literature and barely a mention in the financial press. The reasons are obvious. The difficulties institutions encounter in actually investing the sums entrusted to them would hardly constitute a positive marketing message. Better to give the impression that any and every quoted stock is there to be purchased on your behalf. Liquidity affects investment decision-making and performance to an extent that institutions prefer not to acknowledge.

4 In Britain especially, institutional control of industry is a fact of life. For historical reasons, the UK has an exceptionally high level of institutional equity ownership. Comparative harmony exists now between the City and industry but it is a reconciliation on institutional terms. Chief executives do the things they think will please their owners. In today's business environment institutional investors call the shots. Of that there is no doubt.

But it would be wrong to point the finger at investment managers as being responsible for this state of affairs. Fund managers are simply professionals responding as capitalism dictates to the pressures that clients (institutional or retail) and their advisers, notably the investment consultants, impose on them. Demanding targets are transmitted through the system. The modern obsession with beating the benchmarks means that fund managers need rising share prices and outperformance to satisfy their clients – and are prepared to prod and push companies in which they are invested towards measures that produce the desired result. These actions may – or may not – be good for the companies concerned. Blaming the City for the ills of British industry is a bit like blaming the greyhound for chasing the electric hare.

> Blaming the City for the ills of British industry is a bit like blaming the greyhound for chasing the electric hare.

Anyone wanting to change the behaviour of fund managers needs to look closely at the incentive system within which they are obliged to operate. Industry-standard benchmarking produces industry-standard behaviour, a point made in the first edition of this book and reiterated with some force by the Myners Review of institutional investment six months later. In the pensions field especially, greater benchmark diversity would produce a less uniform approach. The peer group assessment system still used by many balanced funds is little more than a blueprint for herd-like behaviour, imbuing trustees and managers with a finely developed sense of mediocrity. As the shift from balanced to specialist management picks up speed, it is – thankfully – being replaced by index benchmarks customized for each pension scheme. A related issue – also highlighted by Myners – is that the majority of UK pension fund trustees are unsophisticated in investment matters. Plan sponsors' in-house investment expertise is frequently limited. As a result, trustees lack confidence in their dealings with external investment professionals, becoming too reliant on them. This is the source of the deep conservatism exhibited by many boards of trustees.

Amid all the focus on pension funds it is easy to overlook the fact that insurance companies have overtaken pension funds as the single largest owner of 'UK plc'. Insurance company fund managers, especially those running managed funds, can be subjected to performance pressures similar to those experienced by money managers. The big difference is that they are accountable directly to fundholders, not to a board of trustees.

The diversity theme also needs to be pursued on a structural level. UK institutional asset management has too few discrete decision-making units. Rather than a place where new entrants – both outsiders and start-ups – fight and (largely) fail, the industry needs to become a place where, as in the US, skilled new entrants can make the grade. The current trend away from balanced management, with its inbuilt rigidities, towards specialist management on the American model, accompanied by higher levels of professionalism within plan sponsors, is a welcome development. Active fund management is becoming less concentrated, as US asset managers make their mark and homegrown new entrants climb the performance tables. In London, the vogue for hedge funds has created a new set of opportunities, allowing talented professionals to break away from big organizations and pursue their own goals. Against this, however, must be set the countervailing trend towards enhanced scale, as providers are tempted by the benefits of size in the capture of funds.

> Active fund management is becoming less concentrated, as US asset managers make their mark and homegrown new entrants climb the performance tables.

If, as a consequence of these trends, the industry structure can be 'freed up', the result will be a more diverse and flexible set of fund management organizations dedicated to investment in a wider range of assets. A combination of benchmark modification and greater structural diversity offers, at least, the prospect of an industry that is less blatantly homogeneous in its investment decision-making.

CitySpeak – a two-minute glossary

401(k) Easily the most popular US *defined contribution* (DC) occupational pension plan.

active fund management Traditional fund management in that the manager attempts to outperform a *benchmark*, either an *index* or a *peer group* of similar funds.

actuarial consultants Firms of actuaries who advise plan sponsors on pension funds. The actuarial input into *defined benefit* (DB) pension schemes is extremely large. Actuarial consultants have moved heavily into *investment consulting* although not all investment consulting firms have an actuarial origin.

after-market The period of trading immediately after *an offer* or *offering* has taken place.

agent Stock market participants act either as an agent, working for a commission or fee, or as a *principal*, which involves the firm in financial exposure.

alternative assets An American term covering investment in assets outside the mainstream assets of *equities* and *bonds*. Examples are venture capital, *hedge funds* and (in the US) real estate.

American Depositary Receipts (ADRs) A means of packaging a non-US share to look and act like a domestic US stock, making it easier for American institutions (and individuals) to invest.

arbitrage The attempt to profit by exploiting price differences in similar securities in different markets or in different forms.

assets/asset classes Virtually anything can be regarded as an asset for investment purposes. In practice, funds invest predominantly in quoted *securities*. Fund managers invest in classes of assets, the two main ones being *equities* and *bonds*. The Big Decision (as we call it) is the allocation between these two asset classes.

balanced fund management The system of pension fund management much favoured in the UK until recently, in which the trustees appoint a 'balanced' (or 'discretionary') manager who has the freedom to allocate the assets as he sees fit across a range of asset classes. Compare with *specialist fund management*.

basis points Financial jargon for one hundredth of one per cent, e.g. 20 basis points equals 0.2 per cent.

benchmark In investment management, the yardstick, either a widely accepted *index* or a *peer group comparison*, against which the performance of a fund is judged. Funds outperform or underperform, or match, their benchmark.

bond A fixed income security that provides the same cash return in the form of interest each year during the life of the bond (normally fixed at the outset). At the end of the period the sum raised from investors is repaid.

bulge bracket Industry shorthand for the small and exclusive group of leading international investment banks, nearly all American.

buy-side Institutional fund managers and their buy-side (internal) analysts, who use the services of securities firms and their *sell-side* analysts.

capital market Broadly any market where companies and other organizations can go to raise fresh capital via the sale of bonds, equity or any other financial instrument. Also called the *primary market*, as opposed to the *secondary market*. In practice, the Eurobond and Euroequities markets are often referred to as the 'capital markets'.

closet indexing The practice by *active fund managers* of constructing a portfolio that closely resembles the *benchmark* index portfolio against which they are judged, in an effort to reduce the risk of underperformance.

commercial banking The traditional business of banks: taking deposits and making loans to companies and individuals.

core–satellite fund management The approach adopted by many *plan sponsors* in the US and now spreading to the UK, in which a *passively managed* core is surrounded by a group of active, specialist managers.

corporate advisory American terminology covering advice to companies, predominantly on *mergers and acquisitions (M&A)*. In the UK such advice often goes by the misleading term *corporate finance*.

corporate broker A peculiarly British concept in which securities firms act as the interface between quoted companies and the stock market, working in tandem with the *merchant* (now *investment*) *bank* advising the company.

corporate finance In American parlance the many different ways in which an *investment bank* can help a company finance itself. In traditional UK merchant/investment banking, corporate finance refers to *M&A* work and domestic equity capital raising.

cyclical stocks Shares whose earnings and share prices go up and down, usually in line with the economic cycle.

debt The overall term for loans or *bonds* as opposed to *equity*. Both offer an investor regular interest payments and repayment at the end of their life. A company can obtain funds in the debt bank market (a loan) or the debt capital market (a bond). They are conceptually similar and coming closer together.

defined benefit (DB) pension schemes The traditional type of *funded pension scheme* providing the retiree with a pension based (usually) on final year's salary.

defined contribution (DC) pension schemes A *funded* scheme, either employer or individually based, in which the pension received is entirely dependent on the value of the fund accruing to the person concerned at retirement. Also, in the UK, called a 'money purchase' scheme.

derivatives Futures and options.

disintermediation Essentially it means cutting out the middleman. In a financial context it refers specifically to the process whereby companies bypass the banks for debt financing (a loan) and go straight to the debt capital markets (on which they issue a *bond*).

dispersion A fund management term referring to spread of performance figures between different funds within the same organization. Pension fund trustees like to see low dispersion.

distribution Used specifically to refer to the distribution *syndicate* of investment banks and securities firms in an *offering*. More generally, it means the ability to sell large tranches of shares or bonds via a network of salespeople whose main business is broking in *secondary markets*.

equities The generic term for what in the UK are called 'ordinary shares' (or just 'shares') and in the US 'common stocks' (or just 'stocks'). The two terms are interchangeable. Equity is risk capital, with (unlike a *bond*) no guarantee of income (in the form of dividends) or capital repayment.

equity capital markets (ECM) The *primary markets* business of raising new equity from multiple international sources. Also called the 'international equities' market. The equity version of the Eurobond market.

ERISA Employee Retirement Income Security Act. The comprehensive 1974 legislation that underpins the regulatory framework for US occupational pension funds.

Euromarkets The leading international market for capital, originally for *bonds* (hence Eurobonds) but also now for equity that, for historical reasons, happened to develop in Europe. More properly called the 'international securities' market.

financial public relations Financial PR firms assist corporate investor relations (IR) departments in relation to the media and *sell-side* analysts.

Financial Services Authority The new statutory body (it received its full powers on 1 December 2001) responsible for regulating banking, insurance and investment in the UK (in effect, the City of London). It is approximately equivalent to its American counterpart, the *Securities and*

Exchange Commission (SEC).

flotation An equity issue on the *primary market*. Increasingly, the American term *IPO* is used as an alternative description.

funded pension schemes The Anglo-Saxon approach to providing occupational pensions from a fund financed by contributions, so creating a separate and identifiable 'pot' of money for investment and payment of pensions. Alternative approaches rely on current income to pay retirees.

Glass–Steagall The groundbreaking banking legislation in 1933 that imposed a strict division between US commercial and investment banking. Gradually these restrictions have been dismantled and Glass–Steagall no longer applies.

growth stock investing The school of investment that favours buying high-priced stocks on the basis that the share price will follow the expected growth in earnings. Contrast *value stock investing*.

hedge funds Invented originally as a means of risk control in portfolio management, with the aim of producing a consistent annual absolute return (rather than a return relative to a *benchmark*). Hedge funds employ a variety of strategies, including 'short' selling (selling stock not owned in the hope of making a profit by buying it back at a lower price), the use of *derivatives* and quantitative techniques.

high-yield bonds A particular type of *bond* issued by a company or a country. Originally called 'junk bonds', they offer a higher yield in return for the risk that the company may default on its interest payments and/or the repayment of capital.

index/indices A statistical method of measuring the performance of a group of stocks (or bonds). Indices have grown in importance due to their usage as *benchmarks* for fund management performance and for other purposes. The FTSE All-Share Index is the index against which most institutional fund managers operating in the UK are assessed.

indexation See *passive management*.

individual retirement account (IRA) A popular US *defined contribution* (DC) pension plan aimed at those without an occupational pension.

initial public offering (IPO) American terminology, increasingly used in the UK in preference to *flotation*, for a new *equity* issue on the stock market. *Primary market* activity.

investment bank Strictly a bank that raises money for companies on the markets rather than lending money as a *commercial bank* does. Nowadays the term can cover a huge range of activities encompassing *investment banking*, fund management, private equity finance and much else besides.

investment banking In its purest sense investment banking is all about underwriting new issues, about making *offerings*. More and more, it has come to cover most – or even all – of the things that an investment bank does, including particularly capital raising for companies, *securities* broking and trading and *corporate advisory (M&A)* work.

investment consultants Advise *plan sponsors* on the investment aspects of running a pension fund. See *actuarial consultants*.

investor relations (IR) Inside a company, the department responsible for managing the flow of information to investors, especially institutional investors. Sometimes IR departments employ IR consultancies and/or *financial PR* firms to help them in this process.

life funds The funds run by insurance companies containing the premiums from traditional-type 'with-profits' life insurance policies.

life insurance The misleading description for investment-based products sold by the industry, often with an insignificant life insurance protection element.

liquidity A frequently used financial term with several meanings depending on the context. In the text it refers to the ability to trade in and out of shares in large volume without any significant impact on the price paid.

managed funds Funds run by insurance companies for companies and individuals operating on a 'unit-linked' basis, offering much greater transparency than the traditional *life fund* approach.

mandate The financial world equivalent of a contract to perform a particular service, e.g. the management of an investment portfolio, advice on a takeover, etc. In investment management, the term 'brief' is also commonly used.

merchant banking Merchants who turned themselves into bankers became known as merchant bankers. Following American practice, UK merchant banks now call themselves *investment banks*. On Wall Street merchant banking can refer to direct investment by an investment bank in unquoted companies.

merger and acquisition (M&A) See *corporate advisory*.

money manager Strictly a professional fund management firm competing for *mandates* in the institutional (predominantly pensions) marketplace but can be used more broadly.

mutual funds The generic term, used in the US and elsewhere, for what in the UK are called unit trusts. Mutual funds/unit trusts are collective investment vehicles in which the price of the units reflects the value of the underlying assets in the fund.

offer/offering The generic term for any kind of security issuance. See also *initial public offering*.

passive fund management In passive management the manager has a *mandate* to match the performance of an *index*. Also called *indexation* or, more colloquially, tracker funds.

peer group comparison A system of pension fund performance measurement, common in the UK though declining, in which the *benchmark* is the median fund of a group of funds, rather than an *index*.

plan sponsor A useful Americanism referring to the company sponsoring a pension fund for its employees.

pooled pension funds Smaller pension funds often choose to buy units in a pooled fund run by a *money manager*. The insurance equivalent (for institutions and individuals) is a *managed fund*.

primary market The market in which securities are first issued. In the equity market it is called an *IPO* or *flotation*. In *primary market activity* the money raised by selling securities to investors is new money (for the company and/or the founders or backers) not, as in the *secondary market*, a transfer to other investors as payment for the securities they have sold.

principal An investment bank is acting as a principal when it uses its own balance sheet to trade securities, either to facilitate client deals or to make money for the firm (called *proprietary trading*). Contrast with acting as an *agent*.

proprietary trading When an investment bank uses its own capital and trading skills in securities markets in pursuit of profit for the bank. In doing so it is acting as a *principal*.

secondary market The market in which already existing securities are traded by investors – what *securities firms* do on a daily basis. Contrast *primary market*.

securities Evidence of ownership of a financial asset, such as *equities* or *bonds*, that can be bought and sold at will (at least in theory).

Securities and Exchange Commission (SEC) The statutory body, set up in 1934, responsible for regulating the activities of Wall Street.

securities firms What used to be called a stockbroking firm, involved in buying and selling securities on behalf of clients. Securities firms – particularly the larger ones – are often nowadays subsidiaries of investment banks.

securitization The process whereby a loan is converted into a *bond*, so the interest is paid to investors rather than a bank. Or where a bond is raised against an asset, which must have a sufficiently reliable revenue stream to pay the interest.

segregated pension funds A pension fund that is managed separately by an identified fund manager. All large funds operate on a segregated basis. Most smaller funds place their assets in a *pooled fund*.

sell-side Industry shorthand for the securities business, selling their services to institutions (the *buy-side*). An investment or securities analyst is a sell-side analyst.

specialist fund management A system of pension fund management, favoured in the US and gaining ground rapidly in the UK, in which asset allocation is determined by the trustees and portions of the fund are handed to managers specializing in a particular *asset class*, geographic area and/or *investment style*.

style (investment) An American term referring to the investment approach adopted by a *specialist fund manager*, e.g. within equities, 'largecap growth' (companies expected to show consistent growth in profits with a large market capitalization). US institutional investors define themselves primarily by their investment style. Style is a term familiar to US retail investors.

syndicate/syndication When a group of banks come together for a deal because no bank wants to accept the exposure on its own. In *equity capital markets* underwriting and *distribution* are conducted through syndicates.

total return The combination of capital appreciation and income. Commonly used to assess fund management performance in preference to capital appreciation alone.

value stock investing The school of investment that believes in buying stocks that are priced at a discount to their perceived true worth. Contrast *growth stock investing*.

Bibliography and websites

Augar, Philip, *The Death of Gentlemanly Capitalism*, Penguin Books, 2000.

Barker, Richard G., 'The market for information – evidence from finance directors, analysts and fund managers', *Accounting and Business Research*, 1999, 29 (1).

Berger, David, *The Motley Fool UK Investment Guide*, Boxtree Publishing, 1998.

Brealey, Richard A. and Myers, Stewart C., *Principles of Corporate Finance*, McGraw-Hill, 5th edition, 1996.

Butler, Charlotte and Keary, John, *Managers and Mantras: One company's struggle for simplicity*, John Wiley & Sons, 2000.

Cain, P.J. and Hopkins, A.G., *British Imperialism, 1688–2000*, Longman, 2nd edition, 2001.

Chapman, Colin, *How the Stock Markets Work*, Century Business Books, 6th edition, 1998.

Chernow, Ron, *The Warburgs*, Chatto & Windus, 1993.

Chernow, Ron, *The Death of the Banker*, Pimlico, 1997.

Clark, William M., *How the City of London Works*, Sweet and Maxwell, 4th edition, 1995.

Clowes, Michael J., *The Money Flood: How pension funds revolutionized investing*, John Wiley & Sons, Inc., 2000.

Coggan, Philip, *The Money Machine*, Penguin, 3rd edition, 1995.

Cole, Benjamin Mark, *The Pied Pipers of Wall Street: How analysts sell you down the river*, Bloomberg Press, 2001.

Courtney, Cathy and Thompson, Paul, *City Lives*, Methuen, 1996.

Davis, E. Philip, Pension Funds: *Retirement – income security and capital markets*, Clarendon Press, 1995.

Davis, E. Philip, *Can Pension Systems Cope?*, Royal Institute for International Affairs, 1997.

Department of Trade and Industry, *Developing a Winning Partnership: How companies and institutional investors are working together*, DTI, 1996.

Edmeister, Robert O., *Financial Institutions: Markets and management*, McGraw-Hill, 2nd edition, 1986.

Ellis, Charles D., *Investment Policy: How to win the loser's game*, Dow Jones-Irwin, 1985.

BIBLIOGRAPHY AND WEBSITES

Endlich, Lisa, *Goldman Sachs: The culture of success*, Little, Brown, 1999.

Geisst, Charles R., *Wall Street: A history*, Oxford University Press, 1997.

Goldman Sachs, *The Coming Evolution of the Investment Management Industry*, Goldman Sachs, October 1995.

Gompers, Paul A. and Metrick, Andrew, 'Institutional investors and equity prices', National Bureau of Economic Research Working Paper 6723, Boston, September 1998.

Graham, Benjamin and Dodd, David, L., *Security Analysis* (classic 1934 edition), Barbour & Company, 1996.

Greenwich Associates, *Financial Services Without Borders*, John Wiley & Sons Inc., 2001.

Hampden-Turner, Charles and Trompenaars, Fons, *The Seven Cultures of Capitalism*, Piatkus, 1993.

Hobson, Dominic, *Pride of Lucifer: The unauthorised biography of a merchant bank* (Morgan Grenfell), Penguin, 1990.

Hooke, Jeffrey C., *Security Analysis on Wall Street*, John Wiley & Sons Inc., 1999.

Kynaston, David, *The City of London*, Volume 1, *A World of its Own 1815–1890*, Pimlico, 1994.

Kynaston, David, *The City of London*, Volume 2, *The Golden Years 1890–1914*, Pimlico, 1995.

Kynaston, David, *The City of London*, Volume 3, *Illusions of Gold 1914–1945*, Chatto & Windus, 1999.

Kynaston, David, *The City of London*, Volume 4, *A Club No More 1945-2000*, Chatto & Windus, 2001.

Lilja, Robert, *International Equity Markets: The art of the deal*, Euromoney Publications, 1997.

Little, Jeffrey B. and Rhodes, Lucien, *Understanding Wall Street*, Liberty Hall Press, 3rd edition, 1991.

Littlewood, John, *The Stock Market: 50 years of capitalism at work*, Financial Times Pitman Publishing, 1998.

Lofthouse, Stephen, *Equity Investment Management*, John Wiley & Sons, 1994.

Lowe, Janet, *Benjamin Graham on Value Investing*, Financial Times Pitman Publishing, 1995.

Marshall, John F. and Ellis, M.E., *Investment Banking and Brokerage: The new rules of the game*, Irwin Professional Publishing, 1994.

Marston, Claire, *Investor Relations: Meeting the analysts*, Institute of Chartered Accountants of Scotland, 1996.

Morton, James (ed.) *The Financial Times Global Guide to Investing*, Financial Times Pitman Publishing, 1995.

Myners, Paul, *Institutional Investment in the UK: A review*, HM Treasury, 2001.

Owen, James P., *The Prudent Investor: The definitive guide to professional investment management*, Probus Publishing Company, 1993.

Roberts, Richard, *Inside International Finance*, Orion Business Books, 1998.

Roberts, Richard and Kynaston, David, *City State: How the markets came to rule our world*, Profile Books, 2001.

Sampson, Anthony, *The Sovereign State: The secret history of ITT*, Hodder & Stoughton, 1973.

Schumacher, F. F., *Small is Beautiful*, Blond and Briggs, 1973.

Siris, Peter, *Guerrilla Investing: Winning strategies for beating the Wall Street professionals*, Longstreet, 2nd edition, 2000.

Stern, Kenneth A., *Secrets of the Investment All-Stars*, ANACOM Books, 1999.

Taylor, Francesca, *Mastering Derivatives Markets*, Financial Times Pitman Publishing, 1996.

Thompson, Valerie, *Mastering the Euromarkets*, Irwin Professional Publishing, 1996.

Vander Weyer, Martin, *Falling Eagle: The decline of Barclays Bank*, Weidenfeld & Nicolson, 2000.

Wasserstein, Bruce, *Big Deal: The battle for control of America's leading corporations*, Warner Books, 1998.

Weetman, Pauline and Beattie, Aileen, *Corporate Communications: Views of institutional investors and lenders*, Institute of Chartered Accountants of Scotland, 1999.

Websites

Alternative assets **www.altassets.net**
Association of British Insurers **www.abi.org.uk**
Bank for International Settlements **www.bis.org**
Centre for Economics and Business Research **www.cebr.com**
Conference Board (The) (US) **www.conference-board.org**
Corporation of London **www.cityoflondon.gov.uk**
Financial News **www.efinancialnews.com**
Financial Services Authority **www.fsa.gov.uk**
Financial Times **www.ft.com**
FTSE International **www.ftse.com**
HM Treasury **www.hm-treasury.gov.uk**

House of Representatives Financial Services Committee (US)
  www.house.gov/financialservices
Institutional Investor magazine www.iimagazine.com
International Financial Services, London www.ifsl.org.uk
International Monetary Fund www.imf.org
Investment Company Institute (US) www.ici.org
Investment Management Association www.investmentuk.org
Investor glossary www.investorwords.com
Investor Relations Society www.ir-soc.org.uk
Lombard Street Research www.lombard-st.co.uk
London Stock Exchange www.londonstockex.co.uk
National Association of Pension Funds www.napf.co.uk
National Statistics www.statistics.gov.uk
Pensions and Investment magazine (US) www.pionline.com
Securities and Exchange Commission (US) www.sec.gov
Securities Industry Association (US) www.sia.com
Senate Committee on Governmental Affairs (US)
  www.senate.gov/gov_affairs
Warren Buffett's Letters to Shareholders www.berkshirehathaway.com

Index